For King and Kaiser

Scenes from Saxony's War in Flanders 1914–1918

Andrew Lucas & Jürgen Schmieschek

Pen & Sword
MILITARY

First published in Great Britain in 2020 by

PEN & SWORD MILITARY

an imprint of
Pen & Sword Books Ltd
47 Church Street
Barnsley
South Yorkshire
S70 2AS

ISBN 978-1-52674-864-5

A CIP catalogue record for this book is available from the British Library

Layout: Jürgen Schmieschek

Typeset in AGaramond

Printed and bound In India by Replika Press Pvt. Ltd.

Pen & Sword Books Ltd incorporates the imprints of Pen & Sword Archaeology, Atlas, Aviation, Battleground, Discovery, Family History, History, Maritime, Military, Naval, Politics, Railways, Select, Social History, Transport, True Crime, and Claymore Press, Frontline Books, Leo Cooper, Praetorian Press, Remember When, Seaforth Publishing and Wharncliffe.

For a complete list of Pen & Sword titles please contact
PEN & SWORD BOOKS LIMITED
47 Church Street, Barnsley, South Yorkshire, S70 2AS, England
E-mail: enquiries@pen-and-sword.co.uk
Website: www.pen-and-sword.co.uk

Contents

Foreword

This is our second book on the Great War history of the Royal Saxon Army (*Königlich Sächsische Armee*), the national army of the Kingdom of Saxony (*Königreich Sachsen*) – one of four German states to retain its own armed forces in 1914. Despite limiting the scope of our debut work *Fighting the Kaiser's War* (published in 2015) to the Western Front from the La Bassée Canal to the coast we found ourselves struggling to do justice to our subject in the space allowed. The need for adequate coverage of the dozen Saxon (or part-Saxon) divisions and countless smaller units which served at various times in this area forced us to exclude much interesting material and countless photographs, particularly from the best-documented units. Our first attempt to address this was the 2nd Ypres centenary booklet *The Saxons at Zonnebeke*, since revised into chapter 6 of the present volume.

The universally positive response to our work and the many new contacts it generated led us to renewed visits to Flanders and to rich new seams of untapped source material. Our knowledge of – and fascination with – the subject was greatly enhanced, and it was soon clear that we had far more to write about this region of especial interest for Saxon and Englishman alike. The book which you now hold in your hands makes no attempt at the comprehensiveness of *Fighting the Kaiser's War*, aiming instead to explore a selection of notable periods, places and aspects of Saxony's war in Flanders in greater depth. As ever, we do not seek to address the grand strategic issues of the war or to reinterpret history in any radical fashion. Our theme is the war as the Saxons saw and experienced it on this front, from (at most) corps level down to that of the individual *landser* in the trenches, and we hope to enrich the reader's existing understanding of the Western Front with intriguing and moving details from a previously unconsidered direction. Frequent advantage has been taken of the wealth of British primary sources to introduce the perspective of the opposition. Finally we have enhanced the book's value as a guidebook of sorts (provided by the profusion of fully-indexed maps) by drawing attention to surviving traces of the Saxon military presence in the area.

This book first appeared in 2018 in German as *Von Armentières nach Langemarck*. During translation we made numerous corrections and improvements, and took the opportunity to add some particularly choice photos which have since come to light. As ever, our collections and our knowledge of our subject continue to expand!

Providentiae Memor

Jürgen Schmieschek und Andrew Lucas

November 2019

Acknowledgements

As a team we are eternally grateful to the numerous readers of our first book (sadly unnamed here for reasons of space) who have greatly encouraged us, not only by their enthusiasm for our efforts but also by their questions and suggestions, to continue our exploration of the life, suffering and death of our Saxon forefathers in Flanders and to put our discoveries into print.

We also gladly acknowledge the patient support of our publishers Pen & Sword, especially our editor Rupert Harding, and of archival staff both in Saxony and England. We would especially like to thank Jan Vancoillie from Wevelgem (Belgium), who again contributed freely from his collection and above all from his great wealth of knowledge, and Uwe Hänel from Grünhainichen (the present-day recording angel of RIR 244) for his aid in editing the texts.

❖

First of all I must thank my great-grandfather Arno Bierast (*kriegsfreiwilliger-gefreiter* with FAR 48) and his brother Rudolf (*offiziersstellvertreter* with IR 104, probably with service in Flanders) for the family connection to the Royal Saxon Army which continues to inspire my work. Sadly I only knew them through my late grandmother Margot Hemmings (née Bierast), without whose affectionate support I would never have begun my research. I remain profoundly indebted to my parents Michael and Ann Lucas for their unconditional love and support, and for my father's invaluable expertise with British sources. My dearest friend – and now my wife – Diana has stood by me without question throughout my writing career and I love her deeply for it. Lastly I must once again thank my co-author and dear comrade Jürgen, who was the driving force behind this second book and unearthed the great majority of the source material on the ground in Saxony.

Andrew Lucas

❖

I am highly obliged to my dear Ute, who once again had to miss out on a lot of time together for the sake of my work on the book. I would also like to thank my good friend and co-author Andrew for our continued fruitful collaboration.

Jürgen Schmieschek

CHAPTER I

THE BEGINNINGS OF TRENCH WARFARE | JÄGER-BATAILLON 13

A Saxon *jäger* struggles to keep a primitive trench clear. With no cladding to prevent the walls collapsing this would be a truly sisyphean task, even in dry weather. Trailing in the mud, his greatcoat has collected a thick layer of filth to add to the weight of his kit.

The beginnings of trench warfare | Jäger-Bataillon 13

Autumn 1914 at L'Epinette and Pont Ballot

The infantry engagement is usually decided by fire effect and a bold advance on the enemy. However the effectiveness of the fire is increased to its greatest possible extent when we have space to use our rifles comfortably and accurately, to inflict considerable damage on the enemy without ourselves being too much exposed to enemy fire and losses. All these advantages come to full realisation in open order. In this, we do not fight shoulder to shoulder as in closed order, but with larger intervals in between; we form skirmish lines and use all the cover which the terrain affords.[1]

A new recruit reading this pre-war passage, reprinted unaltered in the 1915/16 edition of the *Dienstunterricht des Königlich Sächsischen Infanteristen* (the Royal Saxon infantryman's primer), would find little chance to apply these traditional light infantry tactics in Flanders. The same volume devotes a mere fifteen lines to the 'optional' use of temporary trenches during battle, for which the infantry was plentifully equipped with entrenching tools. While doing so, it also takes severe pains to warn them that *whoever conceals himself in battle* [i.e. to avoid taking part] *is a coward.*[2] What had not been foreseen in peacetime was that the rough trenches scraped out of the battlefield under fire would need to become a semi-permanent fortress system running from the sea to the Swiss border, as the mobile warfare for which all belligerents had planned stagnated into *stellungskrieg* (trench war) due to mutual exhaustion. Only the training of the *fussartillerie* (heavy artillery) and *pioniere* (combat engineers) for siege warfare remained directly relevant. The former found their cumbersome high-trajectory howitzers in constant high demand. The latter, only a battalion strong with each army corps, soon found themselves overstretched as the only troops already familiar with hand grenades, field fortifications, mining, trench mortars and flamethrowers.

Once trench warfare had set in, the Germans were far more willing than their opponents to build for long-term occupation. Bar the 'permanent offensive' in the Argonne and the experimental large-scale gas operations in Flanders, German strategy in 1915 demanded a defensive posture in the west while focusing on Russia. Thus the crude trench lines of 1914, often destroyed in Flanders by flooding that first winter, were rapidly and continually developed with numerous successive lines of defence, multiple dense wire obstacle lines and larger and more resilient dugouts. Due to the high water table, the latter could never be as deep as desired and would rely increasingly on intensive use of concrete. Narrow-gauge railway systems for transporting materiel were brought right up to the front line trench system in 1915, and electricity widely introduced for lighting and pumping water as early as January or February. Fixed telephone networks were established very early, starting with equipment already issued in 1914.

Many ideas were tried and abandoned in the evolution of trench warfare. The cladding or heavy reinforcement of trench walls with wood and even (for instance near the flooded zone north of Ypres) concrete was abandoned, once it was appreciated that under severe shelling the shattered cladding could easily block the trench. Electric barbed wire was a popular novelty which soon proved impractical except for border security. Especially after the Somme trench garrisons became smaller, as notions of holding the front line in strength and refusing to cede any ground were rejected. By the time the British began their 1917 Flanders offensive, the Germans were relying on defense in depth by mutually-supporting nests of resistance, which softened the attackers up for counter-attack by reserves held ready for the purpose. It was accepted that the forward positions would inevitably become a mass of craters, roughly linked together when possible to create battlefield trenches even rougher than those of 1914. By autumn 1917, hulking ferroconcrete bunkers would be the only part of the German trench system on the battlefields around Ypres to survive the combined wrath of the Entente artillery and the weather.

This chapter represents the early stages of this process in the Saxon line south of Armentières during the first months of trench warfare. With the exception of the Christmas picture on p. 17, all of the photos are drawn from a single album belonging to an unidentified member of **2. Königlich Sächsisches Jäger-Bataillon Nr. 13** (JB 13), a Saxon light infantry battalion based in Dresden and initially assigned to 24. Infanterie-Division (24. ID) of XIX. Armeekorps (XIX. AK). Further images from this same album can be seen on pp. 19, 25 and 42 (left).

Rough, irregular trench construction, rudimentary 'funk holes' covered by tent sheets and large trench garrisons are all much in evidence – as is highly irregular clothing, reminiscent of photos from the Christmas Truce. Improvised adaptations to the harsh conditions, the proliferation of homemade knitwear and the difficulty of shaving gave both sides a highly irregular appearance by the time they met in no man's land.

Invasion battles and the 'Race to the Sea'

In August 1914 a regular infantry regiment had three battalions, each around 1,080 (all ranks) strong and comprising a battalion staff and four rifle companies. The three battalions shared the support of the regimental machine-gun company (with six guns plus a spare) and horse-drawn baggage echelon. An active *jäger* battalion however was equipped for independent action with its own machine-gun company, cycle company (*radfahrer-kompagnie*) of 127 all ranks and motor transport column (*jäger-kraftwagen-kolonne*) of ten lorries. Thus JB 13 was mobilised with a strength of 33 officers, 1272 other ranks and 127 horses. It gained a second cycle company at the end of August.

The Royal Saxon Army had a strong light infantry tradition. The *esprit de corps* of its *jäger* battalions and rifle regiment – Schützen (Füsilier)-Regiment 'Prinz Georg' Nr. 108 – was bolstered by uniquely Saxon uniform distinctions (a hunting horn on the shoulder straps and Austrian-style *tschako*). Like all *jägers* they were considered an elite, priding themselves on their standard of marksmanship and receiving younger and fitter replacements than the infantry in wartime. Saxony furnished each of its active corps with one *jäger* battalion (the other being JB 12 from Freiberg, assigned to XII. Armeekorps). Remarkably this was increased in the reserve corps to one per division (RJB 12 and 13 with XII. Reservekorps and RJB 25 and 26 with XXVII. Reservekorps), though these mostly lacked machine-guns at first and never had cycle companies.

JB 13 began the war on detached duty with the army cavalry (Garde-Kavallerie-Division and 5. Kavallerie-Division). Rejoining XIX. Armeekorps on 21 August 1914, it fought in the Battle of the Marne and subsequent withdrawal to the Suippe with 3. Armee. Together with the bulk of the corps, JB 13 was sent marching north from the Champagne to French Flanders on 4 October as part of the 'Race to the Sea'.

After a punishing march of 25–30 km per day in withering heat, the *jägers* reached the Canal de la Deûle west of Lille on 12 October. Here they were welcomed by French civilians who assumed their unusual uniform was British.

A local woman seemingly selling food to a group of *jägers* while they await deployment in the baggage lines with their rifles stacked.

A platoon infiltrated the citadel grounds before being ordered back ahead of the bombardment, and JB 13 remained in reserve at Pérenchies and Englos during the storming and occupation of the city.

Early on 15 October the battalion was sent forward to Armentières. Together with Ulanen-Regiment 18 (one of the corps' two cavalry regiments), it was ordered to fight a delaying action on a roughly 8km-line along the Lys. What may have been the first clash between the British and Saxon armies took place around 7pm at Pont de Nieppe, where 1st Battalion / The Hampshire Regiment was repelled by a single machine-gun of JB 13. On the evening of 16 October the *jägers* were ordered to withdraw and regroup in alarm quarters at Lomme.

XIX. AK now went on the offensive, to prevent British III Corps at Armentières from sending reinforcements to oppose 4. Armee's drive on Ypres. On the night of 19–20 October JB 13 concentrated at L'Aventure farm for the assault on L'Epinette. The battalion history describes this hamlet as a loose collection of farms in a flat landscape without landmarks for orientation. The criss-crossing network of drainage ditches, fences and poplar avenues offered little cover but plenty of obstacles to advancing troops.

The first attack early on 20 October made little progress, and the edge of L'Epinette was only reached by the second attack on the evening of the 21st. Some *jägers* entered the village, but lacked support and finally had to withdraw to avoid being cut off. After the arrival of a shipment of replacements from Saxony, the battalion launched its third attack on L'Epinette on the morning of 23 October. Lacking adequate artillery support, the attackers struggled to advance under intense defensive fire. This was most severe on the right, where 4. Kompagnie gained a few hundred metres before being forced to dig in, making desperate use of hands, bayonets and cutlery in the soft ground. Nevertheless Brune Rue was secured, and Pont Ballot put under so much pressure that it was soon abandoned by the British and occupied by the *jägers*.

The line held by Jäger-Bataillon 13. 'R.K.' is the 2. Radfahrer-Kompagnie, which was 'at times' inserted on the right at Pont Ballot.

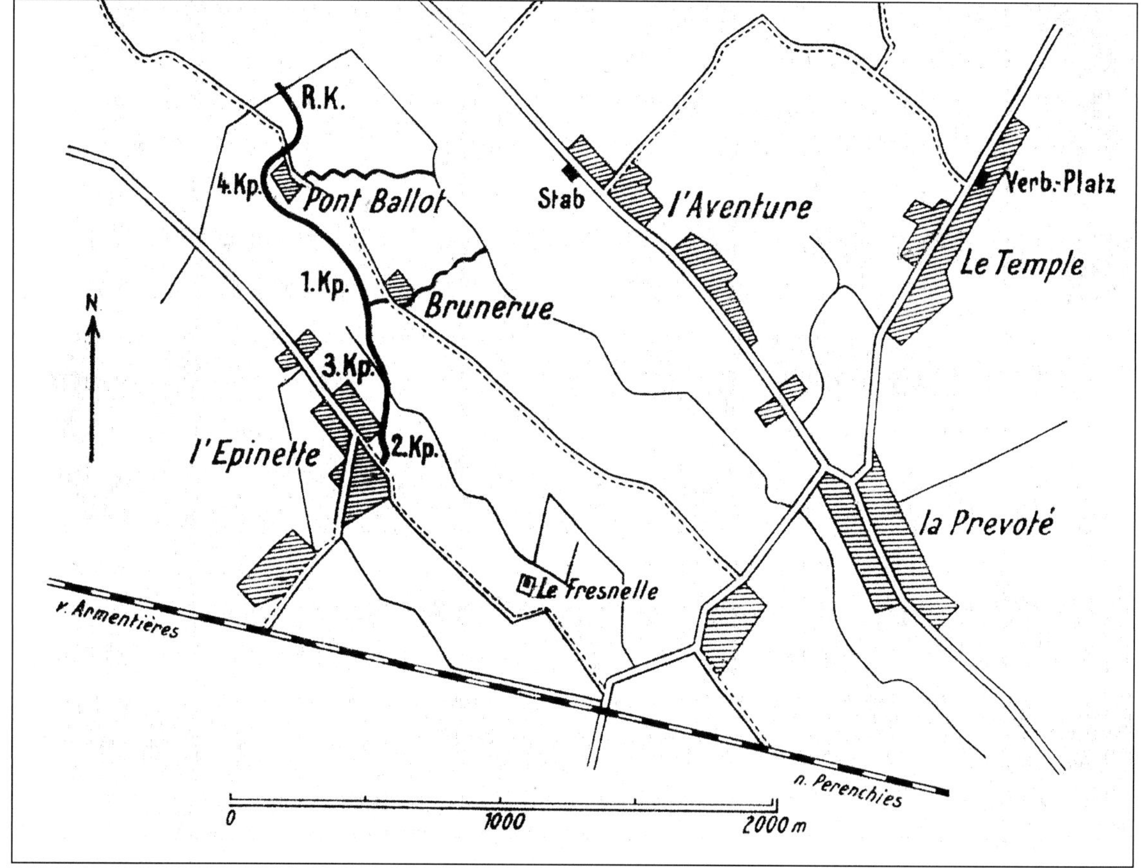

Trench warfare at L'Epinette

This final attack established the line which JB 13 would hold for the next six weeks, at a cost of forty-one dead and many more wounded – including its commander, Major Freiherr von Uslar-Gleichen. The battalion history recalls the onset of trench warfare as follows:

A continuous trench was laid out, which led from there [Pont Ballot] *via Brune Rue to the eastward houses of L'Epinette. The left flank too gained ground. … 2. Kompagnie drove hostile patrols out of the houses to their front, of which one with green shutters was especially conspicuous, and put them firmly under occupation. Thus the* [opposing] *lines here came within a few metres of each other. The houses provided convenient sentry posts from which one could see right into the enemy line.*
From the trenches out of which the enemy had been driven in the course of the fighting, many an interesting and valuable item was salvaged: English rounds, the tip of which could be broken off with a special mechanism on the rifle,[3] *a camera and large tins of preserved meat, the corned beef which would later become so well-known. All forces were directed towards the development of our positions. … At the time we looked upon what we were creating with great pride. To be sure, it would not have stood up to a critical eye sharpened by experience of the subsequent war years. But we knew no other way, and so what was primitive and inadequate, even downright wrong, seemed to us back then magnificent and perfect. The ground and the time of year favoured our earthworks. The heavy clay soil was easy to work and held up well. Thus a man-deep trench soon came into being; admittedly in the 4. Kompagnie line, visitors from the 1. Kompagnie still had to go bent double, if they did not wish to expose themselves to enemy fire. From the trench listening saps were driven forward, and construction of an obstacle line was started. 30–40 metres in front of the trench a smooth wire was laid slightly above ground level as a tripwire. Soon one more and then another were added, and when the obstacle had grown to five wires, it seemed to us almost too much of a good thing.*

Heads and shoulders exposed above the parapet show that this rudimentary and overcrowded trench is not under direct enemy observation.

The traditional tschako of the Saxon *jägers* with its horsehair plume, incongruously combined with homemade woollens. The *oberjäger* above has torn sandbags tied over his boot-tops as a first attempt at puttees, and carries a stick to help him keep his footing in the mud.

A more developed trench section with a high sandbag wall. Note the disposable cloth bandoliers for extra rifle ammunition.

A *gefreiter* cooking potatoes (found locally in abundance at this stage of the war) in his mess tin over a small trench stove.

Dugouts too were created, admittedly neither deep nor concreted. The work had to be done with makeshift materials. No limits were set on the ingenuity and drive of the individual. The easiest way was to drive a tunnel into the earth, following the example of the rabbits, and widen it into a burrow below ground. The ground allowed this. Holes made by earthworms in the ceiling could be plugged with cigarette butts if one desired. More advanced students dug a pit, which they covered with wood and soil. It was certainly dark in there, but nevertheless one had protection from the roughest inclemencies of the weather. The frogs soon noticed this, for they visited the dugouts in large numbers at night.

When it became known that our residence in this position could last a long time, and the weather grew increasingly rough and inclement, it was decided to build more solid dugouts, using the building materials found in abundance in the surrounding shot-up houses. Spacious holes in the ground were covered over and furnished with doors, yes and windows too. What was built back then, would certainly have been described with disdain later as a shack; at the time one felt completely bulletproof in these dugouts, and hence also devoted a lot of love and care to their furnishings and interior decoration. Signs were put up – names were given to the dugouts, and attempts made at poetry. ...

Of course, everything built at that time was, as soon became apparent - fortunately only to those who came after us – completely useless. The unusually dry and cold autumn by local standards had so far prevented us from detecting the main pitfalls of this flat landscape criss-crossed with drainage ditches, which would turn into a swamp under incessant rain in the winter. The 2. Kompagnie had indeed laid their position in a drainage ditch, which they took to be dried up, and which they put great effort into paving. But at this time a severe, if occasionally interrupted, frost froze the ground solid in fine weather.

Thus once the initial furnishings were in place, a merry and restful life ensued in the line. Never again would the food be as good as it was back then. The provisioning of the XIX. AK for six weeks had been imposed on Lille as a contribution at its surrender. But that was not all! The land in front of and within our positions was also turned to good use. Many vegetables, such as red cabbage and Brussels sprouts, grew in the numerous fertile gardens and fields. The stray livestock was particularly appreciated. The chickens, not so rare at first, were soon wiped out. Many a jäger had the expert knack of lopping off the head of the fleeing, loudly cackling kochgeschirr-aspirant[4] *with a bayonet. The herds of cattle, which drifted*

An early trench reinforced only with a few motley sandbags. A *pionier* of Pionier-Bataillon 14 is at work among the *jägers* with his shovel.

freely across the numerous meadows in and in front of our positions, persisted for longer. Admittedly some had fallen in the battles and their distended carcasses tainted the air. It was not a pleasant task to bury them, and for a long time the 1. and 3. Kompagnie argued over the status of a cow that had fallen on their border. But a lot of livestock had survived that period. So the butchers in the ranks of the companies were summoned, and every day each jäger had something he could cook up in the cooking holes. … Eventually of course this delight too came to an end. One day the great farm dog of Brune Rue disappeared and hung neatly slaughtered in place of a calf at the artillery lines in the rear, while at the front in the trenches veal goulash was eaten. The connection between these events remained unclear, but the jägers *were loath to pass by a certain battery position on the following days.*

The 1. Kompagnie had drawn the finest lot with the farmhouse at Brune Rue. … At the pump of the farm there was water, which, like the water in Flanders in general, could not be drunk unboiled because of the risk of typhoid fever. A coal heap which had caught fire and continued to smoulder for a long time relieved them of the effort of making fires. The farm itself was admittedly quite smashed up, and suffered more daily from the continued shelling. But one could nevertheless walk around in the shelter of the solid perimeter walls and stand upright from one's crouching posture in the trench. In a wagon shed the company commander even found a room which was mistakenly reckoned bulletproof and used during the day. By straightforward means it proved possible to render it almost habitable, and as a result it became a favourite object of visits by officers of the neighbouring companies.

And yet service in the trenches was not easy. Besides work on the trenches themselves, sentry duty depleted one's strength. At dawn and dusk, which were reckoned especially dangerous for us, everyone stood to for action in the trench. At night half of the trench garrison kept watch, further reinforced by the Landwehr-Kompagnie Stiefel, which consisted of Lorrainers – some of them French-speaking. One always had to reckon on a surprise attack, and the rifles lay to our front on the parapet. Patrols were conducted against the enemy. Thus on 30 October, Gefreiter Mühlberg of 3. Kompagnie established that the three trenches closest to us were unoccupied by the enemy. The entire battalion held a single trench line without reserves. A breakthrough at any point would have been disastrous.

In the bitterly cold nights, the juniper gin which was provided was very welcome. It burned to be sure, but on the other hand it warmed. When eight days later the order came that it con-

On watch with scarves and gloves. This wooden frame can be covered with *zeltbahnen* (waterproof tent sheets) to protect sentries from rain.

A front-line trench densely occupied by unshaven but alert riflemen, supervised by a pipe-smoking *oberjäger*. Post from home is now reaching the battalion, as the newspaper being perused with interest below indicates.

Woollen knee-warmers for extra warmth. Note the 'funk hole' in the trench wall and sentry with early stick grenades in the background.

tained 90 % alcohol and should therefore be mixed with the same amount of water before drinking, we had already become accustomed to this strength.

Finally our connection to the homeland also grew closer. The post came consistently and in short order, bringing letters, parcels and newspapers. Liebesgaben[5] *arrived in abundance, indeed in overabundance, above all woollens. Socks, cardigans and gloves were very welcome in the cold. ... Back then no-one had any notion of the coming shortages.*

Only one thing was beyond hope; the dirt of the trenches could not be escaped. A thick clay crust fastened itself on the clothing; and to wash thoroughly outdoors in the cold was also not among our amenities. No razor had touched our cheeks for weeks and some wore a handsome beard. The rougher a warrior was on the outside, the better. ...

Our otherwise low losses were increased when a gable of Brune Rue farm collapsed due to storm damage, burying under its rubble the wounded who had been lodged in the shelter of a stable, together with the excellent Sanitäts-Oberjäger Franke (1. Kompagnie). On 23 November the enemy shelled Brune Rue by day. In the fully occupied company commander's dugout a dud threw bricks at the sleeping Oltn. Decker's head and tore the chair out from under another officer; an artillery observation post was also hit. The farmhouse was now finally abandoned. Elsewhere the enemy also began to shell our trenches with his new sulphur shells,[6] which produced a large cloud of smoke upon detonation and stained a wide area around the point of impact yellow.

It was a gratefully welcomed relief when, from 26 November, a quarter of the company at a time (rotated every eight days) was withdrawn to Pérenchies in reserve. Here, where part of the population still resided, one could breathe easily, clean oneself thoroughly, get a whole night's uninterrupted sleep under a roof and take a stroll. Field church services were also held here. ...

At the beginning of December, the weather took a turn for the worse. It began to rain and the clay grew slimy. That was nothing unusual. But the rain did not stop. The water stood in puddles in the trenches and on and on it rained. The umbrellas we had found gave only inadequate protection. It also became uncomfortable to walk through the trenches. The sentries placed a roof tile at their posts so as not to stand in water. Soon a second had to be placed on top, as the flood rose ever higher and the rain kept falling without pause. Anxiously we asked ourselves what this might lead to, but we were relieved of this worry by the 139ers, who came wading through the trenches on 5 December to relieve us. Now we went back, at first to Pérenchies and from there on to Lille.[7]

Sanitäter (first-aiders) playing chess in the trenches of 4. Kompagnie at Pont Ballot.

Besides practical salvage, abandoned houses also yielded sources of passing amusement like this top hat. The unmilitary scruffiness of this cheerful group in their winter woollies contrasts starkly with the menacing shape of a Maxim MG08 on the parapet behind them.

The walls of this communication trench near Brune Rue are already being held in place by wooden boards and posts secured with wire.

Jäger-Bataillon 13 celebrated Christmas 1914 in Lille, mostly in good billets. On the back of this photo however 'Otto' writes: *We spent Christmas Eve at rest in an old shack, where the roof threatened to collapse at any moment. Nevertheless it was a little like being at home.*

Postscript: Jäger-Bataillon 13 at war December 1914 – November 1918

For the next three weeks the *jägers* enjoyed the amenities of the largely undamaged city of Lille, where they celebrated Christmas. On 29 December they relieved JB 10 on the south bank of the Douve near Warneton (see chapter 3), where they suffered the full effects of the winter weather.Three weeks of relentless and still ongoing rain had turned the riverbank into a swamp, and thetrenches were ankle deep (in some places, knee deep) in filthy water and thick mud. Flooded dugouts collapsed, sometimes to deadly effect. Movement in the trenches was near-impossible, and the Christmas Truce tacitly persisted here while both sides focused on the struggle with the weather. Around New Year's Eve newspapers and gifts were surreptitiously exchanged. When Ojg. Blumenstengel and Gefr. Hummel of 2./JB 13 dared to meet the British by day in No Man's Land (in violation of the recent OHL anti-fraternisation order) they got the task of burying a rotting cow as punishment. The truce ended on 20 January when a man from 3.Kompagnie was wounded. Meanwhile a new trench line had been dug under *pionier* direction behind the flooded one, with well-sloped walls and gutters to drain rainwater into the river. Very shallow waterproof dugouts helped to make conditions far more bearable once this line was occupied on 10 January.

In March 1915 the battalion took part in severe fighting for the *Lorettohöhe* (Notre Dame de Lorette, near Vimy Ridge), returning to Warneton from the end of March to 4 May. After a second tour at the *Lorettohöhe*, it again rejoined XIX.AK and held the Frelinghien sector on the Lys (see chapter 2) from 19 June to 25 August. The battalion spent the rest of 1915 at Beaurains near Arras. In 1916 it was recommitted on the XIX.AK front, partly in its original positions near L'Epinette. JB 13 left the corps permanently on 31 July 1916 to become part of the new Saxon Jäger-Regiment 7 (within the likewise new 197. Infanterie-Division) together with RJB 25 and 26. The new division was transported to the Eastern Front to support the Austro-Hungarians in Galicia. After the Russian collapse it returned to the west in February 1918, where it fought in the spring offensive on the Chemin des Dames. The *jäger* regiment subsequently served on the Verdun front and in increasingly desperate defensive fighting near Noyon and later northeast of St Quentin. Here the 197. ID was so badly mauled that it and its other regiments were dissolved, and Jäger-Regiment 7 spent the final weeks fighting with Saxon 241. ID until the armistice.

View of Belgian Warneton from the small French island in the Lys in early 1915, with a Saxon *jäger* relaxing in the foreground.

Chapter 2
The Breweries at Frelinghien

A private soldier and two NCOs of Jäger-Bataillon 13 in the *Südbrauerei* south of Frelinghien village in summer 1915. Although the roof has taken a battering from artillery, the wall behind the *jägers* is still largely intact and has been reinforced with sandbags and beer barrels full of earth.

The Breweries at Frelinghien

... where beer was seldom the main concern

The word 'brewery' immediately evokes beer, but although they both had well-stocked cellars when initially captured, the fame and significance of the breweries at Frelinghien for the men of the Royal Saxon Army had almost no relation to their produce. The reasons are obvious when one considers their positions on the battlefield of autumn 1914 and in the subsequent years of trench warfare.The village of Frelinghien had two breweries, both on the east (French) bank of the Lys north-east of Armentières. Both were extensive and heavily built structures, with capacious cellars offering plenty of safe space for accommodation, storage and amenities such as baths.

The so-called ***Nordbrauerei*** (Northern Brewery–often marked on British maps as a 'dye works') stood beside the main bridge to Le Touquet. Together with most of the town, it fell into Saxon hands during the advance from Lille, and its possession was undisputed while XIX. Armeekorps was in residence. Since the crossing here (soon reduced to a footbridge after the destruction of the original structure) formed the only direct route to the Saxon bridgehead at Le Touquet, the *Nordbrauerei* was vital not only for observation and the accommodation of reserves, but also for the defense of their approach to the front line.

The ***Südbrauerei*** (Southern or Lutun Brewery) lay outside the village proper and was the 'Frelinghien Brewery' known to the British. It was briefly captured by them on 20 October 1914, creating an intolerable threat to Saxon control of the town. This was successfully eliminated on 26 October in a dramatic shock assault supported by two heavy *minenwerfers* of the army *pioniere,* after which the *Südbrauerei* remained firmly in the hands of XIX. Armeekorps throughout its residence.

Both breweries were conspicuous and attractive artillery targets, intermittently enduring the worst shelling the nominally 'quiet' XIX. Armeekorps front had to offer. Despite much damage above ground, their outer walls were still largely intact and their deep cellars secure when the Saxons left for the Somme.

Although the French-style beer from both breweries appealed neither to the British nor the Germans, it won a small place in history at the 1914 Christmas Truce. The famous cask presented to the 2nd Battalion Royal Welsh Fusiliers by 'Count something or other' (probably Hptm. Wilhelm Graf Vitzthum von Eckstädt) of II. Batl. / IR134 almost certainly came from the the *Südbrauerei.*

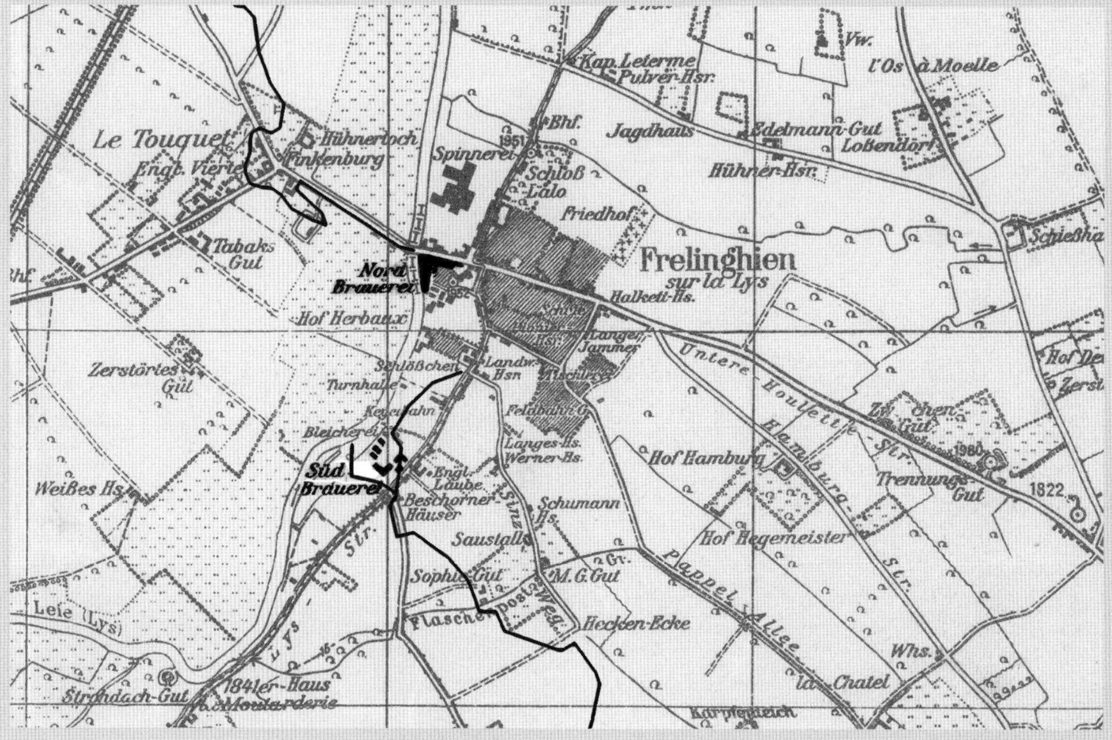

The war reaches Frelinghien

On 15 October, while the cavalry and *jägers* of XIX. Armeekorps were sent to delay the British on the Lys west of Armentières, 24. Infanterie-Division deployed 47. Infanterie-Brigade (IR 139 and 179) to cover Lille; its sister 48. Infanterie-Brigade (IR 106 and 107) would not arrive from Champagne until a week later.

On the right, 40. Infanterie-Division advanced to the Lys between Warneton and Frelingien. When British 10th Brigade / 6th Division advanced from Houplines to seize the town on the 18th, it encountered a trench line lightly held by elements of IR 133 and supported by snipers in the *Südbrauerei* to its rear. The British dug in around the bottom of the map on p. 20, improving their position on the afternoon of the 19th when 2nd Battalion Seaforth Highlanders on their left occupied several houses by crawling along the riverbank. From here they stormed the Saxon trenches on 20 October, taking around fifty prisoners and occupying the brewery and adjacent houses.

This came just in time to stymie the advance of the main body of 89. Infanterie-Brigade (IR 133 and 134) in conjunction with attacks all along the corps front. Initially II. Batl. / IR 133 was committed at Frelinghien, soon joined by II. Batl. / IR 134 from the corps reserve at La Croix au Bois. On the west bank the detached III. Batl. / IR 104 struggled southward from Le Touquet across open swampy ground, where the numerous drainage ditches were filled to the brim with water as much as six feet deep. The regimental history describes how the Seaforths in the *Südbrauerei* further hindered their efforts:

This area is dominated from the east by the large brewery, situated on the other bank of the Lys on a hill close to the river, which is separated from the main part of the village of Frelinghien by a strip of open field 300m in width, and which acts like a castle due to its heavy masonry. The English [sic.] *had firmly rooted themselves there, and by massing their machine-guns had prevented any German advance either against the front of this fortress or on their flanks. Against the massive masonry and the thick, vaulted ceilings, even the heavy field howitzers with the ammunition available to them at the time were not sufficiently effective to render the enemy stronghold ripe for assault.*[1]

The battalions of IR 133 and 134 on the east bank were equally unable to advance within view of the brewery, which dominated the southern part of the village with persistent and deadly accurate rifle and machine-gun fire. Clearly, the village would not be secured until the British had been ejected from the brewery and adjacent houses.

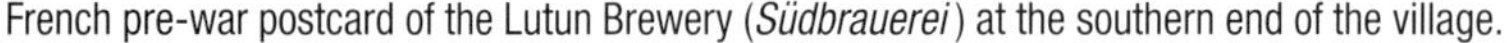
French pre-war postcard of the Lutun Brewery (*Südbrauerei*) at the southern end of the village.

The *Südbrauerei*

The operation to retake the brewery was assigned to Major Johannes Larraß of IR 104, at the head of an ad-hoc Regiment Larraß (II./133, II./134 and III./104). The major became its first casualty on 21 October, killed by a sniper while conducting initial reconnaissance with Obstltn. Vollert of Feldartillerie-Regiment 32. Hptm. Rühle von Lilienstern (II./134) now took command of the renamed *Regiment von Rühle*. It was initially hoped to render the brewery *sturmreif* (ripe for assault) with heavy artillery. The limited number of shells available failed to inflict much visible damage, although the defenders were forced to take cover in the cellars. Finally two 25cm heavy *minenwerfers* were brought up on the night of 25–26 October for an attack the next day. Johannes Niemann (see p. 190) claims in his history of IR 133 that these short-range siege weapons were emplaced behind the *Nordbrauerei* and provides a map (see below). More plausibly, the regimental history of IR 134 places them in the courtyard of Frelinghien chateau.

The defending 2nd Battalion Seaforth Highlanders had never encountered such a weapon and was shocked by the effect of its 97 kg shells:

About 6 am a report was heard and a large shell was observed to drop into a building in the brewery. It did not burst, and on being searched for was found in an outhouse. It measured 3 ft to 3 ft 6 ins in length and was about 11 ins across the base. Very shortly afterwards another dropped, and burst with great effect demolishing a house. The shell could be distinctly seen in the air, and was apparently fired from very close range; it did not fly point forwards, but anyhow sometimes landing on its base and sometimes on its side. As it appeared useless to remain in buildings, the men were ordered into the trenches, and the shelling continued for some two hours doing great damage whenever the shells fell in buildings.[2]

The regimental history of IR 134 states that the bleachery in front of the brewery was obliterated, while huge chunks of wall, iron girders and rooves flew about in the air like feathers. The Seaforths were still struggling to evacuate the brewery when the Saxons attacked.

Sketch of the storming of the *Südbrauerei* on 26 October 1914 from the 1969 history of IR 133 by Johannes Niemann, who received his commission as a leutnant ten days before the attack.

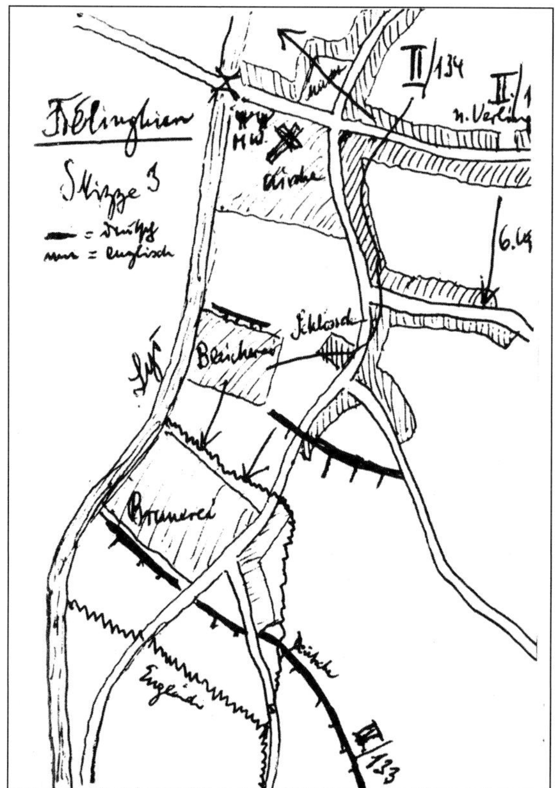

Captured largely intact despite the use of *minenwerfers*, the *Südbrauerei* was subsequently fortified by the Saxons and shelled into ruins by British artillery (see also photos on the following pages).

The last doubts regarding the possibility of success entirely evaporated. A mood of great elation prevailed among all taking part in the assault of 8./134. Unfortunately the brewery itself could not be reached by the minenwerfer *fire and remained completely intact. Two platoons as first wave and a third platoon of men from IR133 as second wave were placed in readiness. The 7./134 had occupied the* [previous] *positions of 8./134. The following assault order was decreed:* [leather] *helmet, buckled equipment without backpack or greatcoat (as it would be necessary to crawl through several wire fences).*

With the final (thirty-second) minenwerfer *shot, two platoons of assault troops stormed forward at the double as far as the gymnasium situated about halfway* [to the brewery], *where the attached* pioniere *and infantrymen equipped with wire-cutters cut through the fences as quickly as possible. Vigorous enemy shrapnel fire ensued from the direction of Le Touquet and Le Bizet. At a sign the third platoon now also followed up. After scarcely a minute the advance resumed, and the storm troops now reached the courtyard of the u-shaped brewery. Furious infantry fire greeted them from the windows of the third storey. Nevertheless in next to no time the doors were broken in and entry was forced. Shaken by the* minenwerfer *fire and surprised by the sudden and energetic assault, the English* [sic.] *were quite stunned, and after a short and desperate melee they were driven out through the windows and exits on the side facing the enemy. They tried to escape by making head over heels for a trench about 100m to their rear. In all probability none of them achieved their goal, as they fell victim to the well-aimed fire of our men. In a large beer cellar full of filled barrels, some Englishmen were on the point of taking numerous large mailbags to safety via the rear-facing windows. Upon catching sight of our men they sprang as if on command through the rear-facing windows, abandoning their mail, and within moments were dispatched by the pursuing fire of our men. The English* [sic] *garrison of the brewery consisted of the well-known 28th Seaforth Highlanders from Edinburgh.* [sic.] *The regiment consisted only of huge, magnificently well-built men and was regarded in England as one of the most prestigious.*

Around 1pm the successful storming of the brewery could be reported. In all manner of chambers within the building the English had established a large stockpile of ammunition, food etc, which fell into our hands. Work was immediately started with all available means on the development of the position. The windows and doorways facing the enemy were bricked up, loopholes built in and a trench dug from the brewery to the Lys.

Credit for the success of the assault with so few men was, besides the excellent effect of the minenwerfers, *principally due to the grit and death-defying bravery of the force, which broke cover without a second thought when the last* minenwerfer *shell was still in the barrel and, by their speed and the impetus of the break-in, drove a significantly numerically superior foe from the huge and completely intact brewery, inflicting very severe losses upon him. Our own losses were acceptable.*[3]

Niemann's history of IR133 adds:

The bombardment was mainly conducted by heavy minenwerfers *emplaced behind the* Nordbrauerei. *Two platoons of II./134 as first wave and a platoon from II./133 as second wave under Hptm. Pechwell stormed forward out of the* Nordbrauerei *and the houses along the Verlinghem road after the last* minenwerfer *shots, despite artillery fire and rifle fire from the three floors of the brewery, and occupied the groups of houses to its front. II./133 held back here while the 134ers stormed further forward into the courtyard of the brewery with Ltn. Enck in the lead, broke in the windows and doors and forced entry into the buildings with their metre-thick walls. The Scots from the 28th Seaforth Highland Regiment* [sic] *were surprised and likely demoralised by the* minenwerfer *fire. They were well-built men and belonged to one of the most prestigious British regiments. The church of Frelinghien had meanwhile gone up in flames. The entire village, including the brewery, now rested in German hands. On the left contact was established with the trenches of IR133, which extended as far as the last houses of Frelinghien.*[4]

Since the British still held the trench taken on 20 October, the *Südbrauerei* now lay in the front line within 200 metres of the enemy. They made no real attempt to retake it, but frequently shelled it to little effect. Despite this, the brewery garden became a favourite venue for morning prayers. On 2 February 1915, 9./IR104 held an evening service in the courtyard. The altar was adorned with duds and shell fragments, and a piano was found. Due to the proximity of the enemy, the volume of music and singing was greatly constrained.

When each division was permanently reduced to three infantry regiments in early March the Lys became the interdivisional boundary. Henceforth the *Südbrauerei* was held by the reunited IR133 as the right flank of 24. ID, with II./134 still attached until the corps was obliged to cede both regiments from its quiet front to army reserve at the end of May, receiving the Prussian 38. Landwehr-Brigade (Landwehr-Infanterie-Regiment 77 and 78) in exchange. LIR78 held the brewery until JB13 returned from the fighting for the *Lorettohöhe* to relieve them on 19 June. The battalion history of the *jägers* remarks how:

... its half-destroyed tangle of fixtures, its huge cellars and machine rooms made it a hard nut to crack. Agitation arose in the middle of August when wooden debris and stock remnants there were set alight, presumably by a flare. The task of extinguishing it was a difficult one, because the site of the fire was difficult to reach and the English disrupted the work. Nevertheless, the fire was successfully reduced to its source.[5]

The *jägers* were irritated to learn that their agreeably quiet new sector was now a showpiece for visitors, similar to the British 'Tourist Line' in Ploegsteert Wood. Extreme standards of order and cleanliness were enforced, and so much as a cigarette end on the duckboards was a punishable offence.

We not only had traffic from front to rear, but also visitors coming forward in the opposite direction. Battlefield tourists who were to be shown something, including war correspondents, artists and others; photographers became a plague.

The otherwise quiet morning hours, which the trench dweller always reckoned particularly good for the nerves to spend sleeping, were occupied with frequent visits by their superiors, who wished to witness for themselves the mood of the troops, the state of the trench and the progress of the work.

NCOs of Jäger-Bataillon 13 in the courtyard of the *Südbrauerei* in summer 1915. Note the overhead telephone lines and heavily reinforced wall.

Nothing escaped their sharp eyes and it would not be tolerated, were the jägers to have stored the previous day's cheese in the waterproof, rat-proof and spacious reserve ammunition boxes.[6] Worse still, since late February low-key mine warfare had been underway near the Houplines road, where No Man's Land was as narrow as 80 metres. On both sides most detonations were defensive, damaging the trenches but inflicting few casualties. The *jägers* were relieved on 25 August by LIR77, a nominally Prussian *landwehr* regiment from the annexed Kingdom of Hanover which had previously filled in for both divisions at Ploegsteert Wood (see p. 48) and Pérenchies. Their tour was disturbed only by largely ineffective shelling, until a British mine detonation on 28 December in front of their line; the crater was immediately occupied by the Germans. On 24 January 1916 the regiment's right flank was severely shelled; two days later it beat off a raid, resulting in a very rare award of the Saxon *Militär-St. Heinrichs-Orden* to a Prussian junior officer, Ltn. d. L. Horst Ritter von Schwarze of 6./LIR77. The main threats remained British snipers and flooding in the winter months which even affected the brewery cellars.

At the beginning of March LIR77 was relieved by IR179, previously on the left flank of 24. ID. The sector was still reckoned safe enough for H.M. King Friedrich August III of Saxony to visit both breweries and the fortified crater on 21 March. To alleviate the mining threat, IR179 launched a major raid on 26 April. This succeeded both in the destruction of dugouts and mine entrances and in the identification of the enemy – 9th Battalion Duke of Wellington's (West Riding Regiment) of 52nd Brigade, 17th (Northern) Division.

This British division was relieved on 13 May by the New Zealand Division, making its Western Front debut. By mid-June the Saxons had noticed that the enemy was significantly more active, and identified them from equipment captured by forward patrols. The regimental history of IR179 describes the New Zealanders as restless, active and bold opponents, surpassing all previously encountered English, Scottish and Irish troops in courage. A significant bounty was offered for a captured New Zealander, and a remarkable 80 marks for a genuine Maori – believed to be 'man-eating savages' by the Germans.

At the end of June the entire corps front became intensely active, as the British sought to prevent the transfer of German reserves to the Somme. Inevitably the *Südbrauerei* and adjacent trenches became a regular target for raids and damaging bombardments, while bombers and long-range guns attacked the accommodation areas in the rear. On 30 June both divisions were subjected to severe shelling and a major gas attack. On the night of 2–3 July, IR179 was forced to eject New Zealand raiders from its trenches.

Despite the enemy's best efforts, on 28 July the order arrived for the transfer of the entire XIX. AK to the Somme, after nearly two years on the Lys. On the night of 1–2 August, Prussian IR22 (from 11. Reserve-Division, itself already badly mauled on the Somme) relieved IR179 at Frelinghien.

Periscope-equipped barricade in the *Südbrauerei*. Despite the proximity of the enemy the garrison seems quite relaxed.

Members of 8. Komp. / LIR 77 in the *Südbrauerei* in September 1915.

The *Nordbrauerei*

Whereas the *Südbrauerei* changed hands twice in October 1914 and remained a bulwark of the front line trench system, the *Nordbrauerei* was a reserve position and was disturbed only by artillery fire. Since it was a safe distance from their own lines, even the heaviest British guns could target it when the necessary shells could be spared. Nevertheless the massive main building would still be standing when the Saxons left, albeit badly holed above ground level.

Due to its strategically significant position beside the main Lys bridge, the *Nordbrauerei* dominated the approach from Frelinghien to the front line at Le Touquet and gave artillery observers an excellent view of the British positions on the west bank. Perhaps even more valuably, its cellars provided copious accommodation for reserves, as the regimental history of IR 104 relates:

The III. Bataillon, of which Hptm. Facius had assumed command at the end of 1914, held a position detached from the regiment under the command of 89. Inf. Brig. (commander since 24 December 1914: Genmaj. Hammer) in the curious bridgehead position at Le Touquet, west of Frelinghien. The left flank of the position was the high embankment of the Frelinghien–Le Touquet road, which runs through the damp meadow area along the river. The accommodation of supports and reserves in trenches was impossible there, because even without heavy rain the high water table caused every spade-cut to fill up with water at once. Only where the houses of Le Touquet began was it possible to dig in by using the structures of the town, and to accommodate reserves right behind the front line. The western part of the village, the so-called "Englisches Viertel" [English Quarter] *was in the possession of the enemy, who were separated from us only by a strip of ground barely 30m in width. The right flank of the position was bent back to achieve contact with the northward-neighbouring IR181, so that again there was no space in depth for the establishment of a reserve.*

The only approach to the position from Frelinghien was the high road bridge, the destruction of which the enemy very soon achieved by hits from heavy artillery. A pedestrian walkway at the foot of the bridge took its place. But since it was still visible to the enemy, and they drew a bead at once on anyone who came into view there, a canvas sheet was fastened as protection from observation in the wreckage of the lattice bridge which lay in the river.

In this awkward situation the only possibility of accommodating a reserve at the disposal of the battalion commander was side-on to the position with good fire effect to the front. The solution was offered by the elevated Nordbrauerei *on the east bank of the Lys, in whose great cellars accommodation proof against both bullets and light artillery was available in abundance.*[7]

The huge cellars not only offered plenty of space for reserves and stores, but also fixtures from its former function which were adapted to create communal baths and a laundry. Regrettably the beer that was found here was even less appealing to the German palate than that of the *Südbrauerei*. It is described as a strong top-fermented brew with a sour flavour and a noticeable laxative effect. Most of it was emptied into the Lys, so that the empty casks could be put to better use. As the regimental history of IR104 relates:

In early January the Lys rapidly began to rise and flooded the broad meadowland on the west bank. The footbridge, the solitary connection [between Frelinghien and Le Touquet] *was swept away. Starting on the left flank, one company after another saw itself driven out of its position by the floodwater, until only the one on the extreme right remained. Working by night, Ltn. d. R. Engler of 2./Pionier-Bataillon 22 used casks from the brewery to construct a floating footbridge circa 400m in length, which even withstood the pressure of the water flooding over the high road embankment and secured the connection between the rear and the last company by the most direct route. With the subsiding of the Lys it was not immediately possible to move into the position; the bailing out of the trenches and draining of the dugouts made for heavy work. However the possibility of new construction*

Pre-war view (looking southward) of the *Nordbrauerei* and the bridge over the Lys. The road to Le Touquet is out of shot on the right.

was ruled out due to the cramped nature of the site, so that it was necessary to make do with the existing structures filled with mouldy air.[8]

A far larger quantity of casks were filled with earth and used both in fortifying the brewery and in trench construction. Many went into the walls of the *Tonnenweg* (Barrel Way) near Ploegsteert Wood, together with oil drums and herring barrels when the supply of casks finally ran short (see also p. 43, map p. 45 and photo p. 49).

Like the area of the *Südbrauerei*, the *Nordbrauerei* and the bridgehead at Le Touquet attracted a steady stream of visitors in quiet periods. Representatives of the German and international press, German politicians and foreign military representatives were all seen here.

The experiences of III. Batl. / IR 104 in early 1915 as part of *Regiment von Rühle* are described as follows in their regimental history:

The construction of the trenches in Le Touquet itself differed very substantially from that in the regiment's trenches in the open ground opposite Ploegsteert Wood. The structures of the houses and farmsteads dictated the course of the line, provided building material and offered the possibility of reinforcing and supporting vaulted cellars to create dugouts proof against splinters and to some extent against light calibre [shells]. *On the other hand, it had to be accepted that the corners, angles and breaches through the building walls made the position confusing and that a newcomer required some time to study the area before he could find his way around the labyrinth. The strange construction of the position here and the unusual approach route from the flank over the Lys attracted many visitors – military and non-military, royalty, war correspondents etc.*

On 22 February the military attachés of the currently neutral powers appeared. The battalion commander Hptm. Facius had singled out the one from the United States for special attention by having a beautiful display of English shell fragments assembled, which clearly bore the maker's marks of the American Steel Company and the Bethlehem Steel Corporation. Regrettably the Herr Attaché evaded this ingenious tribute to his "neutral" homeland by staying away.[9]

An unnamed visitor gave the following impressions of the *Nordbrauerei*:

We enter the ruins of a former brewery. Since October no mash tuns have been in operation here, the bent and rusty metalwork lies scattered on the ground.

We carefully climb a flight of stairs and, unseen by the enemy, look westward through a large hole torn out by a shell. The Lys flows right up to our feet, right now no wider than the Deûle in Lille or the Mulde near Zwickau, but at times of flood several

The paired footbridges erected to restore the destroyed Lys crossing. A wooden fence has replaced the canvas screen mentioned in the text.

View taken from the *Nordbrauerei*, looking across the demolished road bridge toward Le Touquet.

hundred metres wide and a monster feared by the soldiers – because it then fills every dugout and trench in its vicinity with its mud-green water.

The iron bridge that formerly led across the river lies shattered in the water, a twisted barrier, but next to it our pioneers have constructed a boardwalk. So this is the Lys, where so many of our brave men drowned, carrying so much German blood slowly out to sea. And a few hundred metres from the western shore I see the elongated line of the English trenches.

I need only step up a metre from my location to the opening of the wall, then a shot will flash out from an English sniper lying in wait over there and kill me. It is a singular feeling.[10]

The sector lost much of its tourist appeal on 9 April 1915. After an intense bombardment and massed rifle fire, there was a huge explosion under the barricaded positions of 10./IR104 in Le Touquet. Since the loss of their first tunnel (begun at the end of 1914) to the winter rains, the 4th Divisional Mining Party had gradually dug their way from the "English Quarter" along the Le Bizet road undetected by the Saxons. Their first mine detonation had cost 10./104 eighteen dead and twenty-three wounded. The crater was immediately occupied and fortified by IR104, and countermining immediately began under the direction of Ltn. d. R. Hermann Stock – in peacetime an architect from Leipzig, and currently commanding 3. Feldkompagnie/Pionier-Bataillon 22.

To the undoubted relief of its men, III. Batl./IR 104 returned to its parent regiment at Ploegsteert Wood on 20 April and ceded Le Touquet and the *Nordbrauerei* to the neighbouring IR181 (see pp. 57–58). The regimental history sums up their feelings in a verse:

> *We part from you quite painlessly,*
> *For you're undermined, my dear Touquet.*[11]

The brewery continued to endure occasional severe bombardments, notably on 28 December 1915 with what were described as 28cm shells. Nevertheless its walls still stood, and its cellars remained a safe refuge for reserves. Two creative attempts were also made to destroy the vital footbridge while the Saxons were in residence. On 11 March 1915 the British had sent a burning raft floating down the river, which was caught upstream in the wreckage of the lattice bridge where it burned out harmlessly. On 19 May 1916 floating sea mines were spotted in the Lys and exploded by small arms fire before they could reach the crossing.

Together with the rest of XIX. AK, IR181 left for the Somme at the beginning of August 1916, leaving Le Touquet and the *Nordbrauerei* in the hands of the Prussian RIR38 (12. Reserve-Division – again, a unit recovering from the battle).

A HUNDRED YEARS LATER

In November 2008 a memorial to the Christmas Truce was formally dedicated in Frelinghien, and a football match played between a Bundeswehr unit based at Marienberg in Saxony and the Royal Welsh (current successors to the fusiliers). Further matches took place in 2014 and 2018. The venue in each case was Frelinghien's village sports field, situated squarely in the no man's land of Christmas 1914 and right in front of the place where the *Südbrauerei* once stood.

View from Frelinghien across the Lys (and the Franco-Belgian border) towards Le Touquet. This bridge crosses the river at the same point as the lattice bridge destroyed in 1914. No trace remains of the adjacent *Nordbrauerei*.

Chapter 3
At Ploegsteert Wood

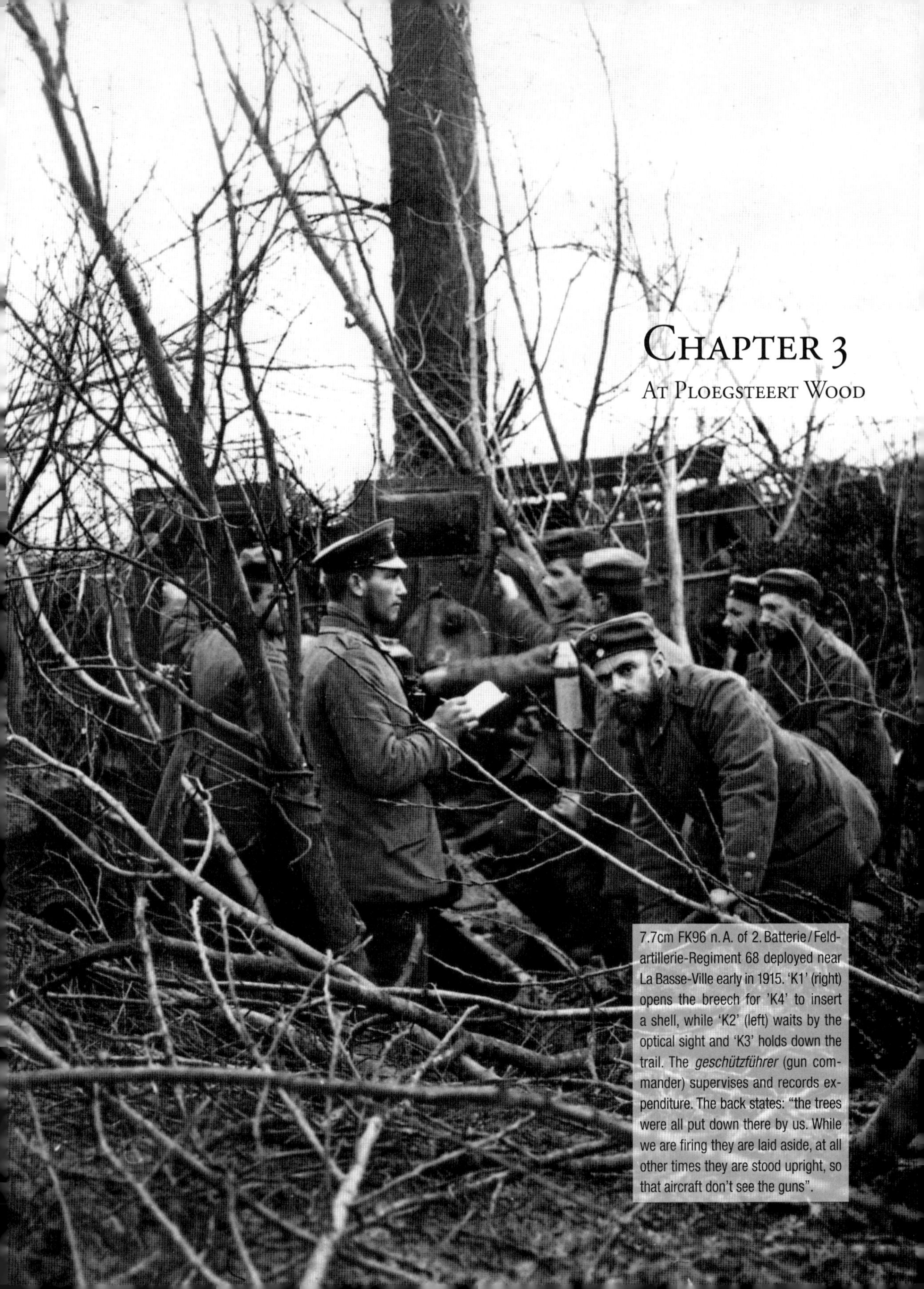

7.7cm FK96 n. A. of 2. Batterie / Feld-artillerie-Regiment 68 deployed near La Basse-Ville early in 1915. 'K1' (right) opens the breech for 'K4' to insert a shell, while 'K2' (left) waits by the optical sight and 'K3' holds down the trail. The *geschützführer* (gun commander) supervises and records expenditure. The back states: "the trees were all put down there by us. While we are firing they are laid aside, at all other times they are stood upright, so that aircraft don't see the guns".

AT PLOEGSTEERT WOOD

Saxon XIX. Armeekorps faces the British 1914–1916

Ploegsteert Wood, the *Ploegsteertwald* of German maps and 'Plugstreet Wood' of British military patois, is modest in size and never held the strategic significance of Messines Ridge to its north or the Lys to its south. It was the scene of major fighting for a few weeks in autumn 1914 and again in 1918, but only in support of larger operations elsewhere. The multiple British cemeteries and Memorial to the Missing (commemorating those left with no known grave as far south as Estaires) nevertheless testify to the thousands of lives lost to the steady grind of routine trench warfare.

The wood looms large in the British folk memory of the war, in part because numerous British (and British Empire) formations gained their first frontline experience in this reliably 'quiet' sector. Thousands of Tommies heard their first shots fired in anger and had their first glimpse of the enemy between the Douve and the Lys. From the arrival of the opposing armies in October 1914 until the end of July 1916 that enemy invariably belonged to the Saxon 40. Infanterie-Division of XIX. Armeekorps, albeit sometimes from a non-Saxon regiment temporarily under its command. Especially during the informal 'live and let live' period of 1915, initial tours here gained a nostalgic glow once units had moved on to more active fronts. This manifested in a peculiar fondness for the Saxons which appears in British personal accounts throughout the war. British anti-German propaganda (unlike that of the French) had always focused near-exclusively on the Prussians, while newspaper coverage of the celebrated Christmas Truce of 1914 strongly emphasised Saxon participation. About half of the truce front' was indeed held by XIX. AK, including the major fraternisation areas of Wez-Macquart, Frelinghien and Ploegsteert Wood. The famous photos taken on Christmas Day by men of the London Rifle Brigade and the sketches of Bruce Bairnsfather (who would go on to develop "Old Bill" while resident in this sector) both depict scenes in the 40. ID sector near the wood. Interestingly, British first-hand accounts repeatedly misidentify non-trucing Saxon units (such as IR 179 on the left flank of 24. ID near Bois Grenier) as Prussian and trucing Prussian units as Saxon. Some Westphalians of VII. AK further south may even have claimed to be Saxon to facilitate fraternisation, suggesting not only that the Royal Saxon Army already had a certain reputation within the BEF but also that other German contingents were aware of this.

Throughout 1915 the Saxon corps turned this reputation to its military advantage, and could easily justify its tacit policy of 'live and let live' by pointing both to its low expenditure of lives and ammunition and to its continual maintenance of a strong body of reserves for use elsewhere. Its 'quiet' front nevertheless saw a steady trickle of deaths from 'routine' shelling, sniping and forward patrols. It also had notoriously dangerous spots, mainly where the lines were close enough for offensive mining by the British. At Ploegsteert Wood the focus was the Le Pelerin salient, known to the Germans as the *Entenschnabel* ('duck's bill') for its shape and to the British as the 'Birdcage' for its dense wire entanglements. The site remains notorious today for its three unexploded mines, prepared for but ultimately not used in what became the Battle of Messines on 7 June 1917 (because the Germans had already retired from this position). From January 1916 onward the British permanently disrupted 'live and let live' on the Saxon front with an aggressive raiding policy, so that the *Entenschnabel* and the British lines on its flanks became repeated targets of raids and counter-raids. South of the wood, the partitioned village of Le Touquet was similarly afflicted by both mining and raiding. By the time XIX. AK finally left at the beginning of August 1916, the sector was marked by frequent artillery exchanges and continual minor operations. On the Somme the corps would go on to earn an entirely different reputation for its relentlessly stubborn defence of Martinpuich, High Wood and later the infamous Butte de Warlencourt.

The Royal Saxon Army would return to Ploegsteert Wood from late May to August 1918, when the old British positions served intermittently as accomodation for reserves of 58. Infanterie-Division (see *Fighting the Kaiser's War* p. 162). This had been formed in March 1915 mainly with units donated by XIX. AK, including IR 106 – which had taken a major part both in the fighting for the wood in autumn 1914 and in the fraternisation there that Christmas.

This chapter focuses exclusively on the experiences of 40. ID in the vicinity of Ploegsteert Wood in 1914–1916. We hope that when our readers visit this popular focus of British front pilgrimages, they may also feel inspired to explore the places where the Saxon garrison lived and fought for the best part of two years. Unusually, many of their graves can also still be seen today at their original resting place – the *ehrenfriedhof* in Quesnoy-sur-Deûle (see p. 242).

The battle for Ploegsteert Wood

The first German troops at Ploegsteert Wood were undoubtedly army cavalry from one of the multiple *höhere kavallerie-kommandos* (cavalry corps) operating to the right of 6. Armee; Hessian Husaren-Regiment 13 of 6. Kavallerie-Division (HKK 4) lost a man killed on patrol at Ploegsteert as early as 8 October. At the opening of the German push toward Ypres on 20 October, this lightly-armed mass of now-dismounted cavalry and *jägers* under the command of General der Kavallerie von der Marwitz had the primary task of holding the line between the flanks of 4. and 6. Armee – respectively formed by the Saxon-Württemberg XXVII. Reservekorps at Gheluvelt (Geluveld) on the Menin Road and Saxon XIX. Armeekorps north of Armentières. The cavalry also actively joined in the offensive as far as its means allowed, attacking between Zandvoorde and Kruiseik from 25 October in direct support of XXVII. RK. It was however soon clear that von der Marwitz lacked the numerical strength or firepower to provide the southern pincer needed to turn the advance of Prussian XXIII. RK at Bikschote (northwest of Ypres) into an encirclement of the city. Hence on 30 October the newly formed *Armeegruppe Fabeck* (with six mainly pre-war 'active' divisions) was inserted between Messines and Gheluvelt. The grievously depleted and demoralised XXVII. RK was now called upon to resume its ruinous attacks north of the Menin Road in support of the renewal of the offensive by von Fabeck's fresh troops (see chapter 4).

Meanwhile on the front of 6. Armee, XIX. AK had stormed the weakly held French fortress city of Lille on 12 October and immediately began to establish defensive positions on the city's western and northern perimeter. On the morning of 15 October, 88. Infanterie-Brigade of 40. Infanterie-Division (forming the extreme right flank of the corps) advanced to form a defensive line on the east bank of the Lys from Frelinghien to Warneton, held mainly by IR 104 with all three battalions abreast. III. / IR 181 held the southern edge of Warneton, and cleared the town of British cavalry on the 17th. For the advance on the morning of 20 October this front was dramatically shortened. I. and II. / 104 crossed the Lys respectively by boat and via the Saxon-held bridge at Pont Rouge to take up position on the railway embankment. IR 181 was inserted on their left between Pont Rouge and the

Situation at Ploegsteert Wood as of 30 October 1914. On the extreme right flank of 6. Armee, Saxon 40. ID attacks the British III Corps in concert with H.K.K.1 (army cavalry). Meanwhile Gruppe Fabeck attacks Allenby's Cavalry Corps north of the Douve.

Le Touquet bridgehead, where III./104 remained in place and thus began an extended period cut off from its parent regiment. Units of Prussian 4. Kavallerie-Division filled in the gap on the right of the reduced 40. ID front, with Jäger-Bataillon 7 south of La Basse-Ville in contact with I./104. The attack was due to start at 9.00 am after a two-hour bombardment, but it was not until 11.00 am that the other units (suffering from heavier going underfoot and less cover) had come level with I. and II./104 on the embankment. Between this line and the wood lay over a kilometre of open ground, criss-crossed with wire fences and hedges which impeded movement while providing convenient range markers for the British machine-guns. With skilled use of fire and movement and supported by their own MGK on the embankment, IR 104 got within 300 metres of the wood by evening and dug in, though the units on their flanks remained bogged down near their start lines.

On 21 October the regiment launched a daring surprise attack with no artillery preparation, creeping forward in silence under cover of morning mist before charging at 6.30 am with the battalion colours of 1870 flying (for the last time in action) and a sudden cry of 'hurra!'. In the wood and at Le Gheer (where 2nd Btn. Royal Inniskilling Fusiliers was overrun) the British were overwhelmed in close combat, while in the open ground south of the wood they were put to flight. Three officers, fifty men and two machine-guns were captured, and the acting regimental commander Obstltn. Eckardt[1] ordered IR 104 to press on. With a much greater distance to cover over treacherous ground, IR 181 and JB 7 had however been halted once again by defensive fire far short of their objectives. Without flank support, IR 104 came under an encircling counterattack from elements of four British battalions. Unwilling to abandon his regiment's gains, it was only after two hours of desperate fighting that Eckardt reluctantly ordered a withdrawal. The flank companies were forced to fight their way free of encirclement with rifle butts and bayonets back to their start line, after which II. Abteilung / Feldartillerie-Regiment 68 pounded the British counter-attackers to a standstill with its 10.5cm howitzers. IR 104 had lost 326 missing, and its sole consolation prizes were the two British machine-guns its MGK had brought back to *Delbecque Ferme* (Loophole Farm). At midday the regiment received I./134 by way of reinforcement and inserted the battalion between I. and II./104, while IR 181 received III./134. Given the division's losses and lack of progress, Obstltn. Eckardt now ordered IR 104 to "*reassemble formations, organise supports and reserves afresh, dig in, the position is to be held; regimental battle HQ is 104er Gut.*"[2]

No further attacks were attempted until 30 October. In the meantime both sides improved their positions as best they

Picture postcard of the British positions at Le Gheer, as sketched from the front line of IR 104 early in 1915.

could, adding reserve trenches, rudimentary dugouts, telephone lines and wire obstacles. Nightly harvesting of the tobacco plants between *Delbecque Ferme* and the front line of I./104 by IR181 (for use in covering their dugouts) proved a mistake as it opened up the view of IR104's main approach route to British snipers. The British artillery was also highly active, and from 28 October gave special attention to the farm almost daily. Meanwhile the German guns were focusing on Le Gheer.

The offensive of *Gruppe Fabeck* on 30 October was to be supported by a renewed push against Ploegsteert Wood. Since 48. Infanterie-Brigade (IR106 and 107) of 24.ID had now rejoined the corps from Champagne, its fresh regiments were used to spearhead the assault. IR 106 was attached to 40.ID on 29 October, and III./106 (plus the MGK/106) inserted that night on the right of IR104. In the next day's attack this battalion advanced over the rough trenches previously held by the cavalry, but soon had to dig in under heavy fire from the wood. That afternoon I./106 was committed from brigade reserve to reinforce the attack of 4. Kavallerie-Division on the right between the St. Yvon and Le Pelerin roads, alongside III./134 and JB 7. Further right, I./134 joined the Garde-Kavallerie-Division on the south bank of the Douve.

Despite two hours of artillery preparation, the attack of 30 October ground to a halt 200–300 metres from the enemy. That night III./106 was reinforced by II./106, forming a new regimental sector under their commander Oberst Kohl (see map p.36). The division elected not to attack on 31 October until the cavalry could suppress British flanking fire from St. Yvon, which failed to occur. For the next attempt on 2 November two heavy *minenwerfers* of Pionier-Regiment 19 (an army-level siege engineer unit) were emplaced on the right flank of IR104. These were most likely the same ones used at Frelinghien, though here they would fail due to faulty range estimation. This resort to siege warfare tactics clearly marked the onset of trench warfare. Among many others, the three successive failed attacks on 2 November cost the life of Obstltn. Eckardt, shot dead in his regiment's front line.

The monotonous regularity of the fighting that would follow in November, the paucity of the gains and the complexity of the ad-hoc formations opposite Ploegsteert Wood can best be exemplified by the following extract from the published history of IR106:

The Abteilung von Eschwege, *henceforth consisting of the II./106, a third of 2./106, 3./106, 9. and 12./134, 1./JB 10, Radfahrer-Komp./JB6 and 10 and MG Komp./JB6 (JB7 and MG Komp./JB10 returned to 3. Kav. Div.) dug in in the newly won positions. Around 4 pm and 8 pm the English pushed forward but were repulsed.*[3]

The first trenches between La Basse-Ville and St. Yvon, as depicted by an anonymous artist serving with IR 134.

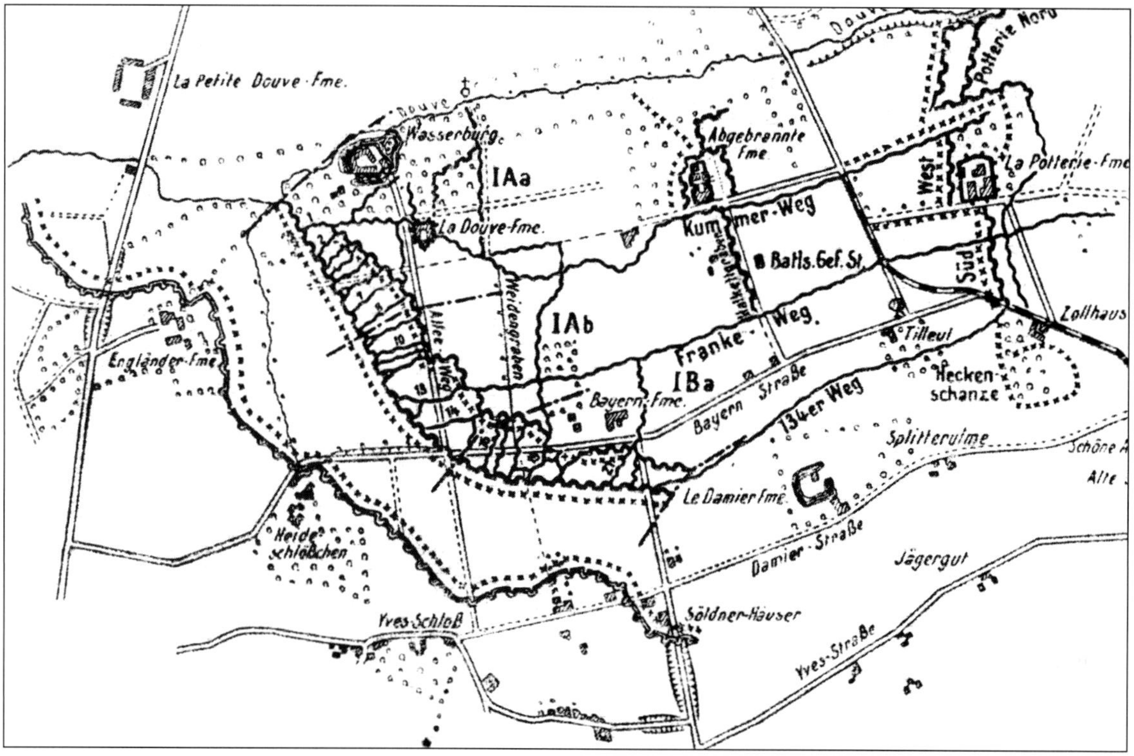

Detailed map of part of the *Detachement von der Decken* (later IR 134) sector, which extended from the Douve down to the St. Yvon road.

Map of the IR 106 sector showing ground gained on 11 November 1914. Much of this *Entenschnabel* salient was abandoned in December due to flooding (see later map on p. 45).

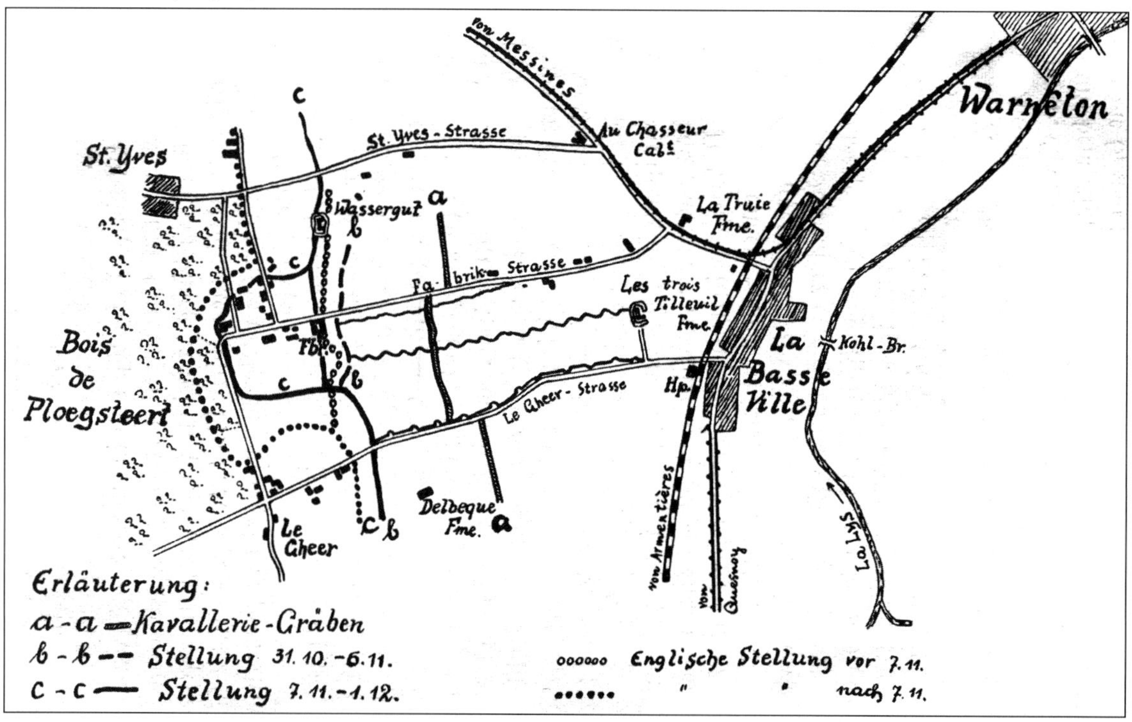

The onset of trench warfare

Just as *Gruppe Fabeck* struggled to gain ground between Gheluvelt and Messines, the supporting actions to their south made minimal progress in early November. Temporary successes like the capture of St. Yvon by I. / 134 on the evening of 30 October were soon undone by counterattacks. In the IR 104 sector, new acting commander Obstltn. Gretschel concentrated on fortifying the position he had inherited on 2 November. Further south, 89. Inf. Brig. went onto the defensive after the storming of the *Südbrauerei* on 26 October (see p. 22). 24. ID made its last attack on L'Epinette on 22 October (see p. 8) and at Rue du Bois on 28 October, after which IR 107 (committed fresh on the 23rd) was too depleted to continue.

Directly east of Ploegsteert Wood however, IR 106 (with II. / 133 now attached) was planning an operation to clear the British from the Le Pelerin area, designated the *Fabrikgelände* (factory site, marked 'Fb' on the map opposite). Throughout 5 and 6 November this position, held by 3rd Btn. the Worcestershire Regiment, was systematically shelled by artillery and heavy *minenwerfers* while fog hindered the efforts of British gunners to locate them. After a renewed *minenwerfer* barrage the Worcesters were overrun around 6.00 am on 7 November, as III. / 106 stormed out of the fog supported by 9. and 12. / 134. Despite strong flanking fire III. / 106 cleared Le Pelerin and gained a foothold in the edge of the wood. Those who pushed deeper were driven back to the edge by counterattacks during the day, and some cut off and captured. On the right the 9. and 12. / 134, supported by JB 10 and 7. / 106 on their flank, had taken the *Wassergut* (Factory Farm) and the British line north of *Fabrik-Straße* (the Le Pelerin road). Although the Worcesters had lost over two hundred including six officers, the attackers had also suffered badly. IR 106 and II. / 133 would continue to do so in holding the resulting salient, exposed to enfilade fire, shelling and subsequent efforts to retake it.

Despite an order of 8 November by the corps commander Gen. der Kav. von Laffert for continued harassment of the enemy, this would be the last German attack of 1914 on his front. Besides the state of the troops, the worsening weather and ammunition shortages made further action unfeasible. A planned operation at Rue du Bois using *minenwerfers* and three large mine galleries was repeatedly postponed and finally cancelled in late November when the tunnels flooded. On 21 November, Genmaj. Kaden of 48. Inf. Brig. (IR 106 and 107) was relieved to record in his diary that 6. Armee had ordered XIX. AK strictly onto the defensive, ending von Laffert's demands for further attacks.[4]

Poor bloody infantry' of 1. / 106 holding a squalid shallow trench on the eastern edge of Ploegsteert Wood in winter 1914–15.

BIOGRAPHICAL NOTES

Oberleutnant Friedrich Olbricht

Born 4 October 1888 in Leisnig, he joined IR106 as a *fahnenjunker* straight from secondary school. By the outbreak of war he was an oberleutnant and regimental adjutant. Already he November 1914 he was awarded the *Militär-St. Heinrichs-Orden* for his performance in this role on the Marne. In April 1916 he was promoted to hauptmann and adjutant of 116. Infanterie-Brigade (58. ID, to which IR106 now belonged). After staff training in January 1917 he served on the staffs of XIX. AK and finally 3. Armee.

After the war Hptm. Olbricht remained in service with the *Reichswehr* in Saxony, and was successfully chief of staff of the 4. Division in 1933 and IV. Armeekorps in 1935. From 1938 he commanded the 24. Infanterie-Division of the *Wehrmacht*, and was awarded the Knight's Cross for his part in the Polish campaign. From 1940 he was a general der infanterie serving in senior staff roles in Berlin, where he devised and on 20 July 1944 carried out the *Walküre* coup plot against Hitler as leader of the military resistance. That night he was the first of the conspirators to be summarily shot in the courtyard of the *Bendlerblock*, followed by the would-be assassin Oberst Claus Schenk Graf von Stauffenberg.

The square in front of the Militärhistorisches Museum der Bundeswehr in Dresden (until 1946, the *Königsplatz*) was renamed after him on 20 July 1991.

Prof. Dr. jur. Peters

Sadly we could not determine the professor's full name or background. Genmaj. Kaden (48., later renumbered as 116. Infanterie-Brigade) writes of him as follows in his diary: *...tenured Professor Dr. jur. Peters from the University of Frankfurt am Main is an expert on constitutional questions, in particular questions concerning trusts. Recently a letter arrived from very senior quarters, stating that Peters must not be exposed to danger, as he is a real authority in certain areas which will come under discussion at the peace settlement, and the only one with a complete understanding of the matter. Peters' doctoral thesis was of such significance, that the requirement for a professorial dissertation was waived for him. Now at the age of 28 he is a tenured professor and* kriegsfreiwilliger gefreiter. *He serves as Olbricht's orderly and right-hand man.*[5]

Oberstleutnant z. D. Kurt von Schönberg
Born 7 September 1864 and semi-retired from IR106 since 1912, he returned to battalion command in November 1914 and regimental command from 15 January 1915 to 11 April 1917. His citation dated 5 June 1915 for the *Ritterkreuz* of the *Militär-St. Heinrichs-Orden* reads: *During the fighting in Flanders as part of 24. Inf.-Div., Oberstl. v. Schönberg took over II. Batl. Inf.-Rgt. 106 under the most difficult circumstances. Over the course of months, under the heaviest artillery fire and in spite of ground water, he developed the position on the factory site at Ploegsteert Wood, the most dangerous post in the regimental sector, to the point where it could be held. This was possible thanks solely to his personal, energetic intervention and to practical measures of his own devising. As regimental commander during the* Frühjahrsschlacht *La Bassée-Arras [Second Battle of Artois] on the* Lorettohöhe *from 11 to 15 May 1915, he seized three trenches of considerable extent back from the enemy, and besides taking forty prisoners and a French machine-gun also recaptured a German machine-gun and* minenwerfer. *Oberstl. v. S. was a model for his regiment of the greatest energy and outstanding bravery.* Obstltn. von Schönberg later received the *komturkreuz* for his leadership on the Somme, and survived the war.

Hauptmann Gerhard Nicolai
Born 27 June 1882, this company commander of 1./106 earned the *Militär-St. Heinrichs-Orden* while opposing the final British attacks of 1914:
At Ploegsteert Wald north of Armentières on 16 December, a section from Hptm. Nicolai's company, which had been deployed 200 metres forward in a house on the edge of the wood, fell back from its position in the face of a superior enemy. Upon seeing this, he leapt from the trench in broad daylight brandishing his sabre, and successfully led the troops forward again despite the enemy fire from the flank... In the same position on 19 December the company was again attacked by numerically superior infantry, after it had been under the most intense artillery and enfilading machine-gun fire for six hours. The personal appearance of Hptm. N. at the endangered points of the trench encouraged the men to hold out, so that despite strong shrapnel fire the enemy did not succeed in overrunning the company. In so doing, Hptm. N. was wounded for the second time.
The photo shows him in the front line in November 1914, carrying his sabre and wearing enlisted man's headgear to disguise his rank from enemy snipers. Although severely wounded in summer 1915 he survived the war.

As the fighting died out in November regular relief cycles were established and XIX. AK settled into the routine of trench warfare. On 28 November it took over the line from St. Yvon to the Douve plus some of its resident units from HKK 2, assigning them to Oberst von der Decken of IR 134. From 7 December, the composition of his ad-hoc *Detachement von der Decken* was essentially as follows: I. and III. / 134 plus the MGK (II. / 134 was at Frelinghien), JB 10, 1. bayerisches (Bavarian) Jäger-Bataillon, MGK / JB 6, 1. bayerische Pionier-Abteilung and Pionier-Abteilung 11. Artillery support consisted of 2. / FAR 32, 2. / FAR 68 and two howitzers of 5. / FAR 68.

Initially its sector extended as far south as the *Fabrik-Straße*; on 29 November IR 106 took over the section south of the St. Yvon road from JB 10, while ceding its own line south of the Le Gheer road to IR 104. The revised IR 106 sector was held by two battalions abreast, with II. / 133 attached and included in the relief cycle. The two 'resting' battalions were housed mainly in La Basse-Ville. This was not ideal, as Genmaj. Kaden noted in his diary on 2 December:

Once again IR 106 had their usual hard luck. They were in the western part of La Basse-Ville, and IR 134 in the eastern part. Because enemy shells were constantly landing in the western part of the town, an exchange of quarters was arranged to give 106 a rest. 106 had scarcely arrived in the eastern part when the enemy redirected their fire onto it.[6]

About the end of November the winter rains set in. The low, shell-churned ground near the wood grew increasingly swampy, and the front line on its eastern edge wholly untenable. On 2 December most of the garrison withdrew to a new line constructed – and heavily wired – by 2. / Pionier-Bataillon 22 around Le Pelerin. This would become the notorious *Entenschnabel* or 'Birdcage'. Outposts were initially retained in the old line on the edge of the wood.

The history of IR 106 describes conditions at the end of November as follows:

Conditions are also bleak in the rest of the regiment's positions. Only by continuous baling and working with hand pumps are the trenches and the few shelters – mostly huts made of boards, which offer some protection against rain, but none at all against enemy shelling – tolerably free of water. Hollowed out by groundwater and worn down by rain, the trench walls collapse. Thousands of sandbags are dug in to hold up the parapet and gradually sink below the muddy surface, or the work of several days is destroyed by enemy artillery fire. To control the primary evil, the groundwater, the construction of a systematic drainage system is in progress from the beginning of December. By making use of the natural ditches which were already to hand, an attempt is made to direct the water partly into the English position, partly into the Lys either by deepening existing drainage ditches or by establishing new ones. However with

Sketch of La Basse-Ville in 1915, looking south-westwards towards the railway station (at the junction of the Le Gheer and Pont Rouge roads).

the meagre gradient in the plains of Flanders this provides no decisive remedy. Consequently the installation of a sump shaft and an efficient electrically driven water pump is in progress behind the front line, and on 27 December this is put into operation for the first time.[7]

From 14 December the British grew active again, shelling both the trenches and rear area of IR 106 as heavily as ammunition supplies permitted. On the afternoon of 19 December their 11th Brigade launched a concerted attack after a preparatory bombardment. This would be the first of many failed attempts to eliminate the Le Pelerin salient over the following years, but its main aim was to deter XIX. AK from sending reserves to oppose French efforts in Artois (as it would often do in 1915). The garrison of the outpost line fell back at once to Le Pelerin. The pursuing battalions, struggling through the mire under fire from their own artillery, briefly broke into the main Saxon position only to be mown down by machine-guns and enfilading fire from the *Yves-Graben* to the north. 11th Brigade retired to its start line, leaving many dead on the wire of the 'Birdcage'. The burial of these unfortunates would figure prominently in the Christmas Truce.

Christmas 1914 at Ploegsteert Wood

Christmas Eve was a still moonlit night. Though snow was lacking, a light frost at least kept the mud at bay. Well supplied with *liebesgaben* from home, the troops in reserve or rest quarters celebrated in traditional style with church services, music and plenty to eat and drink. Those obliged to spend the night in the trenches brought Christmas trees to be decorated with candles and placed on the parapet.[8] Their massed singing famously caught the attention of the British, whose own celebrations were due to begin on Christmas Day. The subsequent trucing and fraternisation not only affected most of the XIX. AK front, but also Prussian (Westphalian) VII. AK on their left and Bavarian 6. bRD on their right. It would however be the Saxons who dominated British press coverage and folk memory of the event, reinforcing their reputation as the least hostile and most amiable of Britain's enemies. British news stories playing up Saxon disenchantment with the war and Prussian leadership would acutely embarrass the officers of XIX. AK (see *Fighting the Kaiser's War* p. 208), especially in light of the strict anti-fraternisation order issued by OHL on 29 December under which all unauthorised approaches to the enemy were to be punished as high treason.

On Christmas Eve the line of *Detachement von der Decken* was held (north to south) by JB 10, bJB 1 and III. / IR 134. According to its battalion history, MGK / JB 6 was at *Damier-Ferme* (despite modern claims that it was with II. / IR 134 at Frelinghien). Opposite them were (north to south) 2nd Btn. Seaforth Highlanders and 1st Btn. Royal Warwickshire Regt. of 10th Brigade / 4th Division. As many British accounts attest, all these units took part in the fraternisation. However the published history of IR 134 states only that Christmas passed 'peacefully' and that of bJB 1 ignores it. The only published German account is that of JB 10 and is surprisingly frank. 4. / JB 10 took over the line about 9 pm on Christmas Eve, bringing their Christmas trees and lights. Contrary to claims by the Seaforths to have begun singing first, JB 10 describes the enemy ceasing fire and calling out in response to German festivities. Hptm. Richter suspected a ruse and ordered his men to fire a volley, which went well over the enemy's heads (probably on purpose). This failed to deter the Scots, and eventually the English-speaking Oberjäger Echte met them at the wire (he was probably the English-speaking German later described by Cpl. John Ferguson of the Seaforths). Surprisingly no British accounts mention JB 10, its Hanoverian heritage or its prominent 'GIBRALTAR' cuff title originally awarded by George III in 1784. On Christmas Day fraternisation continued in conjunction with the burial of the dead (many of them French). Richter's threats of punishment were quashed by his battalion commander, and his company was relieved on Boxing Day. On the night of 28–29 December JB 10 was replaced by JB 13 and bJB 1 by bJB 2, while the British battalions had also been relieved. A tacit truce still persisted into early January, though fraternisation was discretely suppressed (see p. 18).

Numerous British sightings indicate that IR 106 used II. / 133 to hold the half of its line south of the *Fabrik-Straße* over Christmas. Opposite the sector was most of 11th Brigade / 4th Division, with (north to south) 1st Btn. Somerset Light Infantry, 1st Btn. Rifle Brigade plus attached London Rifle Brigade and 1st Btn. Hampshire Regt. Singing seemingly began quite late here. The regimental band of IR 106 under Musikmeister Capitän played at La Basse Ville from about 4 am according to JB 10. Informal contact was probably made with the enemy during the night, since a provisional truce was agreed on Christmas morning with officers of the Somerset Light Infantry and Rifle Brigade for the recovery and burial of the dead between Ploegsteert Wood and the *Entenschnabel*. Capt. Beckett of the Hampshires kept his men in their trenches and simply observed. The history of IR 106 states that:

... on 25th December (Christmas) there ensued with the permission of the generalkommando *a temporary truce for the burial of the dead of both sides, some of whom had been lying between the lines since 20th October.*[9]

Such permission was likely retrospective. Oberst Kohl of IR 106 was clearly anxious to keep contact with the enemy on a formal and militarily permissible basis. On 27 December he ordered a symbolic resumption of MG fire at midnight, of which the Hampshires were politely warned in advance. On the 30th they were told that the Saxons could no longer fraternise, and that symbolic firing might be required. The same day the Rifles received an official New Year truce proposal (preserved in their war diary) signed by Kohl in the name of the *generalkommando*. Although they could not fulfil his conditions in time, the sector remained quiet into early January.

IR 104 lay opposite 1st Btn. East Lancashire Regt. (11th Bde.) and part of 2nd Btn. Monmouthshire Regt. (12th Brigade). Its history describes events very guardedly:

On the first day of the holiday the Englishmen opposite us tried to exploit the peaceful mood with a fraternisation gathering between the trenches, which was prevented by the timely intervention of officers in the regimental sector. At other places along the front, trusting German soldiers who heeded the requests of the English were taken into captivity. Only a short truce was agreed for the burial of a number of the dead from the November fighting who still lay between the lines. This took place on both sides and was an act of reverence to fallen comrades.[11]

Ltn. d. R. Kurt Zehmisch (in front row with peaked cap) was a platoon commander in 11. / IR 134, known for his diary entry on the Christmas Truce.[10] He describes this photo on the back as follows: *Picture from 28 Nov. 1914, after I had received the Iron Cross the day before. In the background our old billets, which were shot up early on 6 Jan. 1915 just as we were about to drink coffee.* This bombardment of La Basse-Ville, which claimed numerous victims, showed that the tacit ceasefire in this period did not apply to the artillery.

British sources unanimously describe a burial truce and fraternisation. According to Lieut. C.E.M. Richards of 1st East Lancashires, his battalion staff took part (much to his disgust) and gave orders that evening to prepare a football pitch in No Man's Land for New Year's Day. The irregular order was never carried out. Sadly two of the Monmouthshires were sniped on Christmas Day, possibly due to the less friendly attitude of IR 181. According to Richards, hostilities recommenced that evening. There are no further reports of fraternisation, though the war diary of 1st East

A photograph taken from the Saxon parapet opposite Ploegsteert Wood, looking across the German wire obstacle line toward the British trenches. Despite the obvious sniper threat such pictures are surprisingly common, albeit rarely of high quality.

Lancashires describes subsequent days as 'all quiet' and only notes that sniping had resumed on the 31st.

IR 181 faced 2nd Monmouthshires and 2nd Btn. Lancashire Fusiliers (12th Bde.). Its published history states that it aggressively rejected all approaches. However some of its men were seen fraternising in the IR 104 sector. 2nd Lancashire Fusiliers certainly fraternised, possibly with III. / 104 at Le Touquet. Accounts from the Lancashire Fusiliers of a German envoy taken prisoner on Christmas Eve (due to a sentry failing to blindfold him before he entered the British lines) may explain the attitude of IR 181 and the reference above to 'trusting German soldiers'.

The first weeks of 1915

As well as burying the dead, this welcome lull was used to improve the trenches. In many places the parapet and parados were raised well above ground level to counter the high water table. Countless sandbags (made from locally sourced fabric of all colours and patterns) were filled, stacked and held in place with wooden cladding. Many old communication and even fighting trenches from 1914 were simply written off due to flooding and replaced with new ones. As construction work grew more complex, the battalions formed semi-skilled infanterie-bautrupps (infantry construction squads) under *pionier* direction. Two platoons of an army-level *eisenbahnbaukompagnie* (railway engineer construction company) were also employed building dugouts in La Basse-Ville.

The detached II. / 133 left the Ploegsteert Wood sector on 5 January and rejoined its regiment. With only its three organic battalions, IR 106 ceded its right flank as far as the *Wassergut* to Detachement von der Decken.

Besides severe shelling of La Basse-Ville and Warneton on 6 January, hostile activity was limited to occasional short bombardments of the front line and suspected traffic hubs in the rear. This allowed work on the trenches to the point where they could survive frost, thaw and days-long rain without lasting damage. On 6 February a new communication trench was completed behind the *Entenschnabel*. This *Tonnenweg* was lined with about a thousand earth-filled casks and barrels stacked two high (see p. 28, map p. 45 and photo p. 49).

Reorganisation and development of the line

After four months opposite Ploegsteert Wood, IR 106 left the sector for good on 5 March 1915. As part of a wider policy of triangularisation (reduction of each division from four to three infantry regiments), IR 106 and 107 plus their parent 48. Infanterie-Brigade left XIX. AK to form part of the new 58. Infanterie-Division. After two months in army reserve (mostly around Roubaix) this was committed on 9 May to oppose the French spring offensive at Vimy Ridge; its later history is discussed in chapter 11.

To fill the gap left by IR 106 at Ploegsteert Wood, the frontage of IR 104 was extended northwards and roughly doubled in size (the map on p. 45 shows the resulting sector boundaries). Incredibly, IR 104 held this sector with one battalion at a time – III. / 104 was still detached at Le Touquet, while II. / 104 was available in corps reserve to aid VII. AK against the British attack at Neuve Chapelle on 10–16 March. This was achievable thanks to the bolstering of the regiment's strength with a fresh intake from Saxony, prepared for front line service by the division's newly established *feldrekrutendepot*. This garrison was reckoned sufficient to oppose any local attack. In the event, the sector stayed quiet enough for a substantial improvement and expansion of the trench system over the following months.

The regimental history of IR 104 describes their original trenches as follows:

For weeks there was scarcely any talk of a supply of suitable building materials – boards, beams, roofing felt and nails – from the vast hinterland of the army; it took a long time for regular

Soldat Gläß (from Muldenberg, left) and Gefreiter Schilbach (from Schirmeck, right) of IR 134 early in 1916 in a well-signposted communication trench near *Jägergut* on the St. Yvon road (see upper map p. 36).

and sufficient supplies of building materials cut to be useable for shelter construction to reach the troops, who therefore resorted to helping themselves and made use of the nearest dwellings for their urgent needs. First came the furniture, then a spacious wardrobe was seen inserted into the trench wall as a bunk. The components of bedsteads, tables and benches were used for the planking of another dugout, whose roof had to be provided by a taut zeltbahn. *The cladding of the slipping trench walls was an equally colourful motley. The harvesting of further timber led to the dismantling of all existing woodwork in the buildings, from roof rafters and roof beams to the floorboards and cellar doors. Liquid manure pumps, household and kitchen utensils were most welcome as tools in the fight against the invading water. We clutched at one stopgap after another. Thus, with the best of intentions, it cannot be said that in the first few weeks there was any system in the technique of construction.*[12]

By early 1915 this 'trial and error' approach had given way to planned construction, fully informed by expert study of ground conditions and tactical considerations. The 'vast hinterland of the army' now delivered plentiful purpose-made construction supplies. In Lille, the textile factories churned out sandbags by the million. Though greatly favoured at this time, these would later be partly replaced by wooden cladding and fascines due to their tendency to rot and stink when exposed to moisture.

The merely rainproof dugouts of 1914 were superseded in 1915 by 'splinter-proof' structures. Protection from bullets and shell fragments was readily achieved by reinforcing wooden planks with (ideally) tree trunks or railway sleepers, covered with waterproof roofing felt and layers of earth. Protection from direct hits by even light artillery demanded concrete, either pre-cast blocks assembled at the front or ferro-concrete cast *in situ.* While such techniques were practical in the rearward defensive lines and artillery positions, it took immense time and effort to create 'shell-proof' dugouts in the front line. Construction material could be brought up the Deûle by hand-pulled barges or a motorboat, but had to be carried further forward. A narrow-gauge railway line from La Basse-Ville to the trenches was not completed until March 1916. Although this soon became a magnet for artillery fire, it helped ensure that the sector was well equipped with concrete dugouts by the time the Saxons left for the Somme.

Electricity was first supplied to the trenches early in 1915 by a generator in Deulemont. After the establishment of electric pumping stations and lighting for the dugouts, there was an attempt to add electrified barbed wire to the defences of the *Entenschnabel.* As in most parts of the Western Front where this was tried, it soon proved hopelessly vulnerable to artillery fire and an impediment to forward patrolling. Another project to harden the line against assault was the installation of an

Prussian trench gun (3.7cm *Grabenkanone*) crew of Schützengrabenkanonen-Abteilung 6 in the 40. ID sector at Quesnoy in July 1916.

electrically-fired underground minefield on both sides of the Le Gheer road. Conventional wire obstacle lines were established early along the entire front and constantly maintained. The nightly wiring parties initially used hammered wooden stakes, inevitably attracting fire. The metal screw pickets which replaced stakes in every army were introduced in 1915.

The line was anchored by mutually-supporting machine-guns, increasing within 40. ID from six MG 08 per regiment in 1914 to ten (plus several captured foreign guns) in summer 1916. In additional a *feldmaschinengewehrzug* (independent MG platoon) was often active in each sector. Further firepower was supplied by rifle grenades, fired from 'batteries' of fixed rifles. The number of *minenwerfers* available to the *pioniere* rose repeatedly in 1915, culminating in the creation of Minenwerfer-Kompagnie 40 at the end of the year (with two heavy, four medium and six light weapons, increasing to three, six and twelve respectively in spring 1916). From January 1916, direct fire support against frontline targets was also provided by the 3.7cm trench guns of Prussian Schützengrabenkanonen-Abteilung 6.

Considerable attention was devoted to the hygiene and good order of the trenches, and strict regulations issued. Latrines were isolated in side-trenches and waste collected in barrels for burial at a suitable distance. Chemical disinfectants were issued and their use monitored. The duckboards covering the gutters in the trench floor were regularly swept clean. Much importance was placed on the cleanliness of the parapet, where rifles were rested. To protect their rifles when out of the firing line, each infantry section dugout received a rainproof gun rack. Orientation within the trenches was aided by numerous signboards, and observation of the enemy facilitated by numerous periscopes, loophole plates and framed sketches of the British line.

The infantry were undoubtedly sceptical of the less obviously essential construction projects, for which they were obliged to supply labour and carry materials. Some ideas were clearly counterproductive, such as a tunnel in the IR134 sector described by Ltn. Illing in the regimental history:

Thus with our limited understanding, it was not yet quite clear what the purpose might be of the tunnel, through which the Kapitalgraben *was directed in the vicinity of the* Jägergut, *and which had given us little joy during its existence. If one had to worry one's way through the tunnel with eight full mess-tins which, owing to the narrowness of the celebrated structure, one must needs carry with outstretched arms to one's front and rear – then one certainly had no particularly pious wishes for the originator of this idea, who had thus created a first-class traffic obstacle. Above all the transport of materials through the tunnel was a task in itself, and thus many sandbags, fascines and squared timbers found a premature and inglorious end there, as they were 'dismantled' in or ahead of it. I can scarcely recall a relief where there was not a prolonged delay in the tunnel – and if it should happen to be hit by a shell, traffic would be brought to a complete standstill. I still believe today that the tunnel was in the wrong place; it should have been built in front of the front line – but not just one, rather as many as possible, one next to the other; then if the Tommies were to come, every attack would have got hopelessly stuck in the tunnel system.*[13]

Ltn. Illing is also predictably critical of experiments with electrified barbed wire:

Tommy was more than a little surprised, when one morning he saw the curious garden fence standing there, consisting of individual panels – made in La Basse-Ville and brought forward complete – artfully mounted on glass feet. He regarded it with little trust and also little respect, as one fine afternoon a little later he was tactless enough to overturn the whole wonderful contraption with a sudden short bombardment. Fortunately we had already experienced the historic moment when it was 'charged' for the first time, a historic moment in that it was also the last time, according to credible canteen gossip.[14]

Despite such later missteps, the establishment of a functional trench system in the swampy ground between Ploegsteert Wood and the Lys in the winter of 1914–15 was an impressive feat. The sketches on pp. 46–47 show what had already been achieved by March 1915. The British reader will surely be amazed that it was possible to buy minimally censored picture postcards of IR104's front line in its battalion canteens!

Detailed map of the IR 104 sector, including locations depicted on the next two pages by Werner Haenel of 4./104. A large series of sketches of the trenches and rear area by Haenel were printed and sold as postcards in March 1915 (with place names partly obliterated).

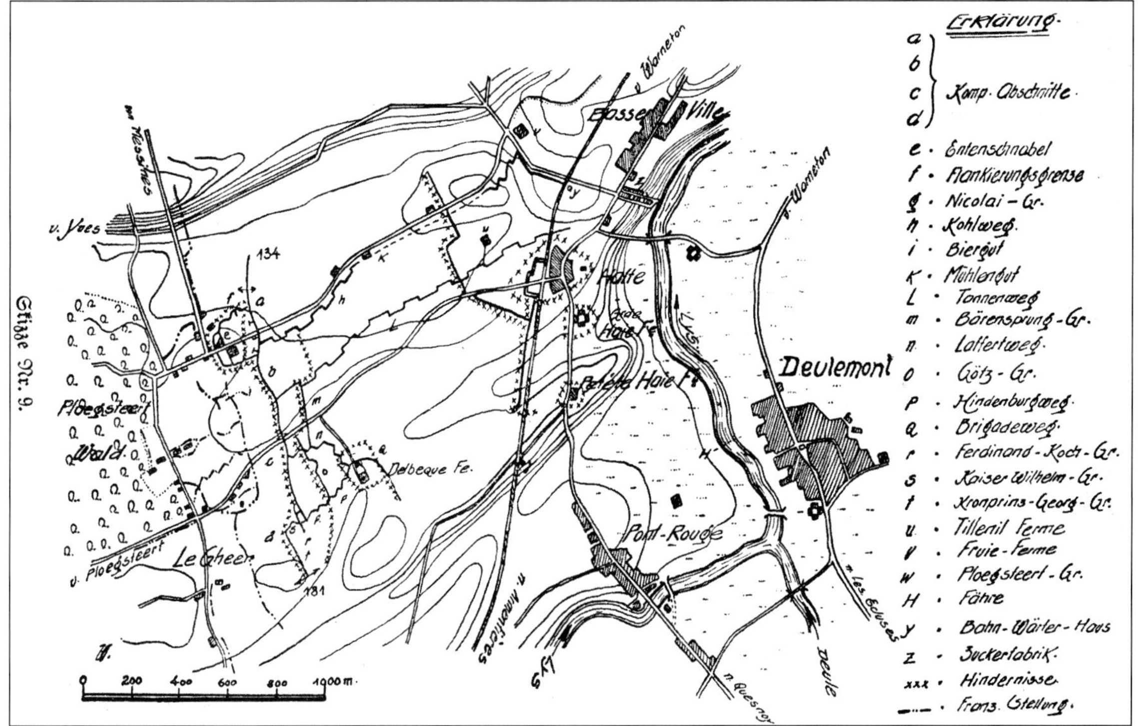

Front-line covered sentry post in the *Ferdinand-Koch-Graben* near the junction with Hindenburgweg (south of the Le Gheer road).

A few hundred metres further back in the *Hindenburgweg* communication trench near *Delbecque Ferme* (Loophole Farm).

Pumpstation C (an electric pumping station) in the *Hindenburgweg*.

Double sentry post with loophole plate in the *Kaiser-Wilhelm-Graben*.

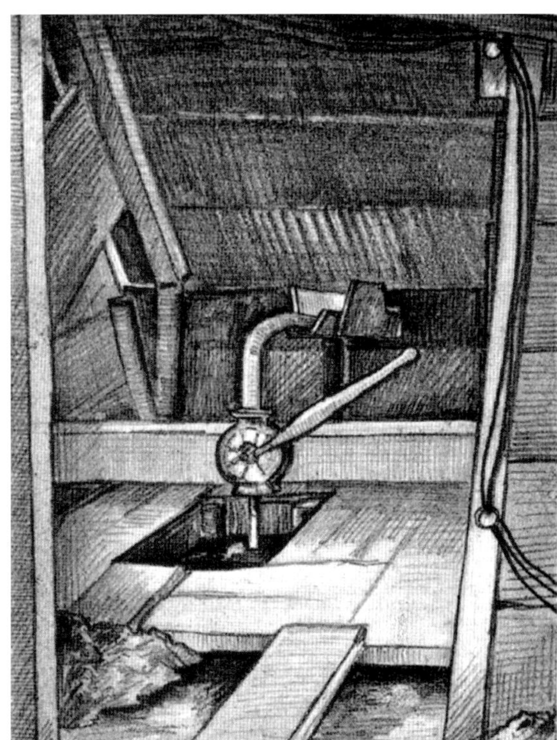

Pumpstation G in *Kronprinz-Georg-Graben* near the border with IR 181.

Open-air toilet over the Warnave stream at *Delbecque Ferme.*

Spring 1915 to summer 1916

After the departure of IR 106 on 5 March 1915 and the ceding of Le Touquet to IR 181 on 20 April (see chapter 2) the 40. ID divisional sector and its three subsectors remained static and consistent. While still held by *Detachement von der Decken*, the right subsector was subdivided at *Damier-Ferme* into a northern section (held by the various *jäger* battalions in rotation) and a southern section (held by *Abteilung Naumann*, comprising I. and III. / 134 in rotation). The central subsector was usually occupied by IR 104 (as per the map on p. 45) with IR 181 on its left.

Throughout 1915, XIX. AK sought to hold its quiet front with the minimum practical garrison – enabling it to serve as a major source of reserves for emergencies further south. As mentioned on p. 18, JB 13 spent most of March fighting at the *Lorettohöhe*. During the British attack at Neuve Chapelle (10–13 March), II. / 104, a composite battalion from 24. ID and nearly half of the artillery were committed. When the Second Battle of Artois opened on 9 May, JB 13 returned to the *Lorettohöhe* and each division again sent its corps reserve battalion to the Neuve Chapelle area. For 40. ID this was again II. / 104 under Hptm. Karl Facius[15], awarded the MStHO for the action in March which had cost his battalion eleven officers and 437 other ranks killed or wounded.

With plentiful replacements for their intermittent losses, the six Saxon infantry regiments of XIX. AK still had the manpower to supply two supernumerary companies each for the formation of IR 183 at Lille on 21 May. Despite recent losses of two officers and 200 other ranks killed or wounded at Neuve Chapelle, IR 104 donated eight officers (including Hptm. Facius) and 400 other ranks. IR 183 was initially billetted in the Lille area and attached to XIX. AK for training and working parties. It left for Cambrai on 8 June, becoming part of the new 183. Infanterie-Brigade (from July 1916, 183. ID) with Prussian and Württemberg units under a Saxon staff. The brigade would see intense fighting in the Champagne that autumn. IR 183 would be one of the first Saxon units committed to the Somme in July 1916, transferring to the Saxon 192. ID in October 1916 after a second tour.

This donation was followed on 27 May by a demand for a brigade staff and two active infantry regiments as army reserve. IR 133 and 134 were chosen, the latter finally reuniting as a result. *Detachement von der Decken* was finally dissolved, releasing JB 10 and both Bavarian *jäger* battalions to join the new *Alpenkorps* on the Italian front. JB 10 left on 20 May, and according to their published history were glad to be leaving:

It was a pleasure to return for the last time through the zig-zag trenches via La Douve Farm. The destroyed farm with the dangerous open side, the dark and stinking henhouse, through which one had to pass before fumbling back down into the trenches again.[16]

In exchange XIX. AK received Prussian 38. Landwehr-Brigade (Landwehr-Infanterie-Regiment 77 and 78), 'lower Saxons' from Brunswick and Hanover who had already served under Saxon command with XXVII. RK from December 1914 to May 1915 (see chapter 6). The brigade remained with XIX. AK until late February 1916, allowing it to maintain its army reserve. LIR 77 initially replaced IR 134 north of Ploegsteert Wood, while LIR 78 replaced IR 133 at Frelinghien (see p. 24). LIR 77 was also able to spare a battalion (III. / 77) to partly relieve IR 139 at Pérenchies from 7 August. Having helped defeat the British and Canadians near Givenchy-lès-la-Bassée on 15 June, IR 134 returned to relieve LIR 77 on 23 August.

On the front of XIX. AK the opening of the Anglo-French autumn offensive of 1915 was marked on the night of 24–25 September with a heavy bombardment and simulated gas attack. Moderate losses failed to prevent XIX. AK from making its greatest contribution yet of reinforcements for the Artois and Champagne fronts – more than half of the *pioniere* and infantry (including all the active brigade staffs), plus a battalion each of field and heavy artillery. 89. Infanterie-Brigade with IR 133 and JB 13 had already been committed from army reserve south of Arras earlier in September. In order to release even more of its infantry, the corps was loaned Saxon 106. Reserve-Infanterie-Brigade (53. RD / XXVII. RK). On 1 October RIR 242 relieved IR 104 at Ploegsteert Wood and RIR 244 took over St. Yvon from IR 134. Compared to their usual sectors, the new garrison found the line well built and initially peaceful. Increasing British activity culminated in a gas attack on 13 October, while RIR 244 was celebrating its first birthday. Crude *atemschützer* respirators were donned and burning straw piled on the parapet. Thanks to this and the rising sun, the gas floated harmlessly overhead.

At the end of October the rains began in earnest, flooding dugouts and low-lying trenches, and both visiting units were glad to be relieved by the usual residents on 16 November. RIR 244 alone left twenty-one dead at the *ehrenfriedhof* in Quesnoy-sur-Deûle (see p. 242) from this 'quiet' period. Meanwhile I. / 104 had fought the British at the *Hohenzollernwerk* near Auchy from 28 September to 19 October. From the beginning of October IR 134 and the rest of IR 104 had opposed the French offensive near Givenchy-en-Gohelle. The returning regiments would now remain at Ploegsteert Wood until the whole XIX. AK was sent to the

The famous barrel-lined *Tonnenweg*, running north of (and roughly parallel to) the Le Gheer road from La Basse-Ville to the front line.

Major Dörffel, battalion commander of III. / 104, and his adjutant Oberleutnant Ehrhardt in front of their HQ dugout in spring 1915.[17]

Unidentified leutnant (left) and fähnrich of IR 104 in a trench visibly built up well above ground level with sandbags.

Retouched and obviously posed photo (from the published history of IR 104) depicting the *Entenschnabel* / Birdcage position in 1915.

Picture postcard of the 'Saxon-Bavarian border' (between XIX. AK and II. bAK) near the Douve, produced by Uffz. Dorfer of 1. / IR 134..

Relaxed infantrymen of IR 134 in cosy surroundings at Quesnoy-sur-Deûle, where the regimental reserve was housed. Rest quarters for regular troop rotation in the regimental sector were at La Basse-Ville, and later also in the newly built *Naumann-Baracken* on the Lys.

Somme at the end of July 1916. JB 13 was intermittently included in regimental relief cycles as a fourth battalion – serving from 15 to 27 March, 7 to 19 April and 15 to 27 June in the IR 134 sector and from 9 to 24 July that of IR 104.

Apart from mining at the hotspots and brief bursts of activity for the Entente offensives, enemy activity throughout 1915 was largely restricted to routine 'ritualised' artillery fire, sniping and cautious forward patrolling. Neither side could afford to waste ammunition outside of battles, and the tacit 'live and let live' arrangement benefited both. XIX. AK could reliably despatch multiple full-strength active regiments to emergencies elsewhere, while the British had a 'nursery' sector to introduce new units to the Western Front. An unintended side-effect was the proliferation on the British side of the Saxon reputation for amiability and non-aggression.

The quietness of Ploegsteert Wood in 1915 is attested by the time and effort available for leisure activities once the winter floods had passed. Not only vegetables but also flowers were grown in small decorative gardens. Much trench art was produced, especially vases made from engraved shell cases (an activity later suppressed due to the need to recycle strategic metals). Sketching and photography were wildly popular, and favoured examples were printed in Saxony as postcards for sale at battalion canteens. By spring 1915 regular relief cycles were in place, and whole battalions at a time could 'rest' at Warneton, Deulemont and Quesnoy-sur-Deûle (nicknamed 'Genua' by the Saxons), where baths, canteens, estaminets and even field bookshops were available. The lengthy residence of the Saxons among the remaining civilian residents and the relatively low level of hardship for both parties at this time allowed the development of comfortable and even friendly relations.

However 'quiet', front line service was never pleasant or safe. While the British were often inactive the plentiful rats and lice persistently plagued the trench garrison. Artillery and trench mortars could still kill even when following a predictable timetable, and the careless fell prey to snipers at the quietest times. Although low-key compared to the raids of 1916, both sides also regularly patrolled forward of their lines at night to gain intelligence, and ideally booty or prisoners. Details of enemy trench routine and especially of unit composition were priceless – the Saxons aiming to identify new formations and the British to determine when regiments of XIX. AK were withdrawn from this front. Such intelligence could also be gathered by less

On the reverse, a soldier of IR 104 writes from La Basse-Ville ('La B.') on 6 June 1915: *this card is by a soldier (photographer) of a Prussian Regiment 77 (inftr.). This regiment has been in the line there and now that 134 is away is in this part of the line near us. I don't know yet when we're going to get away, it could be any day now. Now imagine, dear Helene, about 11am today the English again exploded* [a mine] *by the 5. Komp.,* [and] *half an hour away where we are the earth shook violently. Once again there are a number of dead, lightly and severely wounded.*

bloody if less 'sporting' methods, as the regimental history of IR104 illustrates:

After the English [sic.] *had already made the attempt at the beginning of August 1915 to engage our sentries in conversation by shouting in German ('Do you have beer? What kind of beer do you have? Give me a bottle! So you are Bavarians after all? Why are you fighting for the Prussians? Has Warsaw really fallen? Why don't you answer? You're already asleep? Good night! Sweet dreams!') from the mine crater opposite the flank trench, on 23 August they proposed a mutual exchange of newspapers. Gefr. Held of 4. Komp. responded to the proposal with the intention of identifying the opposing unit. After taking off his tunic he approached as far as the English forward wire and was handed a Canadian newspaper dated 30 July 1915 in exchange for a German one.*

Since four Englishmen [sic.] *were now approaching from over there, Soldaten Stein and Kinzler of 4. Komp. clambered out of the trench in their shirtsleeves. Stein asked for a shoulder strap and a tunic button as souvenirs. Before any of his opponents had a chance to express their agreement, Stein had snatched and cut off both of the desired items. Under the pretext that they wanted to fetch them a similar souvenir from their dugout, the men of 4./104 quickly withdrew, highly satisfied with this success. The members of the 34th Canadian Regiment waited in vain for the German return visit. In order to blunt all enemy attempts at fraternisation, a regimental*

The text on the reverse reads as follows: *June 1915. A mine detonation conducted by the English in front of the position of Saxon Inf. Regt.104, accompanied by a small earth tremor.*

Aerial photo of the trenches at Ploegsteert Wood taken by Saxon Feldflieger-Abteilung 24. The two British mine craters of 6 June are visible at the northwest corner of the *Entenschnabel*, as are the German craters of 10 and 14 June to its south and north respectively, both now connected to the British trenches. Since only one crater is visible opposite the southern face, this photo presumably predates 30 June, when the Saxons blew a second mine alongside it (injuring three men holding the original crater). On the northern side a British camouflet was blown beside the existing crater on 28 June, but with little effect on the surface.

order prohibited unauthorised leaving of the trench without the permission of the company commander.[18]

The mention of a mine crater brings us to the most persistent and dreaded threat to the relative peace at Ploegsteert Wood. The recently formed 174th Tunnelling Company RE took over existing workings at Trench 121 opposite the northwest corner of the *Entenschnabel* in April. This salient, around 150 metres deep and 200 wide, was of obvious value for forward observation. Inevitably it was also a focus for every form of enemy aggression – especially at the corners, where it came closest to the British lines. Enfilading small arms fire, trench mortars and rifle grenades were all employed against its defenders. Mining was suspected from underground sounds early in 1915, and countermining begun by *pioniere* aided by seconded infantrymen with mining experience. As a result, the British tunnellers soon grew concerned at the increasing volume of German underground activity. After sighting blue clay (evidence of deep mining) on the German parapet on 28 May, and suspecting the use of a boring machine, they armed and fired two 2,500 lb black powder charges early on 6 June. The northwest corner of the *Entenschnabel* was obliterated, killing twenty-seven men of the trench-holding 5./104 and another five from a working party of 10./104. This horrifying reverse would not be repeated, though both sides would blow many 'defensive' mines in no man's land around the *Entenschnabel*, mostly at the northwest corner. The *pioniere* blew their first mine on 10 June near the southwest corner, creating a crater which was occupied by the British. A second mine near the northwest corner on 14 June collapsed two British galleries, temporarily trapping several tunnellers and costing them weeks of work. Despite these and subsequent countermining efforts, the 171st Tunnelling Company RE (having relieved the 174th) would finish laying four charges containing a total of over 100,000 lb of explosives in galleries running under the *Entenschnabel* from the northwest in April 1916. The men of IR 104 remained blissfully unaware of this, and after a major demolition raid from the southern face on 13 May 1916 (described in detail in *Fighting the Kaiser's War*, pp. 114–117) falsely believed they had destroyed the entrances to the main British galleries. In the event the 'Birdcage' mines were never used; one was triggered by lightning in 1955 (killing a solitary cow), while the others remain unexploded today. After its second tour on the Somme in October, IR 104 would unknowingly spend another seven months above similarly enormous mines at Spanbroekmolen. It was relieved just in time to be out of the immediate blast area on 7 June 1917.

The winter of 1915–16 brought the expected struggle with the water, and snow as late as March. The Lys again broke its banks, rendering the low bridges at Warneton impassable. Drainage work was hampered by the greatly increased activity of the British artillery and the retaliation of the German guns, which would ensure that the XIX. AK sector was never as quiet in 1916 as heretofore. The accommodation villages of La Basse-Ville, Deulemont and Warneton were now regularly targeted, and the remaining civilians were evacuated. Sniping and raiding likewise grew increasingly intense. Already in January IR 134 recorded considerable success for its observer / sniper teams. On the night of 25–26 March raiders from 10th Btn. Argyll & Sutherland Highlanders were caught on the Saxon wire and repelled with hand grenades; IR 134 was able to take two wounded prisoners and identify 9th (Scottish) Division. A previous raid attempt against IR 104 near the Le Gheer road early on 12 March had been equally unsuccessful.

April was quieter, except for the highly active German artillery. Ploegsteert Wood was heavily shelled due to the suspected presence of gas cylinders, and La Basse-Ville temporarily evacuated in case of retaliation. The British started to shell more heavily in May, and attacked the divisional *pionierpark* and Warneton railway station with super-heavy artillery; some relief was gained after the downing of a British spotter aircraft by a German fighter. In June the British guns systematically leveled every tower or chimney usable for observation by 40. ID, and mock gas attacks were repeatedly used to lure the Saxons to the parapet for bombardment with shrapnel.

With the Somme offensive imminent, the British escalated their diversionary raiding. On the night of 28–29 June 1916 a well equipped force approached the lines of IR 134 on both sides of the *Bayernstraße*, but was soon beaten off with hand grenades. The gas intended to support this attack was discharged the following night. On 30 June the whole trench system of 40. ID was shelled throughout the day and badly damaged. About 11 pm gas was discharged all along the line, followed by numerous raiding parties from 41st Division.

Group from three arms of service in the front line near St. Yvon in autumn 1915. From left: infantry *scharfschütze* (sniper) Hermann, artillery Uffz. Wietzniok, *pionier* Gefr. Vogel (seated), infantry Uffz. Ehrentraut (behind Vogel), a clerk (infantry?) and artillery Uffz. Heinicke.

Roster of telescopic-sighted sniper rifles (including civilian hunting rifles) on issue to men of IR 134, one of whom is a Gefr. Hermann.

Infanterie-Regt. 134
Nr. 8728.

28.2.1916.

Nachweisung der Zielfernrohrgewehre und Buechsen .

Lfde. Nr.	Gewehr-Nr.	Name des Schuetzen	Komp.	Art des Gewehrs	Wo befinden sich die Gewehre
1	4361 h	Utffz.Munzert	1.	Gewehr 98	Jn Stellung
2	4399 h	Gefr.Tröger	1.	"	" "
3	2692 h	Sold.Heinrich	1.	"	" "
4	337 a	Gefr.Kämmer	2.	"	" "
5	3221	" Röschter	2.	"	" "
6	274	" Lotter	4.	"	" "
7	718	" Sammler	4.	"	" "
8	957 b	" Schuricht	9.	"	" "
9	2911 a	" Wunderlich	9.	"	" "
10	2250 h	" Wagner	9.	"	" "
11	6620	Sold.Luderer	10.	"	" "
12	3445 a	" Kühn	11.	"	" "
13	8242 F	Gefr.Schmidt	12.	"	" "
14	51 i	" Queck	12.	"	" "
15	8998 G	" Jakob	12.	"	" "
16	977 b	" Buschner	11.	"	bei Wachtkomp.XIX. z.Rep.abgeg.26.2.16
17	7401	"d.Res.Böscher	5.	"	Jn Stellung
18	6983	Sold.Wunderlich	5.	"	" "
19	1561	Gefr.Bölke	6.	"	" "
20	7273	" Giessner	6.	"	" "
21	7626	" Uhlmann	6.	"	" "
22	8361	" Brückner	7.	"	" "
23	1386	" d.Res.Schlimper	8.	"	" "
24	5397	" Stuhr	8.	"	" "
25	1253	" Hermann	1.	Jagdbüchsen f.Mun.88	" "
26	0897	Sold.Sandner	2.	"	" "
27	158	Gefr.Fuchs	2.	"	" "
28	0818	" Preissler	3.	"	" "
29	146	Utffz.Glass	9.	"	" "
30	4330	Gefr.Petzold	4.	"	(bei Wachtkomp.XIX.
31	0982	Sold.Helm	12.	"	(z.Rep.abgeg.26.2.16
32	4509	" Franz	10.	"	(" "

G.K.O. 4550 II c. 28.2.16.

Soldat Richard Bohm of 1./IR 104. On the reverse is a dedication (dated 20 April 1916) to his civilian hosts of 1914.

Lightly equipped infantrymen of IR 134 in the trenches near St. Yvon in February 1916.

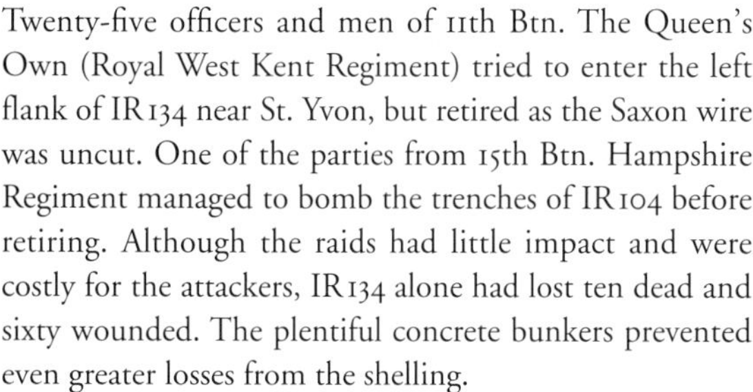

Twenty-five officers and men of 11th Btn. The Queen's Own (Royal West Kent Regiment) tried to enter the left flank of IR 134 near St. Yvon, but retired as the Saxon wire was uncut. One of the parties from 15th Btn. Hampshire Regiment managed to bomb the trenches of IR 104 before retiring. Although the raids had little impact and were costly for the attackers, IR 134 alone had lost ten dead and sixty wounded. The plentiful concrete bunkers prevented even greater losses from the shelling.

Another burst of activity began on the night of 9–10 July with a successful raid by 32nd Btn. Royal Fusiliers on IR 134, whose line had been smashed up with mortars during the day. Three failed attempts and a mock raid followed in the St. Yvon and Ploegsteert sectors between then and 16 July. Despite all this plus frequent shelling and gas, 40. ID managed to commit III./104 to Fromelles on the 19th (in the event, it was not needed). After an extended lull, 41st Division made a final major raid with two full companies on the night of 26–27 July. The trenches of IR 104 were pulverised by heavy artillery and trench mortars for several hours, before a company of 10th Royal West Kents overran a forward patrol of 2./104 and invaded their trenches near Le Gheer; the raiders withdrew on schedule pursued by a counterattack, leaving their wounded behind. This operation did nothing to hinder the transfer of the entire XIX. Armeekorps that began on 3 August.

The regimental history of IR 104 offers monthly casualty totals for November 1915 onwards, illustrating the increasing lethality of the Ploegsteert sector.[19]

November 1915	32 dead and wounded
December 1915	52 dead and wounded
January 1916	57 dead and wounded
February 1916	92 dead and wounded
March 1916	92 dead and wounded
April 1916	79 dead and wounded
May 1916	90 dead and wounded
June 1916	141 dead and wounded
July 1916	110 dead and wounded

The regiment's subsequent ordeal at *Fourreauxwald* (High Wood) on the Somme would produce losses to dwarf these, and make the survivors positively nostalgic for Ploegsteert Wood.

South of Ploegsteert Wood

From October 1914 to July 1916 IR 181 held the sector from Pont Rouge to the Lys, with the exception of the Le Touquet salient, held by III. Batl. / IR 104 until 20 April 1915 (see chapter 2). IR 181 had dug in where its attacks had bogged down in open ground south of Ploegsteert Wood, and was forced to defend and redevelop these crude trenches over the winter. The line ran across open fields interspersed with hedges and drainage ditches, with a clear view of Ploegsteert village and Armentières, and was crossed diagonally by the Warneton-Armentières railway line.

Beginning in May, Husaren-Regiment 19 (divisional cavalry) formed *grabenkommandos* of fifty men per squadron for trench service. Initially individual hussars were attached to the infantry. Later, HR 19 received a company subsector – usually, the undesirable left flank at Le Touquet.

To combat the known mining threat there, IR 181 formed an ad-hoc *miniertrupp* under Ltn. d. R. Jürgens, a civil mining engineer. This was supervised by Ltn. d. R. Stock of 3. Feldkompagnie / Pionier-Bataillon 22, awarded the *Militär-St. Heinrichs-Orden* for his actions following the British detonation near the Le Bizet road on 9 April 1915 (see p. 29):

… On the occasion of the first English mine detonation at Le Touquet on 9.4.1915 he rapidly built the position back up into a defensible state despite the reaction of the enemy. As a countermeasure against the English mineworks, the 3. Komp. Pi.-Batl. 22 under the direction of Ltn. Stock, among other things, drove a gallery towards the signalman's house in front of the German position.

About 5 pm on 20 April, British 4th Division miners near the railway reported the flash of electric lamps. Saxons had broken into a branch off the main British gallery, and a nightmarish underground firefight ensued.

Ltn. S. immediately satisfied himself in person of the state of affairs. Rapid action was essential. He therefore ordered the necessary explosive charges to be brought up as quickly as possible. The enemy intended to break into the German tunnel system and smoke out the miners with incendiary bombs. When Ltn. S. rushed back to the gallery after completing the initial arrangements, the first victims of [carbon monoxide] *gas poisoning were being carried out. He immediately took over the direction of the rescue operation and eventually descended himself. He managed to recover the last of the gas casualties and was the last to return to daylight. Thanks to his self-sacrificing action and his swift and courageous decisions, it was possible to blow the gallery the next day.*

1st Btn. King's Own (Royal Lancaster Regiment) in the trench above the mine reported that the Saxons in fact blew their charge at 7.30 pm on the 20th, when the British had almost sealed the breach. One British miner died underground and several were hospitalised with gas poisoning,

Remarkably relaxed and unarmed infantrymen of IR 181 in a fortified position among the houses of Le Touquet in summer 1915.

but their main gallery was mostly undamaged. The next day Saxon miners were heard within two yards of a British gallery on the Le Bizet road, which was blown early on 22 April. IR 181 lost one dead and British observers believed they had breached a drain under the road. The Saxons retaliated with heavy artillery, and a counter-mine nearby that night. Another Saxon countermine was blown near the railway on 13 May. An attempt two days later to blow up the signalman's house failed unnoticed, but Major Dove of 2nd Btn. Sherwood Foresters was shot dead and his battalion endured a sharp *minenwerfer* and artillery bombardment. Stock's men had a major success on 13 June, bringing down two houses in Le Touquet (the British admitted to one), ruining a British gallery and capturing a tunneller. The British retaliated on the night of 18–19 June with five mines near the railway line accompanied by a sudden barrage, inflicting serious losses on II./181 and following up with a small raid.

IR 181 endured gas attacks on 24 September and 13 October, occasional heavy bombardments and attempted raids on the night of 28–29 December by multiple battalions of British 74th Brigade. On the afternoon of 19 January 1916 the same brigade attacked the Le Touquet salient on a scale not seen since 1914. The four-hour bombardment included 12-inch howitzers and trench mortars, concluding with gas on a 500-yard front north of the railway and smoke on the actual attack front. In the salient many of the defending 2./181 were killed, wounded or buried alive. Their trenches were so ruined that the raiders (over 200 all ranks, mainly from 2nd Btn Royal Irish Rifles) could find no mine entrances before aggressive counterattacks, a counter-bombardment and their own thirty-minute time limit forced them to withdraw, taking eleven prisoners. The raid had cost IR 181 twenty-two dead, eight-eight wounded and twenty-two gassed, and won Ltn. Joseph Grohmann of 2./181 the MStHO for his part in the defence.

The regiment beat off smaller British raids on 21 and 25 February, taking prisoners on both occasions from the recently arrived 9th (Scottish) Division. Hostile forward patrols on 22 and 29 March and on 23 June were beaten off by Saxons in no man's land and several battalions identified. Raiders from British 41st Division entered the front line of IR 181 on the nights of 30 June – 1 July and 8–9 July, but found it empty and had to retire; on the second occasion they were ambushed by fire from loopholes in the second line. On the night of 12–13 July two parties from IR 181 raided the British near the Lys, taking four prisoners and other booty with no Saxon losses; a British raid two days later was defeated by defensive fire. Despite a final British attempt on the night of 26–27 July, IR 181 was successfully relieved by RIR 38 on the night of 3–4 August 1916 and sent to the Somme.

The *Burghof* at Le Touquet on 20 January 1916, in the aftermath of the previous day's trench raid by 2nd Btn. Royal Irish Rifles.

The artillery

As an active division, the 40. ID had a full brigade of field artillery. In total 40. Feldartillerie-Brigade (Feldartillerie-Regiment 32 and 68) comprised one *abteilung* (battalion) of 10.5cm light field howitzers (II. Abt. / FAR 68) and three of 7.7cm field guns. Each *abteilung* had three six-gun batteries, each of three two-gun züge (sections). A gradual reduction of existing regiments to four guns per battery began in spring 1915, with 'spare' *züge* used to form regiments for new divisions. In XIX. AK, a few six-gun batteries survived until mid-May 1916. The full strength of its artillery was however never committed on its front. Within 40. ID, an abteilung of FAR 32 served from March 1915 as reserve and fought in spring and autumn 1915 at Neuve Chapelle and Arras. From November 1915 this reserve reinforced the weak 117. ID to the right of 40. ID; from 30 March 1916 it was attached to XXVII. RK.

During the fighting of October 1914 an ad-hoc organisation was adopted based on the *'gruppe'* (group) of all batteries within an infantry regimental sector, typically under an *abteilung* staff. *Gruppe Weihmann* (later *Rabe*) was assigned to *Detachement von der Decken*, usually including 2. / 68, 2. / 32 (later 4. / 32) and a *zug* of 5. / 68. *Gruppe Partzsch* (later *Krohn* and *Stuhlmann*) supported IR 104 (and IR 106 until its departure) with 3., 6. and the rest of 5. / 68. *Gruppe Haberland* (later *Henker* and *Schulze*) supported IR 181 with 1. and 4. / 68. The other two batteries of FAR 32 were in the Frelinghien sector. In November 1915, FAR 68 redeployed as per the map on p. 60.

Until the end of the 1914 fighting, field artillery batteries changed positions repeatedly as per their doctrine of mobile infantry support. Trench warfare turned them into ad-hoc siege artillery firing from fortified positions, a role suited only to the 10.5cm howitzers. Concrete gun bunkers began to appear in spring 1915.

At the onset of trench warfare, the artillery on both sides was hampered by low ammunition stocks. The Saxon guns would only fire if enemy action demanded it. It was only in 1915 with better orientation in the terrain, more stable gun positions and restocked munitions that the artillery could actively engage threats to the infantry. However the ongoing need of both sides to save ammunition for emergencies and offensive operations limited its activity throughout the year. The weather could further hamper it by impeding observation and even flooding gun positions. As a rule the German guns were more active before noon and the British after, as observation was easier with the sun at one's back. Major enemy operations elsewhere on the Western Front were invariably accompanied by more intense exchanges, as the British sought to conceal the location of the attack and deter the release of reserves. Beyond routine 'ritualised' shelling, the artillery of XIX. AK outside these brief periods focused on

A junior officer of 2. Battr. / FAR 68 (standing third from left) celebrating Christmas 1914 in billets with NCOs and men of his battery.

preserving the 'quietness' of its front by punishing enemy aggression. Targets engaged at the request of the infantry were typically significant points in the British trenches, such as forward observation posts, support weapon positions, strongpoints and approach routes. At their own discretion, the artillery targeted batteries, observation posts, rear-area traffic and billeting areas such as Houplines and Armentieres with the aid of aerial observation.

The corps had the use of a modest amount of heavy artillery. Initially 7. Batterie of Saxon Fußartillerie-Regiment 19 (II. Batl. / FußaR 19 being a corps asset) was attached to FAR 68, but replaced by 5. / FußaR 19 under Hptm. Rudolf Uth in November. Lacking much choice of higher ground, Uth's observers made regular use of the 35 metre high chimney of the Pont Rouge sugar factory; the building's upper floor had already collapsed. The chimney was finally hit by a British shell on 12 April 1915, Sergt. Konrad Niemz barely escaping with his life. The British finished off the chimney the next day. For their long and valuable service at this hazardous post Niemz received the war's first award of the rare *Goldene Militar-St. Heinrichs-Medaille* (the highest Saxon award for enlisted men) and Ltn. d. R. Joseph Schaak the *Militär-St. Heinrichs-Orden*.

5. / FußaR 19 was relieved by Prussian Fußartillerie-Batterie 233 (with six guns but no limbers) on 13 May 1915. A Saxon Fußa. Battr. 430 (obsolete 9cm guns) was formed in September, and in November a battery of long-barreled 15cm guns and Bavarian Mörser-Batterie 257 (21cm howitzers) were added.

Fire positions (*feuerstellungen*) and observation posts (*beobachtungstellen*) of Feldartillerie-Regiment 68 in November 1915. Inexplicably the bulge in the German line at the *Entenschnabel* is omitted. Note that 4. / 68 has been subdivided into a three-gun section and a lone gun.

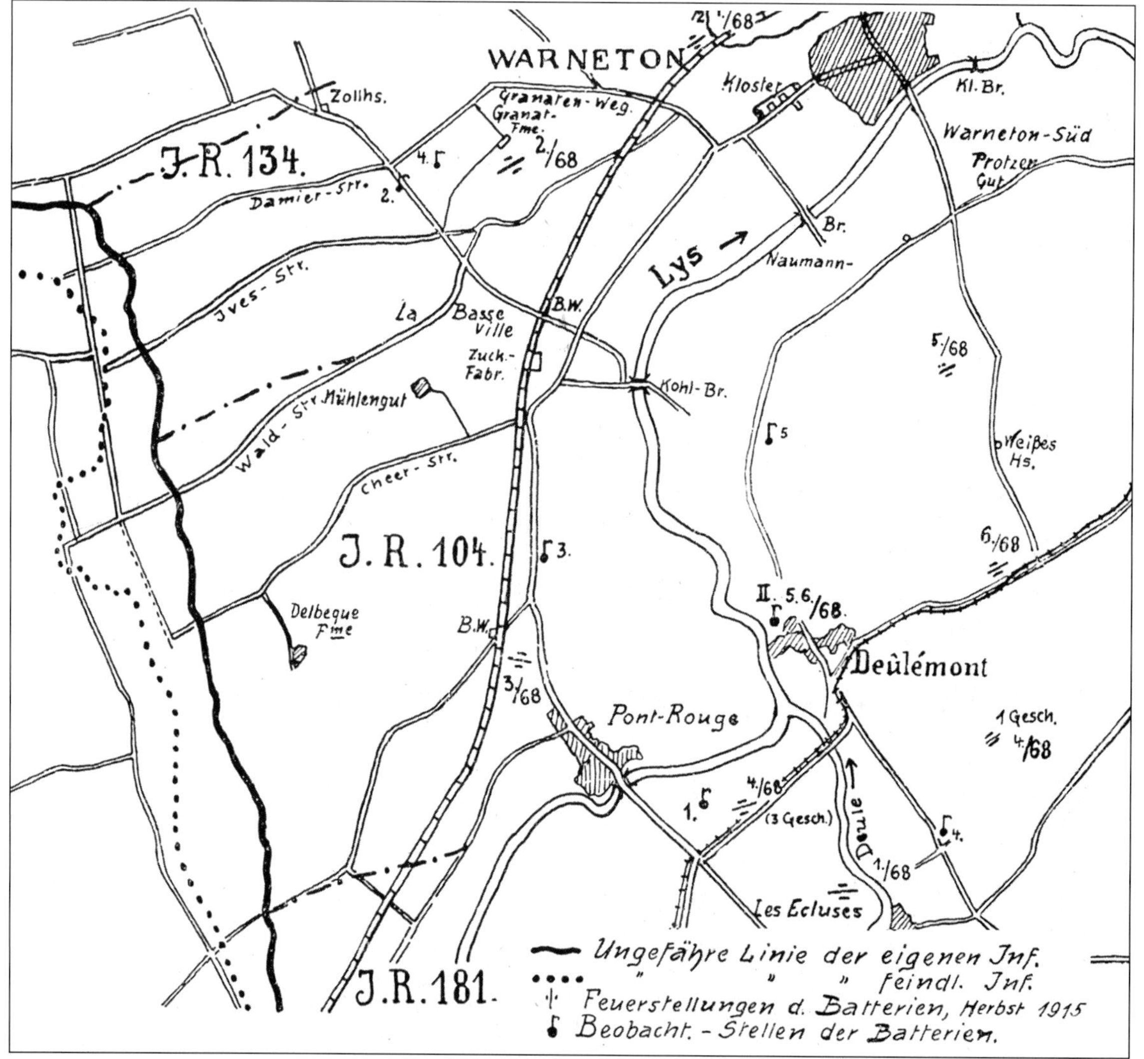

'Water closet' behind the billet for the officers of 2. Battr. / FAR 68 in Warneton, during a period of flooding in the winter of 1915–16.

Enlisted men's accommodation of 2. Battr. / FAR 68, one of several farmhouses they inhabited northwest of Quesnoy and east of Warneton-Sud.

Fire position used by 5. Battr. / FAR 68 at the farm on the road south of Warneton-Sud (Waustine Farm on British maps).

Detached kommando of II. Abt. / FAR 68 with one of their 10.5cm IFH 98 / 09 howitzers at an artillery repair workshop in Hellemmes near Lille.

Feld-Luftschiffer-Abt. 27.

Geschaeftsstelle: **Lille, rue d'Isly 2.**
Fernsprecher: **Amt Lille No. 74.**

No. 155

Ballonbildmeldung

Richtg. PLOEGSTEERT WALD (südl. Teil)

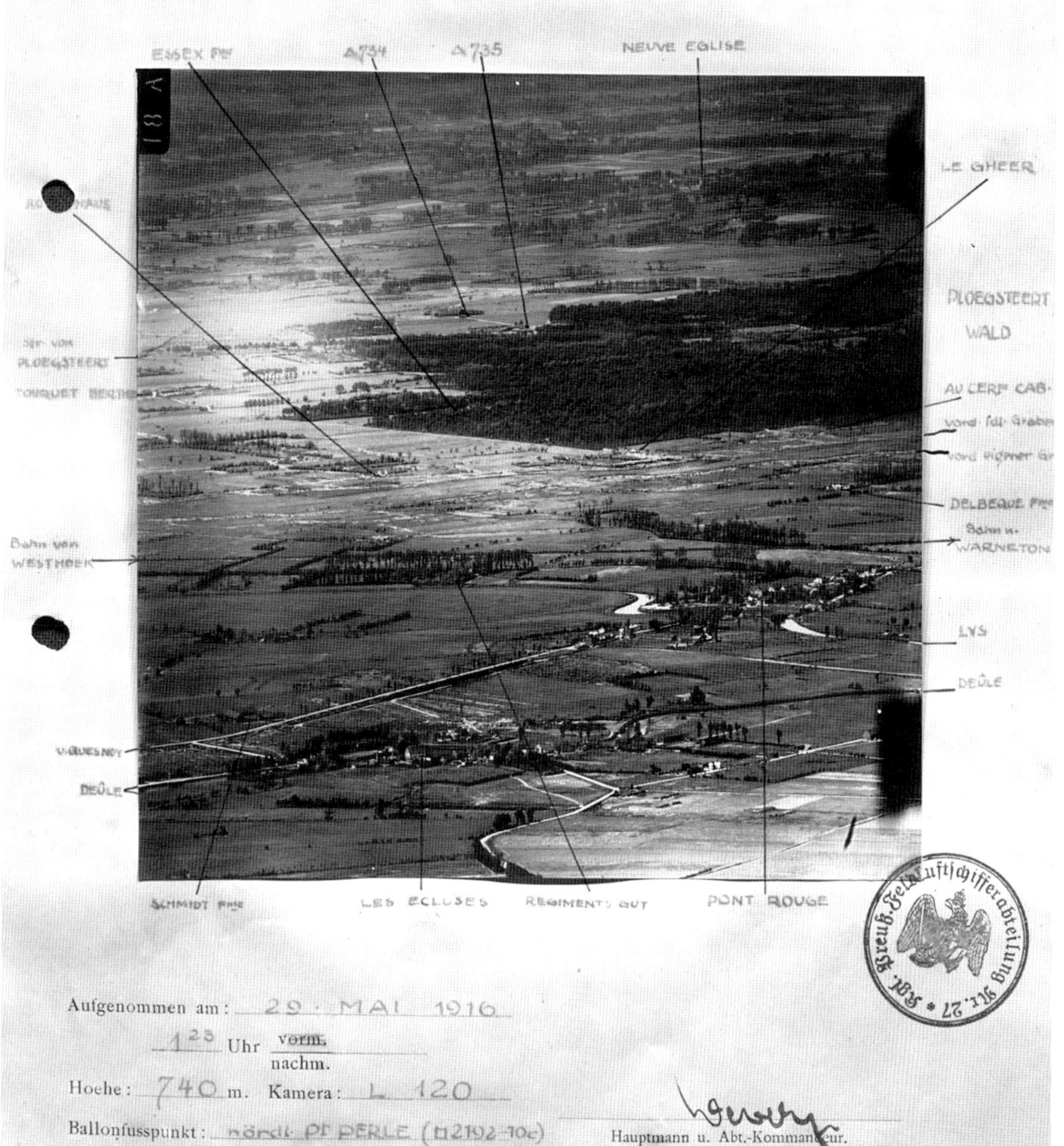

Aufgenommen am: 29. MAI 1916
1[23] Uhr ~~vorm.~~ nachm.
Hoehe: 740 m. Kamera: L. 120
Ballonfusspunkt: nördl. P^T PERLE (□2192-10c)

Hauptmann u. Abt.-Kommandeur.

A HUNDRED YEARS LATER

Original and current grave crosses for Gefr. Kurt Zill of 1./IR 104, KIA at Le Gheer on 2 November 1914, in Quesnoy-sur-Deûle (see p. 242).

According to his brother, Soldat Kurt Bechler from Crimmitschau (12./IR 181) was shot in the head and killed around 6.30 pm on 17 January 1916. His Christian name is recorded as Albert by the Volksbund Deutsche Kriegsgräberfürsorge and on his current headstone at Quesnoy-sur-Deûle.

Chapter 4
The First Battle of Ypres | Reserve-Infanterie-Regiment 245

Unteroffizier Heinrich Schmidt of 3. Kompanie / Reserve-Infanterie-Regiment 245 sent this photo home from Coblenz (Koblenz) during the train journey from Leipzig to the front on 13 October 1914. Schmidt was wounded early in the battle and never returned to the regiment. He wears the *Zentenarmedaille* awarded to everyone in active service on the 100th birthday of the late Kaiser Wilhelm I (22 March 1897), indicating that in 1914 he was probably in the older classes of reservist like most of the regiment's NCOs. As per peacetime regulation for NCOs he wears white gloves, and his brand-new boots are fitted with *Fußschoner* (additional leather straps) to help ensure a good fit.

The First Battle of Ypres | Reserve-Infanterie-Regiment 245

In the words of the regimental commander Major Alfred von Heygendorff

Alfred von Heygendorff.

Alfred von Heygendorff was born at Bad Elster on 1 March 1868 into minor nobility. His great-grandmother was the actress and singer Karoline Jagemann and his great-grandfather the Grand Duke of Saxe-Weimar-Eisenach, who ennobled his mistress as Freifrau von Heygendorff. Alfred's grandfather Karl had been a Saxon generalmajor and his father Bernhard (who died in 1916) a senior police officer. Alfred was privately tutored at home from the age of six and accepted into the prestigious Königliche Gymnasium in Dresden in 1878. After a break for several years in which he studied at the Großherzogliche Gymnasium in Weimar instead, he received his *abitur* (graduation certificate) and joined Leibgrenadier-Regiment 100 as a *fahnenjunker* in March 1887. He received his officer's commission as a leutnant the following year. His promotion to oberleutnant followed in 1893 during a secondment to the Kadettenkorps (1892–1894). In May 1894 he was married in Dresden to Elsa von Wittern, herself daughter of a Saxon *oberst*. This marriage produced a daughter and two sons, both of whom in turn became officers with Leibgrenadier-Regiment 100. The elder, Egon, was tragically killed in the Battle of the Somme two days before Alfred himself while serving as his father's orderly officer. The younger, Ralph, survived both world wars having reached the rank of generalleutnant in the Wehrmacht.

From 1898 Alfred held the prestigious post of personal adjutant to HRH Crown Prince (and future King of Saxony) Friedrich August for three years, after which he became a company commander in Grenadier-Regiment 101 with the rank of *hauptmann*. He reached his final pre-war rank in 1911 as major on the regimental staff. In 1913 he became a battalion commander in the likewise Dresden-based Infanterie-Regiment 177 (32. Inf. Div.), with which he went to war the following summer.

While lying in the firing line at Perthes in the Champagne on 1 September 1914, Major von Heygendorff was wounded by a shrapnel ball and had to cede command of his battalion, but insisted on remaining with the regiment in the field. Due to heavy officer losses he reported fit for duty again a few days later, although his wound was not healed and had to be freshly bandaged every day. On 2 October he was given acting command of Infanterie-Regiment 178 (23. Inf. Div.), which was down to a strength of two companies. The regiment was refilled with replacements a few days later and von Heygendorff became one of its battalion commanders. On 22 October he was awarded the Iron Cross 1st Class. The next day he was sent to take over Reserve-Infanterie-Regiment 245 with 54. Reserve-Division of the Saxon-Württemberg XXVII. Reserve-Korps, then heavily engaged in the First Battle of Ypres. His exemplary and energetic leadership of this undertrained and demoralised volunteer regiment in truly appalling circumstances earned him the *Ritterkreuz* of the *Militär-St. Heinrichs-Orden* (the highest Saxon and oldest German gallantry order) on 17 November. Without exception the surviving writings of his officers and men describe him with great affection, often calling him the 'soul of the regiment'. As the division's senior regimental commander he was also well regarded by his superiors and entrusted with a critical role in the Second Battle of Ypres (see Chapter 5). His popularity even seems to have overcome the mutual distrust between the Saxon and Württemberg elements of his division. Promoted to oberstleutnant, he was killed on 12 September 1916 by a direct hit on his regimental HQ dugout in Rancourt during the Battle of the Somme.

Extracts from his private diary were later provided by his widow and surviving son to the regimental veterans' association and serialised in its newsletter *Was wir erlebten* ('What we experienced'). Written at the time and neither edited nor intended for publication, these entries provide a shockingly frank and immediate account of the chaotic situation Major von Heygendorff faced in Flanders on October 1914.

From the diary of Major Alfred von Heygendorff

24. Oktober
We travel right through the night. There is no thought of sleep. The route goes via Maubeuge and into Belgium between Ostend and Ghent. In Tielt we report to the AOK, where we learn that our Reservekorps – four have been formed – are not advancing due to a lack of active leadership[1], the dreadful losses taken immediately upon entering the battle and their composition from *landwehr* and war volunteers. ... We proceed to Dadizeele and report to the *generalkommando* (General v. Carlowitz). I am appointed regimental commander of RIR 245, belonging to the 54. (Württemb.) Division (Exz. v. Schäfer) and then head off to find my regiment, which has been scattered and engaged in combat since Monday (today is Saturday). In Becelaere I meet the acting brigade commander Oberst v. Roschmann, who briefs me but emphasises the hopelessness of the situation. So now I'm standing here in the town with no troops (they are out in front, I. Batl. is detached), no horses (they are swimming in northern France), no baggage (it was left at the *generalkommando*), no nosebag (my orderly has disappeared with it), no billet and no hope. The street is teeming with stragglers from all regiments, who have come out of the trenches to fetch some food (as they have received nothing since Monday) or to bring in the wounded (which they are not authorised to do for themselves). I search them out in the houses and cellars. The complaint is always: we have no leaders and no food. ... Finally I have 1½ platoons together and deploy them behind the village, since the place is coming under a great deal of artillery fire.

25 October
The fun lasted until 2 am, then I laid down deathly tired on the bed in the brigade guardhouse. Crazy rifle fire during the night. ... The next morning I insist that my II. Batl. (v. Wachsmann) be put back at my disposal, so that I can relieve the forward firing line and get my sub-units in order. Around midday the regimental adjutant Ltn. Bachmann and battalion adjutant Ltn. Wienicke turn up, having spent three days stuck in a house with the English lying only 30 metres away. They managed to sneak past. I gather that the [previous] regimental commander Oberst Baumgarten is wounded, the battalion commander Oberstltn. Haeser has fallen and Oberst Hesse is wounded.[2] As v. Wachsmann and his officers are receiving orders from me, a shell strikes the house. Splinters fly everywhere. And now a bombardment is let loose which beggars all description. There are surely spies there who have betrayed our position, as the most frenzied fire is directed at the staff quarters. I have destroyed a telephone line, had a windmill burned and cut the guyropes of a factory with wind catchers which struck me as suspicious. Naturally we relocate. About 5 pm I receive an order to advance with my 'reserves' as protection for the artillery deployed to our north, because the 53. Reserve-Division fighting on our right is retreating from an English breakthrough. Thank God our heavy artillery shoots exceptionally well and commits no fratricide. The breakthrough fails. I would have been unable to do anything about it, since I have only found about 30 men. I go back home. The relief takes place. Around 1 am I have the I. and III. Batl. together, in total 350 men! Major Franz[3] has also been sent to me – now despite it all there is some sort of order. Torrential rain.

26 October
I got to bed at ½ 2 o'clock[4] but was disturbed continually by messages and orders. Yesterday the scoundrels shot up the church, where the wounded lay – appalling chaos.[5] The amount of rifles and ammunition left lying around defies all description. ... Due to the shortage of war-experienced leaders division into unit sectors and cohesion are impossible. The bombardment continues, we are outgunned in artillery. To remain alive is almost out of the question. And on top of that an attack order has already been issued, which has however been postponed for the moment. In the afternoon very heavy shelling from heavy artillery. It is intended for us staffs. In the evening we find a spy, or at least a very suspicious fellow, whom I have escorted to divisional HQ.

27 October
Beautiful peaceful morning after a well spent night. At noon the 'blessing' of the artillery kicks off, at first harmlessly, then a fearsome cannonade begins. Almost all the houses in which we are residing are shelled. Several shells hit the brewery where my 6. Kompagnie is staying. 6 dead, 8 wounded. The new brigade commander, whose roof has been penetrated, goes to Molenhoek. My house is low-lying and comparatively well protected. Nevertheless, the windows are blown in by the air pressure – so it is a 'castle in the air'! In the evening we move to our old apartment and eat well and plentifully. My 6. Kompagnie digs itself a cover trench behind a hedge.

28 October
A dreadful day – since the English most definitely want me out of Becelaere, they fire 500 shells at us. They shoot up the church steeple in the hope that it will fall on us. The shells come hailing down all around us, everything is shaking, all the houses are shot ablaze so that mine – which until

then they could not get a fix on – becomes visible. Due to the burning houses everything possible starts to burn – debris, tent sections, corpses. Finally a tent section on which several thousand cartridges are lying catches fire. These begin to explode. We douse the hot cartridges so everything else is not endangered, a task which is not entirely without risk. We go from time to time into the cellar of the brewery, as soon as it dies down we go back to the chateau. Suddenly a shell hits the adjoining room. The air pressure hurls us out of the doorway. A safe saves our lives by taking the force of the blast. It is no longer safe for us to stay there. We retire to the brewery and together we – v. Wachsmann, Bachmann and myself – play an 'explosive' round of skat out of desperation. While I am still pondering where I should retire to next, an order comes from the brigade commander Oberst Mühry[6] that I am to come to Molenhoek. It is done. A Major v. Holzhausen has fallen and is to be buried together with a Leutnant v. Uslar.[7] Since the furious fire has prevented us from burying about 60 corpses, he is still lying there. finally his groom, who has been looking for him for days, comes with some comrades and carries him away. The body is to be taken back to Germany! ... My current orderly Landwehrmann Müller frets over me most touchingly, he cares for me like a son. Lately I met a 15-year-old boy scout named Fritz Lehmann, who lies in the firing line, joins in the shooting, has a textbook fury toward the English, fetches food and transports the wounded. Now he has got himself a uniform from the dead and received the Iron Cross.[8]

Picture postcard of Fritz Lehmann in *pfadfinder* (boy scout) uniform, showing the wound he received at Dinant in August 1914.

29 October

Already yesterday evening an attack order came from our new corps commander Exzellenz Schubert, successor to Exz. v. Carlowitz.[9] ... Exz. Schubert wishes to attack without artillery preparation. RIR 245 must rush forward out of its trenches, which lie 20–200 metres from the enemy in one great surge and take Gheluvelt. A further battalion of Bavarians is to be subordinated to me.[10] This arrives an hour late at the place where it is to report (Becelaere) and since the time of the attack is fixed, a thorough briefing is impossible. We are to storm Poezelhoek, a hamlet that has a completely dispersed layout. I place the Bavarians behind my right wing in reserve. When I come under fire on the left flank from the eastern houses of Poezelhoek, I give a Bavarian platoon the order to take these houses. So three companies rush forward in a disorderly manner in long bounds, going south rather than west, and suffer appalling losses. A fourth company still held in reserve rushes off to the front – I am left out on a limb. I manage to get one Bavarian platoon in hand, which I put in a trench. Since I find Poezelhoek empty when scanned with the binoculars, I go in there and very soon find myself under fire from three sides. I try to get the platoon to come closer, which succeeds only to the extent of getting ten courageous men out in front who hold a single trench in check. Now there is nothing for it but to retire, as my death would be of no benefit to anyone.

Together with Ltn. Bachmann I crawl 500 metres through a wet cabbage field, bound into the wood and make my escape. Now I proceed to my left wing, coming under furious shrapnel fire and upon reaching Westhoek under shellfire. I see the appalling tragedy on the left wing. The whole field is sown with the dead. The wounded wail, many are hit again by the shells. Still I assemble two companies from all regiments, receiving the 26th Jägers[11] (one company) in addition and am thus able to hold my old line. Only the 26th Jägers have gained some ground. I watch as 100 Englishmen are taken prisoner on my left wing. The forming up of units without leaders trained in peacetime is a Sysiphean task. I sleep again in Molenhoek.

30 October

In the night a fresh attack order arrives. … Of my company commanders Hptm. Kaeubler has fallen, Halbauer and Arnold are wounded.[12] I had a search party out for the latter last night. The attack is not making progress due to insufficient artillery support (this is difficult in woodland). The 26th Jägers have only been able to gain ground on the southern edge of Poezelhoek by night. The XV. Armeekorps on our left is also not advancing. Therefore there is a relative lull. The greatly superior English artillery fires all day long. The rascals are somewhere different every day; ours are always standing still, get discovered by aircraft and are vigorously bombarded as a result. I have four companies in the front line and one in reserve. The division has taken four companies away from me, so that unfortunately I have scarcely any depth. In the afternoon I go back to Molenhoek and am connected to the front by telephone. My horses and batmen turn up. At last, after fourteen days – a change of clothing and a thorough wash! Naturally no post yet, it is too sad; finally a good night's sleep for once.

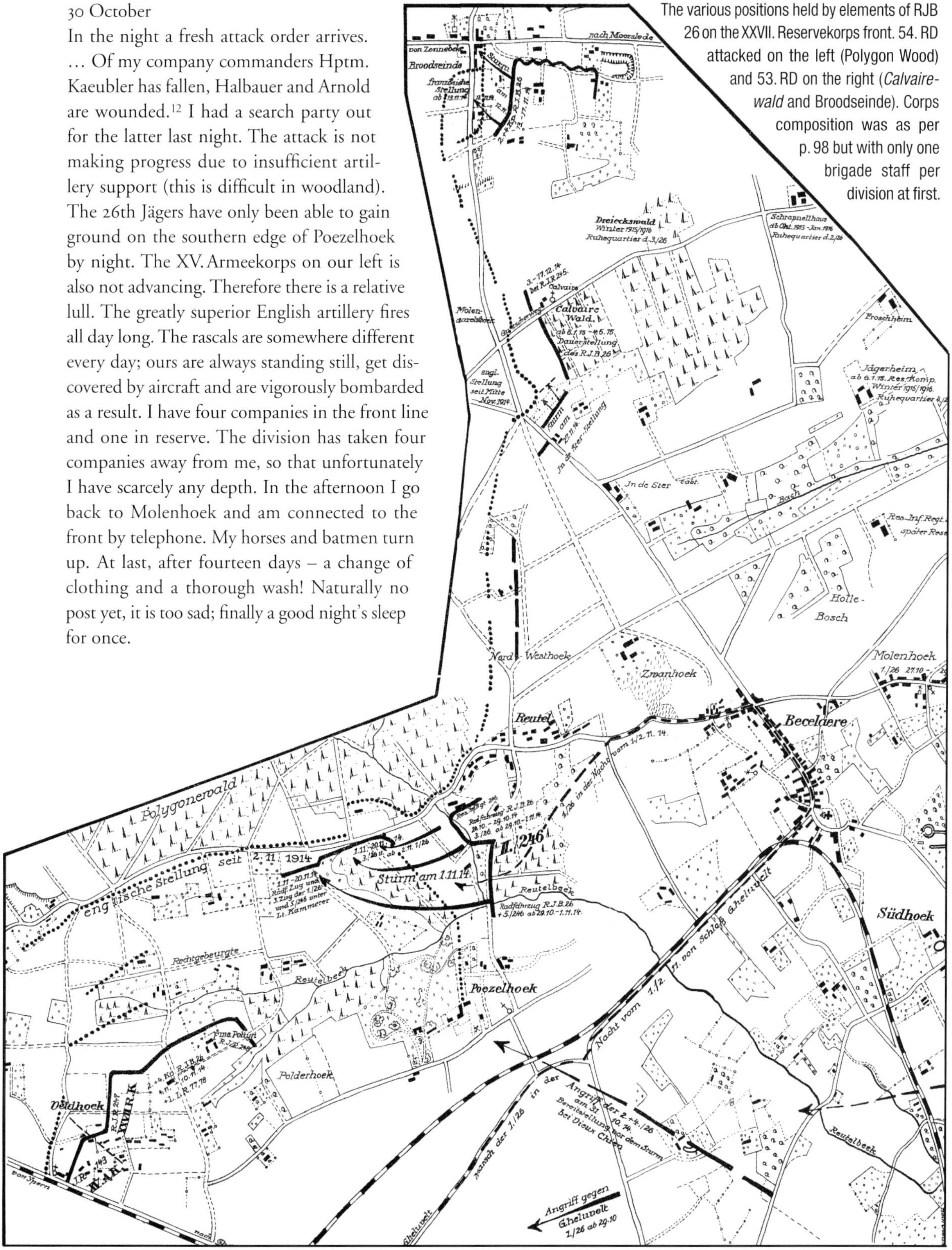

The various positions held by elements of RJB 26 on the XXVII. Reservekorps front. 54. RD attacked on the left (Polygon Wood) and 53. RD on the right (*Calvairewald* and Broodseinde). Corps composition was as per p. 98 but with only one brigade staff per division at first.

31 October

Heavy artillery bombards the well dug-in enemy. Order to attack Poezelhoek, applying pressure from left to right. – Artillery effect is zero. The corps commander is insistent. Frontal advance almost impossible. A thrust by the Bavarians subordinated to me (II./RIR16) costs them two company commanders. When I go to my left wing in the evening to issue the attack order for the night there is dreadful disorder there. 245., 247., 248., Res. Jäger 26 and Bavarians are standing around. No-one knows whose command he is under, or how far forward the regiments are to be found. Whole platoons which were sent forward have disappeared somewhere. I announce my battle plan: to take Pozelhoek via pressure from the left to the right flank from the bend in the road southwest of Becelaere. I then go back to Molenhoek to ask Oberst Mühry for clarification of the situation. I get all the troops which lie within a particular part of the battlefield subordinated to me, divide it up into three sectors and give a clear attack order which reaches the troops at 12 o'clock. I then lay down to sleep. Among the wounded is a 15-year-old boy who has taken a headshot – not my friend Lehmann. The composition of my staff is comical, all of them – clerks, *tagebuchführer*[13], chauffeur (using his own car) and telephonists are educated men, engineers, lawyers etc. A hotelier (Friese-Adolf) from Venice is in charge of the kitchen wagon. The cook has never worked in Leipzig.

1 November

Sunday! I arrive early in my cover trench, where my Bavarian reserve company is supposed to be – vanished. I go searching and find a lost platoon in the wood. finally the Bavarian company also turns up, which in turn has mislaid another platoon. Here the lack of peacetime trained leaders makes itself felt; our training also needs to pay yet more attention to the NCOs. Thanks to the efficiency of my group commanders - v. Wachsmann, v. Aspern[14] (former officers) and Franz (active) – a tidy advance ensues. We win Poezelhoek and Polderhoek, from which the English have withdrawn due to a threat on the right wing. For the moment we stop there, so as not to press on alone. My old cover trench is graced with rapid shellfire (750 rounds) in the course of the battle, but we are not at home. – In Poezelhoek we find the corpse of Oberstleutnant Haeser, which is buried. In the evening I go back to Molenhoek, after I have handed three companies over to v. Wachsmann as reserve.

Aerial view looking northwestward from the rough vicinity of Polderhoek Chateau across the German trenches toward Polygon Wood.

Major Gustav von Aspern, battalion commander of I./245.

2 November

I have a severe coughing fit which well-nigh suffocates me. In the night an order arrives that I must hand over a company to my right-hand neighbour Res.-Inf.-Regt. 246. I send the company of 26th Jägers. In the course of the day I go into the line. The brigade has relocated to the southeastern edge of Becelaere. I also settle there (at Westhoek). Prior to this I hand out 26 Iron Crosses, among others to Major von Wachsmann. Since we only have to hold our position it is relatively quiet. My right-hand neighbour asks for help again and receives my Bavarian company as well. I'll soon be out of reserves. I eat together with the brigade commander Oberst Mühry. In the morning I visit the grave of my brother's friend Oberleutnant Arnold,[15] who succumbed to his injuries. The grave is very prettily decorated. In the afternoon the XV. Armeekorps makes an attack on Veldhoek. Suddenly a cry for aid reaches me – I have to help because the English, reinforced by the French, are launching a counterstroke. If my regiment advances it will come under enfilade fire from Polygonewald – so I decline and point out that Oberst v. Hügel will have to be on my left. The latter is intervening too with RIR 247 and 248. A heated struggle breaks out, which we observe

Polderhoek Chateau after the battle, showing the scars of artillery fire and the graves of some of the fallen.

from Westhoek. Now the message comes that Veldhoek is lost! I go forward into the line and manage to determine that the southern edge of Veldhoek is in our possession. RIR 248 links up with us. In the evening I visit Oberst Mühry.

3 November
Quiet night, slept until ½ 9. Peace reigns; we have no determination to attack, the enemy even less so. A glorious sunny day and yet gloomy at heart – I receive no letters and see no possibility of winning a decisive victory. Hope for our cause is running out. In the evening I eat with my six medical officers who have been decorated today and sit together with Oberst Mühry afterwards.

4 November
Quiet night. Our heavy artillery must have been shooting tremendously near us, as the English made a thrust west of Veldhoek – in which they got a bloody nose – and I heard nothing. I grow steadily weary. The horror associated with the knowledge that there is nothing that can be done about the heavy losses (the attack on 29.10. brought my regiment over 50 % losses) and the lack of news from my family paralyses my courage. I regard our cause as hopeless. We can no longer deliver any great blows; we lack the men for it, especially leaders. England cannot be suppressed – so, a bad peace. In the morning I go into the trenches and give dispositions for the further advance against *Polygonewald.* We have to work our way forward little by little. Today a new mortal threat crops up. The English have identified the position of the heavy artillery behind Westhoek by aircraft – who knows whether the bombardment of Westhoek will come off now. In the evening a letter comes from my wife and my father. Thank God. I receive a visit from Rittmeister Lampe-Fischer, who heads my baggage train. He and Oberst Mühry eat at mine. The catering is excellent. Due to the resourcefulness of my agents, I have a nicely laid table and enough lighting.

5 November
Slept until ½ 9. However orders always come during the night which require work. So one has to catch up during the day. Tomorrow Rechtgebeurgte must be occupied. I have the impression that the English are falling back, in order to dig in afresh further back. Then the work will begin anew. The heavy artillery is relatively quiet. It could also be a trap.
Today Major v. Wachsmann is going back to the homeland due to intestinal bleeding. I'll miss him very much. I have the dead buried and their things gathered up. Hundreds of

Crude trenches near Reutel in November 1914, with the *Dreieckwäldchen* in the background and a mass grave marked with 'duds' in the foreground.

thousands of cartridges are still lying all over the place from the fighting. Millions in value are lying in the street. In the evening a cosy dinner with guests. Whoever is hungry comes to see me.

6 November
Slept until ½ 9. Nothing going on. Trench warfare. The English artillery is firing less. Rumour has it that the English are pulling out, as they have worries on account of the insurrections in India, Egypt and the Cape. If so then peace cannot be lacking for much longer.

7 November
My little daughter's birthday! I wanted to be home by then. As usual I go to the firing line, give commands, hand out decorations and try to raise the mood of the men. Apart from that I work and write a great deal. The English are said to have withdrawn. It looks that way too; as there is a lot of shooting and the bullets are striking near us. This is how the French shoot, they do not aim. Bachmann presented me with roses 'for Wera'.

8 November
A glorious sunny Sunday, since the November rains have stopped for a long time and the aircraft stay away. The English have been quite silent for the whole night. We have got 30.5 cm heavy howitzers at Vieux Chien.[16] There is no advance anywhere. *Korps Beseler*[17] is also unable to apply pressure on the right wing. In front of us the English have disappeared. One notes the rafales, the more vigorous shooting and the bullets going high, which are more dangerous to us in the rear than in the firing line; for the French shoot badly. I have the stray pieces of equipment gathered up, so that thousands of marks worth of kit is not lost.

9 November
Nothing new. Hauptmann Reimer of Res.-Feldart.-Regt. 54 eats with me. In the afternoon I am at his place for cocoa. Very nicely arranged. Reimer plays the piano. I receive all the post still addressed to Inf. Regt. 177: 23 letters, 11 cards, 12 parcels. One relishes so much love.

10 November
An attack order arrives during the night. A *Garde* division which is deployed on our left is to advance against the *Nonnenwald* northwest of Veldhoek.[18] We are to support the attack. Thanks to the lessons of the latest battles it's being done cautiously. Today there is crashing and banging everywhere. Ypres railway station is said to be destroyed and the withdrawal of the English scheduled. May it be true!

Before the war Hauptmann Kurt Reimer (left, with Leutnant d. R. Goehle) was the most junior battery commander in Germany (with FAR 78). After the loss of its first two commanders on 24 October 1914, he took over the I. (sächs) Abteilung / RFAR 54 at the height of the battle, was awarded the *Militär-St. Heinrichs-Orden* on 17 November and led his *Abteilung Reimer* (from April 1917 redesignated as III. / RFAR 32) for the rest of the war.

English prisoners are said to have stated that our attack on 29 October was known in advance. So we are surrounded by spies! But we are also too trusting. Not me, though; I'm having the whole population taken off to Dadizeele. Unfortunately there is a certain tension between Württembergers and Saxons. Hptm. Reimer breakfasts with me; I'm round at his for cocoa in the afternoon. I write a lot of letters and stick to the house apart from my visit to the firing line, as the weather is cold and damp and I must go easy on myself as much as possible. In the afternoon a Prussian Maschinen-Gewehr-Abteilung[19] turns up, which is to reinforce our thin line. We hear nothing at all of the bigger picture. All the more though we are driving world politics.

11 November
This morning the *Garde* division wishes to attack on our left. To this end all available artillery has been brought together to fire on the *Polygoneveld*. It is frightful. The ground trembles, it roars so much that one cannot hear oneself speak. I'm glad I'm not an Englishman. One could really pity the rascals. And still they hold out. As parts of my regiment advance this afternoon to keep pace with the Prussians,

they shoot my company commander Ende[20] – a very dear fellow – and five men dead. The advance continues this evening. This morning Feldgeistliche v. Funcke[21] held a beautiful service in Becelaere. This, the death of Ende and the cold November day put me in a very melancholy mood. In the evening a bottle of champagne in the usual circles with some guests puts me back in order. A thunderstorm in the evening.

12 November
The attack continues. My regiment works its way up to within 120 metres of the enemy. The order to 'take the southern edge of *Polygonwald* by 11 am' looks good in writing, but is not achievable due to the wire obstacles, behind which death is lurking. The divisional commander calls on me, he is in full agreement with my assessment and my arrangements. Hptm. Reimer and a Ltn. Wilhelm from the Prussian M.-G.-A. eat breakfast at my place. In the afternoon I am at Reimer's, he plays the piano most prettily. It's beautiful to be able to forget one's misery for a few hours. In the evening we mark Oberst Mühry's wedding anniversary. Bachmann has composed a nice poem. This afternoon there are fresh pancakes baked by a man of my staff.

13 November
A rainy day. I am sick at heart for my poor fellows in the trenches. Rheumatism and intestinal ailments are appearing. The advance progresses steadily, but only very slowly. I report to my superiors that I do not wish to advance, as we are within 100 metres of the edge of the wood, have a good field of fire and cannot assault because of the wire obstacles. The bombardment of the wood yesterday has torn down the trees, so that movement through the wood is impossible.

14 November
Wet weather! My poor men! The trenches are full of water. Rheumatism and diarrhoea. 100 sick from a rifle strength of barely 700! Nonetheless morale is good. In the afternoon our fellows capture seven men as well as three people who returned to their homes and may well have brought about the shelling of Becelaere. I turn them in at Dadizeele with a sharply worded delivery note. In the evening the medical officers eat at mine. Stabsarzt Bücking develops his ideas regarding the war. I ought to be venting the fury which I have toward the English, due to the wretches verifiably shooting with dum-dum bullets,[22] not against our miserable opponents but rather against their government. Since I can't throttle the government though I will stick to its instruments.

The main street of Becelaere looking toward the church, showing the extent of the damage inflicted in October and November 1914.

15 November
Storm and rain; it's enough to drive one to despair! I present Major v. Aspern with the Iron Cross. Today we catch 5 men and 7 women. An edict announces that from all now on all those we catch will be shot. Hopefully the influx will stop now. Besides this, nothing new.

16. November
We are working our way forward again as per divisional orders. … It is so peaceful early today that one could almost think that peace talks were underway. This afternoon we have the usual fun. It is cold and damp. At times it snows. Combat strength today 554 rifles, 100 sick. Where will this lead? Am highly despondent today; have had it up to here with it all. Homesickness is setting in.

17 November
On today's morning stroll a shell explodes not far away from me. God graciously protects me. Already in the night between 1 and 2 am heavy shells came flying to Becelaere, probably because the Württembergers who have been in the village since yesterday carelessly lit candles. … In the afternoon a pretty girl of about 18 is brought to me, who has cooked for the Germans in Lille and wishes to continue doing so with us. I send her off to Dadizeele. Much post in the evening. About 200 replacement men have arrived, so I can reorganise into six companies and permit two companies the blessing of being relieved.

18 November
I welcome the new arrivals with a rousing speech and divide them up. Then I go into the trenches with the six new *offiziersstellvertreters.* Otherwise the day passes like any other. The yearning for peace is growing.

19 November
The day proceeds according to routine. It is snowing and bitterly cold. For the men though the cold is better than the damp.

20 November
At half 7 in the morning shells come down again in the village. The Württembergers who are staying in Becelaere with us are so careless that the aircraft must see everything. … Much work during the day as RIR 246 is coming in with a battalion and I must find billets. The arguments with Oberst R[oschmann] are not settled without a struggle. The sectors at the front also shift. 248 und 245 move 100 metres rightward to take pressure off 246, which must hand over a company of Reserve-Jäger-Batl. 26 and ninety 247ers. The battalion commanders all come for coffee and I talk everything over with them. Then I write a lot of letters. In the evening I am with Oberst Mühry and Ltn. Wilhelm (of MGA 9) at Hptm. Reimer's, where all the artillery officers are eating, 15 gentlemen in total. After dinner there is beer. In addition a battery quartet and a soloist from the Prague Opera sang beautifully – sounds of home, which one might never get the chance to hear again.

Oberst a.D. (later Generalmajor) Alfred von Roschmann of RIR 246, killed by a shell commanding 107. Res. Inf. Brig. on the Somme on 13 September 1916, the day after von Heygendorff.

21 November
The English are now shooting at the village with heavy siege howitzers. The crack of our long 10cm guns sounds harsher in these very cold nights, so that sleep is scarcely to be thought of. In the morning I feel shattered. Inspection of the new sector, with which I am very satisfied, especially as the cover trenches are very fine. In the afternoon I write letters.

22 November
There has been little noise of battle all day. Rumours of armistice and wishes for a separate peace have been buzzing about of late. The English 'grumblers'[23] have thrown up a lot of new craters in the past few days, so that my battalion commanders no longer feel safe in Poezelhoek and move closer to the firing line. Oberst Mühry feels unwell. … While I am going to see him in the evening, my escort has his upper arm smashed by a stray rifle bullet – a metre behind me.

23 November
While I'm in the front line, my sector comes under heavy artillery fire; however no harm is done. The night is quiet.

24 November
I don't come out into the trenches, because the divisional commander Exzellenz von Schäfer is convening a great council of war at Becelaere. He wants to have the *Polygonenwald* bombarded. This would need to happen on a daily basis – then the fellows would be ground down. Sadly we have too little ammunition. After the conference I go for a stroll for an hour with Oberst Mühry. Only two ricochets whizz past us.

25 November
A local attack by the neighbouring division is called off – for their sake though I must stay with the reserves. *Liebesgaben* arrive from the photographer Patitz (Dresden) and from Leipzig. In the line of 246, which lies very close – 6 metres – to the enemy, a Frenchman calls over that they have no desire to continue, the English are gone. Thereupon a German writes a letter stating that they should give themselves up. He declares himself ready to take the letter over if the French refrain from shooting, which also happens. Halfway across Frenchman and German meet. Both try to see as much of the other side as possible. The Frenchman is amazed at how strongly occupied our trenches are. The letter is handed over, at 1 o'clock an answer is made out. This reads dismissively: 'The invitation is a bad joke. The opposite would be more likely.' The negotiators disappear, lively fire starts up. So it may take a long time yet.

26 November
Nothing new. Bad weather. I get hold of a larger dugout for my staff and myself, i.e. a row of dugouts 37 metres long – because the shooting is getting increasingly uncomfortable. Sadly everything is drowning. There is an appalling amount of water here. The day passes uneventfully like so many.

27 November
At ½ 1 am orders come and with them the *Heinrichsorden*. Cheers! Hauptmann Reimer receives it too. He ate at mine but has already left. So off to see him, parade march in front of his window. Afterward everyone goes back to my place, where we celebrate together. In the afternoon an attack by the 53. Division is scheduled, which brings it as much as 300m closer in places. In the night there is a gigantic cannonade along the entire line, which disturbs us, achieves nothing and does no damage.

The graves of those killed in the final assault of RIR 243 on 14 November bear witness to the appalling price of securing the dense and tangled *Calvairewald*. RIR 245 took over the wood and the front line on its western edge on 2 December.

Oberstleutnant Wilhelm Lüddecke, commander of RJB 25 and (from February 1915) RIR 242. He was awarded the *Militär-St. Heinrichs-Orden* on 27 May 1915 for his part in the Second Battle of Ypres, became an oberst in 1917 and survived the war.

28 November
The French are getting cheeky. They shoot by day too, wasting a lot of ammunition and thank God not hitting much; but all the same it is annoying and grates on one's nerves in the long run. The brigade commander Oberst Mühry is really not at all lively. His stomach and nerves are giving out. There is a frenzied cannonade during the night which won't let me sleep. Finally I get up. While it rained like mad in the evening, there is now a glorious starry sky. It goes quiet at 2 am, after we have counted about 1000 shots. It cannot be determined who, whether friend or foe, has fired so much.

29 November
First day of Advent! Honoured by the French in so far as they shoot like mad with their artillery. Zero hits on us, but in Becelaere it is as if a deer hunt is underway – 'the game is lively'.

30 November
Professor Hans von Hayek from Dachau near Munich and Leutnant Engelhardt of Luftschifferabteilung 2 (currently with Feldwetterstation 6 of AOK 6), the former in civilian dress as a war artist, came to Becelaere yesterday and were taken for spies as they asked our men about every possible subject. I searched them thoroughly, especially the professor, who was painting Becelaere church. To make amends I invite them to

In late November Uffz. Walter Flor of 11./245 sent his wife this pre-deployment picture of his *korporalschaft* (section), noting that only five of them are left. He has marked the casualties on the photo as dead (x), wounded (*verw.*), missing (*vermisst*) or sick (*krank*).

breakfast. Leutn. Engelhardt talks most interestingly about our Zeppelin airships, the 42cm guns and the general situation. Well, we are all going to put down roots here. The enemy artillery shoots more and more, ours has no ammunition. It's enough to drive one to despair. The evenings grow increasingly dour, as no-one is in the right mood any more.

1 December
Quiet night, but I sleep badly. My nerves are giving out. Field church service at 9am, given by a Württemberg *hilfsgeistliche* in the school. A shell strikes nearby, but it turns out to be the only one. At midday the steeple in Becelaere is demolished by *pioniere*, as it is an aiming mark for enemy artillery. In the afternoon I have a factory chimney pulled down for the same reason. 125 French deserters are said to have come over to the 53. Division. Oh, if only yet more come!

2 December
The day begins well! Divisional council of war: new sector allocation, as elements are being pulled out for other employment. 245 gives up its position south of *Polygonwald* and occupies the western edge of *Calvairewald* and eastward thereof to an extent of 1000 metres!
March off at ¼ 3pm to take over the new position. First of all to RIR 243. Here I meet my old regimental comrade Kurt v. Holleben [see photo p. 121] who commands this regiment as oberst. He has had gunshot wounds in the stomach and back on top of his gout, but is still his old self. His position at *Calvairewald* is splendid, brilliantly constructed. I then go to see Oberstleutnant Lüddecke of RIR 242 [see photo p. 77] who conducts me into his sector. The route goes through a swampy trench, where we sink in past the knee. In the mean time it has got dark. I sit down

Trenches and dugouts in *Calvairewald* in December 1914. Note the trenches named after officers (e.g. *Major-Höckner-Straße, Aspernstraße*), fancifully named dugouts (e.g. *Die goldene Zwölf* – 'The Golden Twelve'), aid post (*Verbandplatz*) and *minenwerfer* (MW) position.

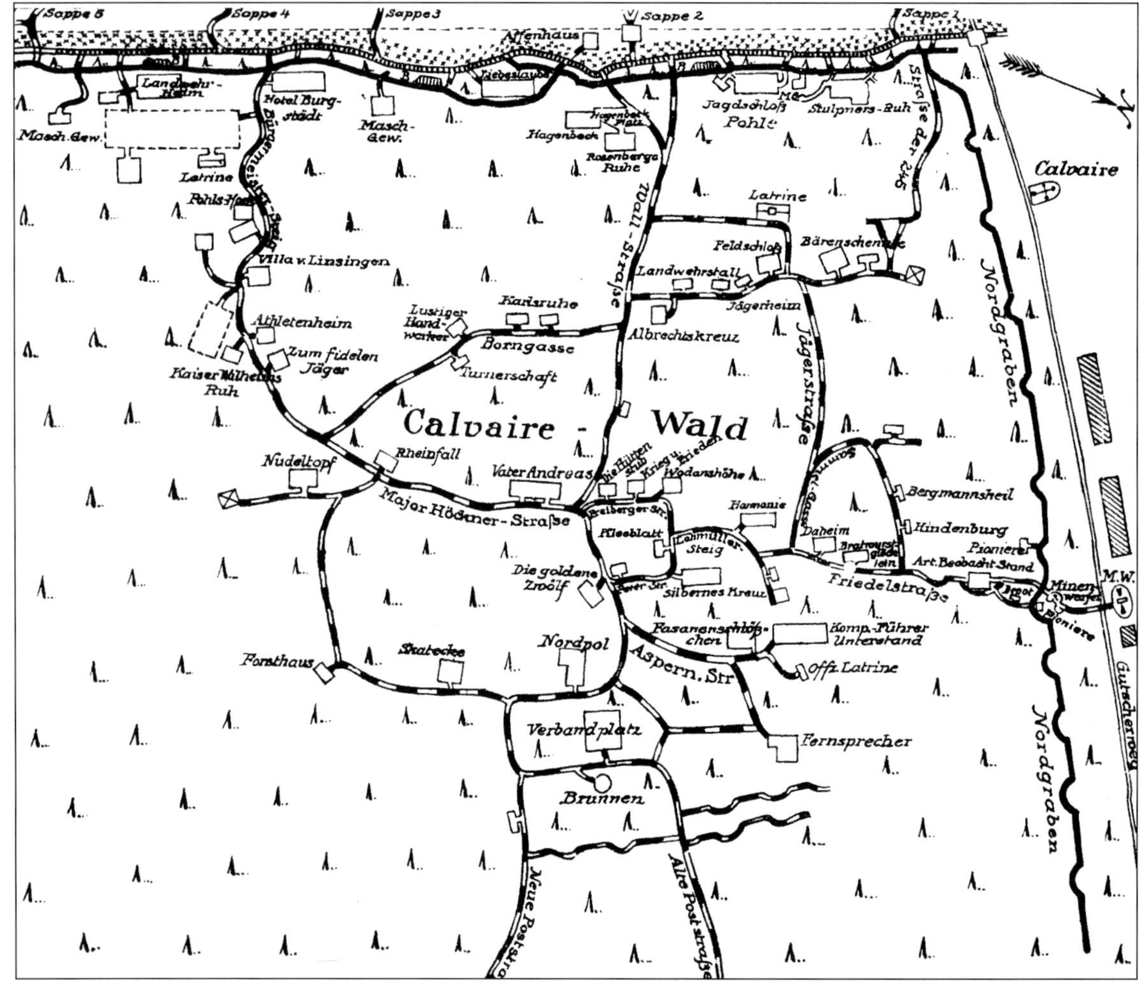

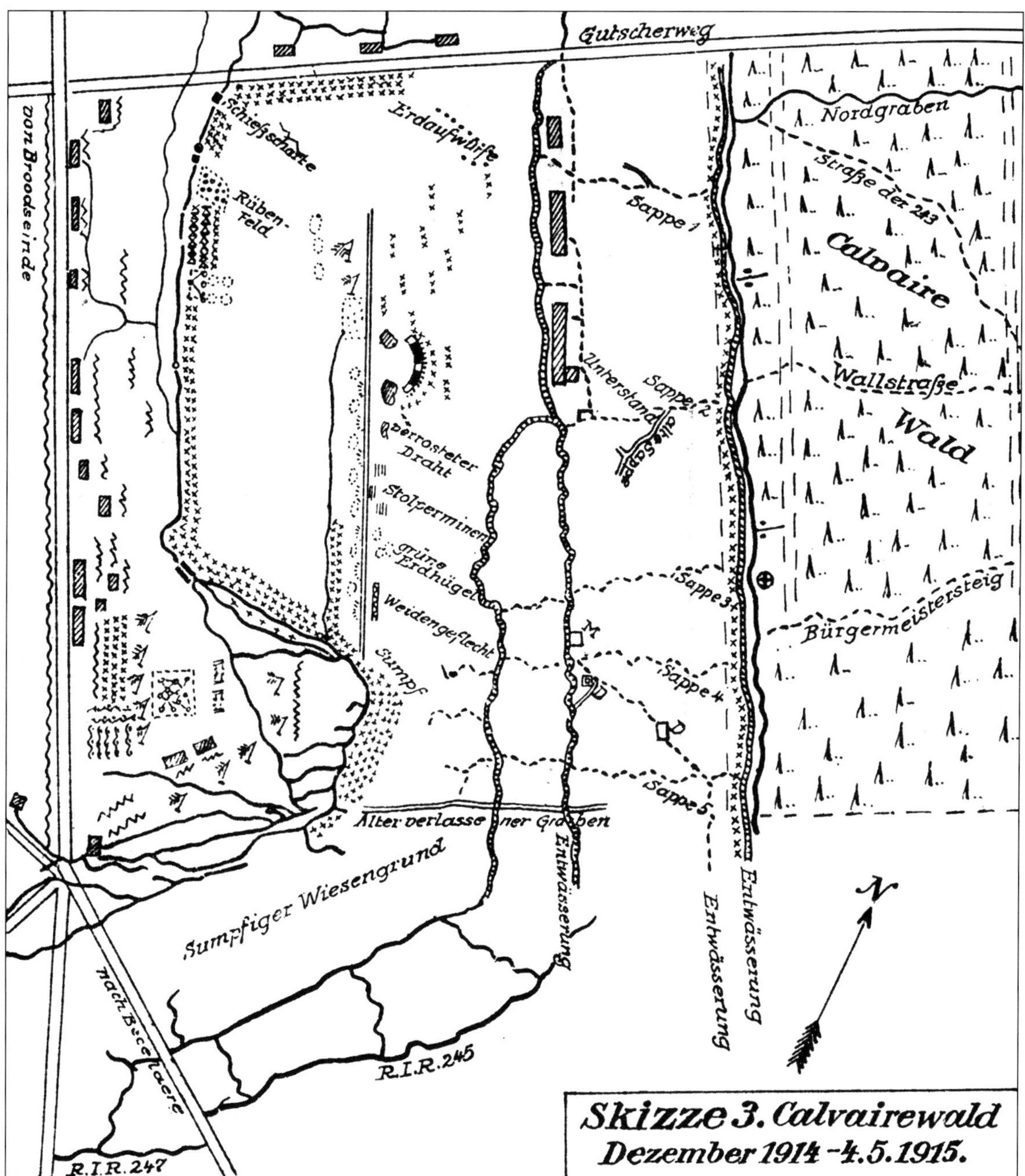

Opposing trench systems in the partially flooded field between *Calvairewald* and the Passchendaele–Becelaere road in December 1914.

in despair in the front line and forgo any further inspection. At ¾ 8 pm I am 'at home' – i.e. in Becelaere for supper at Hauptmann Reimer's.

3 December

At 9pm I head out to look for a new 'castle' in the new sector. East of *Calvairewald* I find a filthy house that has not yet been shot up. Oberst Mühry, Major Dörtenbach and a few others come to a farewell breakfast. Oberst Mühry gives a touching speech, calling me the 'soul of Becelaere'. At ¼ 4 o'clock I decamp with part of my staff and go into the northern half of my sector. The trenches are cleverly laid out, but lack comfort for the men. At ½ 8 pm I retire to my shack, as sick at heart as an outcast.

A NEUTRAL VIEW

The following purports to be a critical assessment of German fighting methods by an anonymous (probably military) observer of undisclosed neutral nationality attached to the British Army. It frankly describes the serious tactical and operational deficiencies exhibited by the undertrained and ill-equipped reserve divisions in their baptism of fire at the First Battle of Ypres.
A copy of this document was found among the papers of Major von Heygendorff and printed in Was wir erlebten *in the 1920s alongside the above diary entries.*

Ypres, 23 October 1914
As a citizen of a neutral country who is embedded as an observer in the English camp but sympathises with the German cause, I would hereby like to give a short description of how the German attacks appear when viewed from over here, and do not doubt that it will yield a few hints which may be of use to the German troops. …
The bravery of the German infantry is the subject of universal praise over here also. However it almost gives me the impression that the infantry assaults have achieved few successes other than setting new records for bravery. I have often been downright amazed, with what unheard-of recklessness the foot soldiers have been sent into the battle line against the defences on this side, in the absence of even the slightest prospect of breaking through with the assault. Evidently reconnaissance has been lacking on the German side, since the low losses of the English infantry and artillery alike suggest that many German thrusts were driven forward 'into the blue'. …
It seems incomprehensible that the Germans do not follow the French method for the storming of villages, which thus far has almost never failed against the nevertheless undoubtedly steadfast German foot troops, namely to subject the buildings in question to a well-aimed shellfire.
The generally prevalent opinion here of the mobility of German foot soldiers is not a favourable one. – However since I have found on occasional visits to German gymnastics festivals that the Germans are second to none in terms of agility, I have therefore taken a closer look at the German infantrymen and now cannot help but place the principal blame for the slowness of their movements on unsuitable equipment – with a 20 to 40 pound pack on the back sprinting is out of the question, to say nothing of the fatigue which must already be setting in on the approach march. No-one here can understand why a German infantryman takes spare clothing etc. (but no food!) with him in his backpack into the trenches, where he certainly can't make any use of it.
There is no doubt that leaving the backpack behind would greatly improve mobility, especially in woodland, when leaping over trenches, swimming canals, etc., and would considerably reduce losses. What a waste of materiel it must be when the backpacks of thousands of dead and wounded men are left lying in the fields or fall into the hands of Germany's enemies (the effect on morale!).
A beet field provides passable cover from observation for a line of prone riflemen. However as soon as the towering superstructure of backpacks and mess tins appears on the backs of the riflemen, the position is given away. ...
The battle could surely have taken a far more favourable, if not decisive, turn for the Germans, if machine-gun fire (which is intensely feared by everyone fighting on this side) could have been used instead of massed rifle fire. … Shouldn't it likewise have been possible for the Germans to set machine-guns up in trees to shoot into the enemy trenches?
Given the intelligent German human material, it should not be difficult to increase the number of machine-gun teams by making use of long-serving foot soldiers. What I have been able to observe so far of the effectiveness of the German artillery unfortunately gives little grounds for congratulation. It is no longer the German artillery of Lüttich, Namur, Maubeuge! On every occasion I have been able to discern that observation and reconnaissance are lacking on the German side. I am inclined to believe that especially at the start of the battle the German foot troops must have been severely thinned out by their own artillery. Nowhere have I been able to observe any use being made of the field telephone. Otherwise there would not have been such an obvious lack of coordination of the artillery and infantry attacks. The stubborn resistance encountered proves that all this has not gone unnoticed on the English side.
The German trenches do not offer enough protection! French and especially English use of cover is worth emulating. Haystacks and treetops often hide spies, who become quite usefully active, often remaining undetected for a long time. Farmhouses too (attic corners and cellars) are often not searched carefully enough on the German side!
I will also try to smuggle through my further observations on the battle which is currently raging, but I cannot say when or if there will be another opportunity to do so. If by the above hints one thing at least can be achieved, namely a reduction in the terrible loss of life on the German side, I will consider my actions sufficiently rewarded; and if fate should lead me into German captivity, I will argue for chivalrous treatment. I will perhaps not neglect to refer to this document.

Chapter 5

The Second Battle of Ypres | Reserve-Infanterie-Regiment 245

On the way to the front at Verlorenhoek via the former forward positions in May 1915. The leading man has wrapped the action of his rifle in rags and covered the muzzle to keep the mud out; purpose-made muzzle caps did exist, but (unlike this homemade cover) would have to be removed before firing. Also clearly visible here is the so-called '*riechpäckchen*' ('smell packet') worn in its waterproof pouch on the left shoulder. This first German 'gasmask' was merely a cloth pad stuffed with cotton waste, with tapes to tie it in place over the mouth and nose. The pad was soaked in hyposulphite solution immediately before issue and returned for re-soaking after action.

Zweite Flandernschlacht | Reserve-Infanterie-Regiment 245

In the words of Hauptmann Curt John, acting commander of II. Bataillon, and Major Alfred von Heygendorff

After spending December 1914 at *Calvairewald* (see map p. 79) together with RJB 26, the regiment ceded the wood itself to the *jägers* in early January 1915. Henceforth it held the 'In de Ster' subsector, extending from the appallingly swampy southern edge of *Calvairewald* to meet RIR 247 east of Polygon Wood. It crossed the Becelaere–Passschendaele road via a tunnel in the front line and a rear communication trench near the ruined estaminet of In de Ster Cabaret. The most exposed spot was on the left flank at the *Hexenkessel* (Witches' Cauldron), a sharp corner by a group of ruined buildings where the enemy was no more than fifteen metres away and hand grenades a constant threat. The regimental history records how *"the Frenchman throws over his explosive-filled tins and the German sends him discus grenades in return. Both types of close combat materiel are equally effective, as both seldom explode."*[1] Both sides soon shielded their trenches here with wire mesh anti-grenade screens, after which gossip and verbal sparring were exchanged instead. When a Belgian unit took over the trenches opposite and won the sympathy of the Germans with lively abuse of the hated British, complete peace briefly reigned until the Belgians were again relieved by the French.

Hauptmann Curt John.

The regiment was still holding this sector when the III. Bataillon was temporarily detached on 23 April 1915. Together with two Württemberg battalions of 54. RD (II. / RIR 247 and an ad-hoc three-company battalion from RIR 246) it joined a composite regiment under the command of Major von Heygendorff which was initially assigned to corps reserve. This *Regiment von Heygendorff* was subordinated to the likewise composite *Sturmbrigade von Schmieden* and billeted in Wallemolen. On 25 April the composite regiment stormed the so-called *Erdwerk* ('earthworks' – not to be confused with the *Erdwerk* near s'Gravenstafel) on the north bank of the Strombeek, taking 300 prisoners and four machine-guns. Early the next morning it secured the crossroads on the Gravenstafel Ridge. Temporarily withdrawn on 1 May, the regiment was committed again two days later. Its attack on 3 May overran Berlin Wood and the nearby *Erdwerk*. Although not completely ejected from the ridge, the British were nevertheless forced to retire from the untenable eastern end of the Ypres Salient during the night.

Meanwhile at In de Ster Cabaret I. and II. / RIR 245 had simply been tasked with pinning the enemy in place. Once the British overnight evacuation of Polygon Wood had been discovered early on 4 May, II. / 245 immediately joined the pursuit which halted that afternoon at the new British defences on the line Arrêt–Eksternest. Our account here of the period from 22 April to 1 May is provided by Hauptmann John, while from 1 May onwards we return once again to Major von Heygendorff.

Curt John came from Burgwenden near Sömmerda in Prussian Thuringia. His surviving writings indicate that he came to Flanders with II. / 245 in 1914 as a formerly retired leutnant and was the only officer of the battalion left standing after the First Battle of Ypres. After briefly serving as battalion adjutant of I. / 245, he was promoted to *oberleutnant* and given acting command of the replenished II. / 245 on 2 January 1915 until replaced by Major von Schulz. Having reached the rank of *hauptmann* and again taken acting command of the battalion, he was severely wounded in the thigh during a relief on 14 November 1915. The amputation of his leg three days later failed to save his life, and Hauptmann John died on 21 November 1915 at Reserve-Feldlazarett 94 in Ledegem. Known and much-loved in the regiment for his sense of humour and love of nature, his loss was marked in von Heygendorff's diary with the mournful words *"what a crying shame about this splendid fellow"*.

From the diary of Hauptmann Curt John
(taken from the veterans' newsletter *Was wir erlebten*)

In the trenches, 22 April 1915
It seems that the English were very annoyed with us yesterday. At 12 noon they began a fearful shooting, as though they intended to ensure that nothing was left of us. One could scarcely hear oneself speak. It lasted ¾ of an hour. We have not determined what its reason and purpose were. Not a single one of us was hit. We did not retaliate at all, so finally they desisted. Tomorrow we'll be going back to Waterdamhoek.

In the trenches, 23 April 1915
We will not be relieved today; yesterday afternoon the 26. [Reserve-]Korps attacked toward Ypres from the north and reached the line Boesinghe–Zonnebeke. As a result, the sack around Ypres has been drawn much tighter. To the south our lads are at St. Eloi. It's only 10 kilometres from there to Boesinghe, so it may get too cramped for the English near us. To ensure that they don't simply withdraw on the quiet while we are being relieved we must remain here until tomorrow, possibly even until the day after that. That's most agreeable for us, since the units which are right behind us must brace themselves to be sent who knows where. The corps commanders will probably organise a general race to see who gets to Ypres first. Unfortunately, we and ours will miss out on the honour. Yesterday field guns were captured too, and numerous Englishmen and blacks taken prisoner. We do not yet know the full details. – Earlier on we watched two aircraft shoot at each other. In the end they both flew away.

In the trenches, 24 April 1915
We are still in the same position as yesterday, which means that we are still not being relieved today. Our I. Bataillon[2] stands in corps reserve with three others at Moorslede, where I too have spent half a day. Von Heygendorff leads this reserve and Major Franz the regiment. Yesterday 1,600 prisoners and thirty artillery pieces were reported. We have just heard that the attack from the north is making good progress. We are behaving here as if we too intended to attack at any moment. This morning between 1 and 8 am 180 *minenwerfer* bombs were sent over, and every so often we shoot like men possessed. In between we let our bayonets glitter in the sunlight and loiter around the assault ladders, naturally so that it can be seen from over there. The enemy seems to have only two guns at his disposal for us, and earlier on he fired one of them into his own trenches. After that he desisted entirely. The prisoners are unfortunately more French than English. If this continues we will soon be approaching Ypres. In any case they are attaching very great importance to this success up there. –

The so-called John-Hof, headquarters of II. Bataillon / Reserve-Infanterie-Regiment 245 in Waterdamhoek.

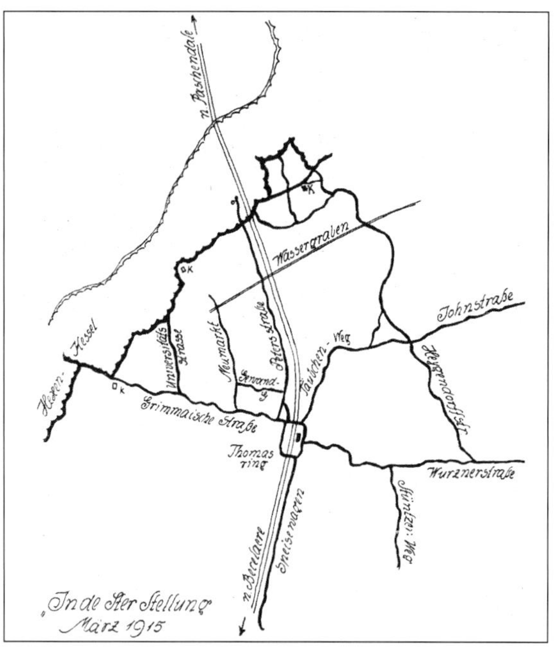

The In de Ster sector in March 1915, showing trenches named after familiar streets in Leipzig and officers of the regiment (including our diarists). *'Wassergraben'* indicates a drainage ditch.

Last night was very unsettled. At 2 pm the orders for today and the mail arrived at the same time. Major Franz came at 4, and the *Stabsarzt* at 6. In between Lorenz had to use the telephone etc. Then the spectacle began. At the moment we are all sitting together in my dugout. The others read the paper and I write while smoking a pipe. I hadn't furnished myself with enough cigarettes for so many days in the trenches, and only have one left. It seems that I will probably never return to our *kasino*, built with so much love and art. If we reach Ypres in exchange for that, it will be fine with me.

In the trenches, 25 April 1915
It is said that today is Sunday – this is probably the case, we just don't notice it. The situation today is still the same. Yesterday once again some prisoners and five guns were captured. This morning Heygendorff will probably have attacked with his reserves to the north of us. Yesterday evening we shot an enemy stockpile of rifle ammunition and mortar bombs up in flames, that was beautiful. Our losses are few, the war is now being waged with entirely new means.[3] While all the commanders are sitting in a dugout and waiting to fall in for our stroll to Ypres, the photographer has just sent me ten pictures of the princes and one of yesterday's batch of prison-

Birthday well-wishers for Major Aspern of the I. Bataillon at the *Froschheim* (see map p. 69) on 10 April 1915.

The *Froschheim* east of *Calvairewald* housed the staff of whichever battalion was currently in regimental reserve.

ers. We have rapidly consumed all our provisions. Everyone is smoking my Bismarck cigars. Today we received three bottles of red wine, which we can't take with us either. Such are our problems now. And yet it appears increasingly likely that we will still be sitting here tomorrow. It is now ¾ 4 pm[4], so there is not much time left today. Ulbricht has just turned up as well, so now there are ten of us. We are packed in like herrings – I'm having some coffee brewed now. We don't have enough cups though, so some will have to drink from glasses like they do in Karlsbad. Dr. Lomer and Eppert are also coming now, so it will be too cramped to continue writing.

In the trenches, 26 April 1915

Not much has changed. We are to be relieved today and will go to the *Froschheim*. For how long, we do not know yet. I'd rather stay here at the front. The regiment wants us relieved though, as we have already been in the front line for seven days and the frequent sentry duties are overexerting the men. By my estimation though they would quite gladly remain here. But orders are orders. To the north of us the advance slowly pushes on, and we wait for it. Heygendorff took 100 prisoners yesterday, besides which there are said to be many dead, and Englishmen at that. Hopefully everything continues to go well. – Today our regiment is 245 days old. The party in the *kasino* won't happen now. No harm done!

Froschheim, 28 April 1915

We probably won't get our turn now. The English attacked us during the night but were soundly greased. It is said that Major von Heygendorff wants another two companies, one from the I. and one from the II. Bataillon. The order is not there yet, so we will probably be doomed to sit and watch. My tunic has just turned up – hopefully I can get it altered, it is now much looser than in August. The hedges here are completely green, magnolias, cherries, apples, pears and plums are all in flower. Sadly the muse is lacking to pay proper tribute to the beauty of nature. – I alone have four woolen blankets, two greatcoats and a cloak, that demands space. – Yesterday evening at 11 o'clock I heard that the divisional staff wanted to talk to me, I already thought I would be heading north, but it was only Adolf who wanted to enquire after me. – Our losses are low.

Froschheim, 29 April 1915

There's nothing new to report. We are still setting here in our HQ at *Froschheim* and waiting for whatever is to come. The III. Bataillon will return to Waterdamhoek on the 2nd, it has 25 dead and 107 wounded. Tomorrow we will be back in the trenches once more, after which the relief cycle will be divided up afresh. How, I don't yet know. Now perhaps I will see the casino and my freshly decorated apartment again after all. I paid nigh on 10 Marks for paints etc. – At noon today after dinner we lay on the lawn in the sun, and later we played skat in the summerhouse.

In the trenches, 1 May 1915
It is very pleasant outside here, everything is dry and the weather is splendid. The enemy has only four field guns left and no shell for them, he only shoots with shrapnel now. That's a cosy feeling. It is ½ 9 am, I am sitting in my roughly patched-up palm garden. To our right the guns are already thundering again. Yesterday it was frightful to hear, the guns positively roared from 4 o'clock in the morning until late at night, all in the direction of Ypres. – At noon today I am invited to dinner with Baring, it is his birthday. – Tomorrow we will be relieved, this time it'll be completely different. We will now be alternating reliefs with Regiment 247 every 14 days. Hence we are going back, the whole regiment into corps reserve. One battalion to Waterdamhoek, one to Slippskapelle and one to Dadizeele. As the most junior I will probably have to take the latter. No-one is keen on going to D. as the *generalkommando* is based there, besides which it is the furthest from the regimental staff. This kind of relief is more pleasant in so far as the regiment always remains together and cannot be so split up e.g. as it was lately at Langemarck. At Langemarck they picked up some beautiful souvenirs again, sadly we weren't with them up there. The English have lost very many killed. Prisoners have stated that they had intended to attack us in a few days. Now we have pre-empted them. They are now down 63 field guns and 50 machine-guns, on top of many thousands dead.

From the diary of Major Alfred von Heygendorff
(taken from the veterans' newsletter *Was wir erlebten*)

1 May 1915
My son Egon is going into the field. God protect him! My poor wife! Visit of Exzellenz v. Schäfer, whom I conduct through the trenches. To our right it thunders the whole day. At 9 o'clock in the evening I am told that I am to be relieved at 10, Regt. 245 is to be relieved from the line so it can go into corps reserve for 14 days' rest. I schedule the march out of Wallemolen for ½ 11 pm, but have to wait another hour as the relief takes a very long time. Finally part of 246 goes astray, which I leave to its fate. On the way a nightingale sings in a copse. The feeling of freedom is delightful. The regimental band awaits us at Moorslede railway station. Waterdamhoek welcomes us in festive style. A dress rehearsal for Leipzig!

Major von Heygendorff on his mare Fortuna and accompanied by Leutnant von Vahl in front of regimental HQ in Waterdamhoek. Originally head of the regimental despatch riders, the critical shortage of officers saw von Vahl appointed as von Heygendorff's adjutant.

Major Artur Franz (right) as acting commander of RIR 245 in von Heygendorff's absence, with his adjutant Leutnant Wienicke in early May 1915. Franz left to take acting command of RIR 243 on 11 May, a loss von Heygendorff could ill afford.

I bid farewell to the Württembergers. Party at the *kasino* until ½ 5 am. My chair is garlanded.

2 May
Slept until 10 am. While I am taking a footbath General v. Erpff[5] visits me. Morning drinks in the *kasino*. Ride in the afternoon to division at Dadizeele. Exzellenz v. Schäfer fetes me with a glass of champagne. Suddenly an order: *Regt. Heygendorff* to be reformed and march to Wallemolen, it will be subordinated to the 53. I.D.[6] So I rush off to Passchendaele on horseback without eating anything. As per orders subordination to the 53. Div. in Wallemolen. I must leave my poor boys to sleep outside in the rain; I myself find makeshift accommodation in a heavily occupied hut.

3 May
Waited all morning in the cold for orders. 53. I.D. is to take Gravenstafel: I. Batl. at the disposal of *Brigade v. Schmieden* (*Batl. Mügge*, Regt. 247), ½ hour later: the whole *Regiment v. Heygendorff* sent there. Advanced into trenches of 241 between Mosselmarkt and Gravenstafel. I reconnoitre, discuss everything with Bachmann. Northwest of Gravenstafel in front of a copse is an earthwork, which must be stormed. With difficulty I get hold of the artillery. They only shoot after vigorous coaxing. Finally from ¾ 4 to 4 pm a rolling salvo ensues every minute. Meanwhile my 247ers advance. At 4 they go in. The enemy flees into a wood but – because we don't have enough shrapnel – is able to hang on in a flanking trench to the northwest, which spits death and destruction on the battalion of 247, now reinforced by two companies of 245. On our left 243 does not come with us, but contents itself with shooting us in the back. Finally I direct the artillery fire and am assisted by Bachmann in the observation. The enemy loses his grip and abandons his position in the evening. Still during the night we capture the heights. Part of III./245 takes the evacuated and badly shot-up Zonnebeke. Ten minutes after I leave my observation post, my orderly Mälzer falls – *A bullet came a-flying, Is it my turn or yours?*[7] – I spend much time with Oberstleutnant Reußner at the battle HQ of Regt. 241 and pass the night in a dugout in the firing line.

4 May
The next morning the regiment is withdrawn and pulled back to the Broodseinde crossroads as corps reserve. This was the key point of bitter fighting and is therefore terrifically devastated. Huge craters from the German *minenwerfer*, hundreds of unexploded hand grenades and desolate ruins bear witness to bloody combat. I accommodate the regiment in the trenches of the German and English lines. The latter stinks abomin-

The abandoned ruins of Wallemolen (a windmill destroyed in 1914), jumping off point for the advance of *Regiment von Heygendorff.*

The front line of RIR 245 in the In de Ster sector, built up far above ground level with sandbags due to the high water table.

MG emplacement of RIR 246 at the southern edge of Polygon Wood.

Sniper of RIR 246 aiming through a loophole plate at Polygon Wood.

ably of corpses, as the 'culture-bearers' have buried their fallen comrades right in the walls. I myself lie tightly cramped in a trench section adapted into a dugout.

5 May
We are honoured by a crowd of senior battlefield tourists in a car. The head of the *Armeeoberkommando* Duke Albrecht of Württemberg expresses his thanks and appreciation to me for the achievements of *Regiment Heygendorff*: *"you've got the stone rolling"*. I have become a dedicated tour guide: the Crown Prince of Bavaria (who gives me a cigar), the commander of the Marinekorps, Exzellenz v. Hüllsen[8], whose escort hands out cigars and tinned food to my men. In the afternoon the regiment is alerted and brought forward to Zonnebeke, as the attack on Frezenberg is not making progress. From the 'Kleine Molen' windmill I observe the fighting. Nothing comes of our intervention and we go back to the trenches; I try to be clever and settle down in Zonnebeke to get some peace for once. Instead heavy shells and shrapnel come flying into the hamlet all night long.

6 May
Regiment Heygendorff is dissolved. III./245 moves to Westhoek. I go to see my regiment at Eksternest. The position is still in a bad state, since we have only just taken it. Most of the

Leutnant d. R. Karl Hotz from Frankfurt/M. was with 8./245 from 1914 until his death on 11 September 1916 at Rancourt on the Somme.

men have to camp out. Thanks to the kindness of my friend Martini, commander of Reserve-Jäger-Bataillon 26, I myself find shelter in a cellar. Many losses to sulphur shells.[9]

7 May
Go into the line. Attack tomorrow. A lot of meetings and preparations.

8 May
Artillery barrage at 7 am, which is very effective. I. Bataillon takes *Höhe 38* west of Eksternest, 1. Komp. under Leutnant Schunke breaks into the English trenches on the railway, is severely enfiladed and exhausts its ammunition. The English attempt an envelopment; the company has to go back, goes to ground at the railway embankment and returns during the night. Regt. 247 on our left does not advance due to flanking fire. I commit the III. Batl. here from the north. The ensuing flanking fire from the right forces us into a frontal attack, which is brought to a standstill. I go into a ruined house in the front line to get an overview. At this moment 100 Englishmen attempt a counterstroke, which our artillery easily repels. A further advance is impossible – so now trench-digging, regrouping of sub-units and establishment of three lines. I go into my cellar again. 150 casualties.

9 May
Sunday. Further development of the position. Splendid weather. A wounded 'Englishman' is brought in, and turns out to be a Rumanian who was sent to Canada due to involvement in a pogrom against the Jews and forcibly recruited into the army there. He curses the English in no uncertain terms. Artillery barrage from 3.30 to 5 pm, then a renewed assault which gets us 400m forward. Is it worth the sacrifice? The English still resist with colossal tenacity. They are masters in flanking defences and make use of their light MGs.

10 May
The position is held. A great deal of enemy artillery fire. Acting company commander Leutnant Krauß falls. I go into the line, whose new defences are the cause of much work. There is much to do 'at home'. My 'parlour' is mother nature; if it rains Martini will have to take me into his dugout. We're building ourselves one here too. In the evening skat with Martini over a pilsner. As ever I am left without cash.

11 May
Go into the line, which is coming along. Great preparations for a cylinder attack. Much visiting, hence little time. In the evening skat at Martini's.

The British strongpoint known to the Germans as the Erdwerk near s'Gravenstafel, stormed by III. Batl. / RIR 241 on 3 May 1915.

British dead amid the debris of battle in the shattered *Erdwerk*, already picked over by looters and awaiting burial.

12 May
The wind has changed, so the attack is called off. I go into the line. The firing has stopped there, instead Westhoek is covered in shell and shrapnel. A shell hits a small arms ammunition wagon in Haanebeek, the fragments of which are scattered over a 100m radius. Attack tomorrow, hence preparations. Unfortunately Major Franz has acting command of 243 since yesterday, and I have an even greater shortage of officers. Ypres is burning every day now. The towers are being targeted as there are artillery observers sitting there. A pity about the beautiful city. In the evening skat at Martini's.

13 May
A critical day of the first order. Rain, muddy ground. At battle HQ in Eksternest at ½5am. Artillery barrage from 5 to 7.50am to little effect as adverse wind makes observation impossible. Hence the general assault collapses under the machine-gun fire of the English. Everyone remains in the trenches or flees back to them. The platoon on my right wing along the railway disintegrates. After some hours I see through the scissors periscope that a few are crawling back, but half of them are dead or wounded. About noon at least a battalion of the English appears in the *Eierwald* opposite. *Fußartilleriebataillon Welter* and *Kanonenzug Schneider* throw a hail of iron into it. Trees collapse, fountains of earth fly into the air, there must have been terrible losses. Later we fire with artillery on the dugouts along the railway, in which the English must wait out the heaviest artillery fire in order to enfilade us afterwards. They are really tough nuts. Unfortunately we are always faced with fresh troops, while we send in the same long-suffering men again and again. In the afternoon the English launch a counterstroke against my right flank and the 53. I.D. on our right. We manage to ward off the danger with artillery. Two regiments of 53. I.D. rush backward. I throw the II. Bataillon and two machine-guns into the right flank. 26. Jäger and I. Bataillon 248 place themselves behind my right wing. I get the artillery to enfilade the English. As a result they remain stationary. We are able to hold our old line, but casualties (almost 300) are pointlessly sacrificed. In the night the 26. Jäger relieve my first line; I have nothing to do at the front for two days, for the first time since 1 October after recovery from my wound.

14 May
Slept for a long time. Worked, as there is much paperwork left to do. The rest does me good.

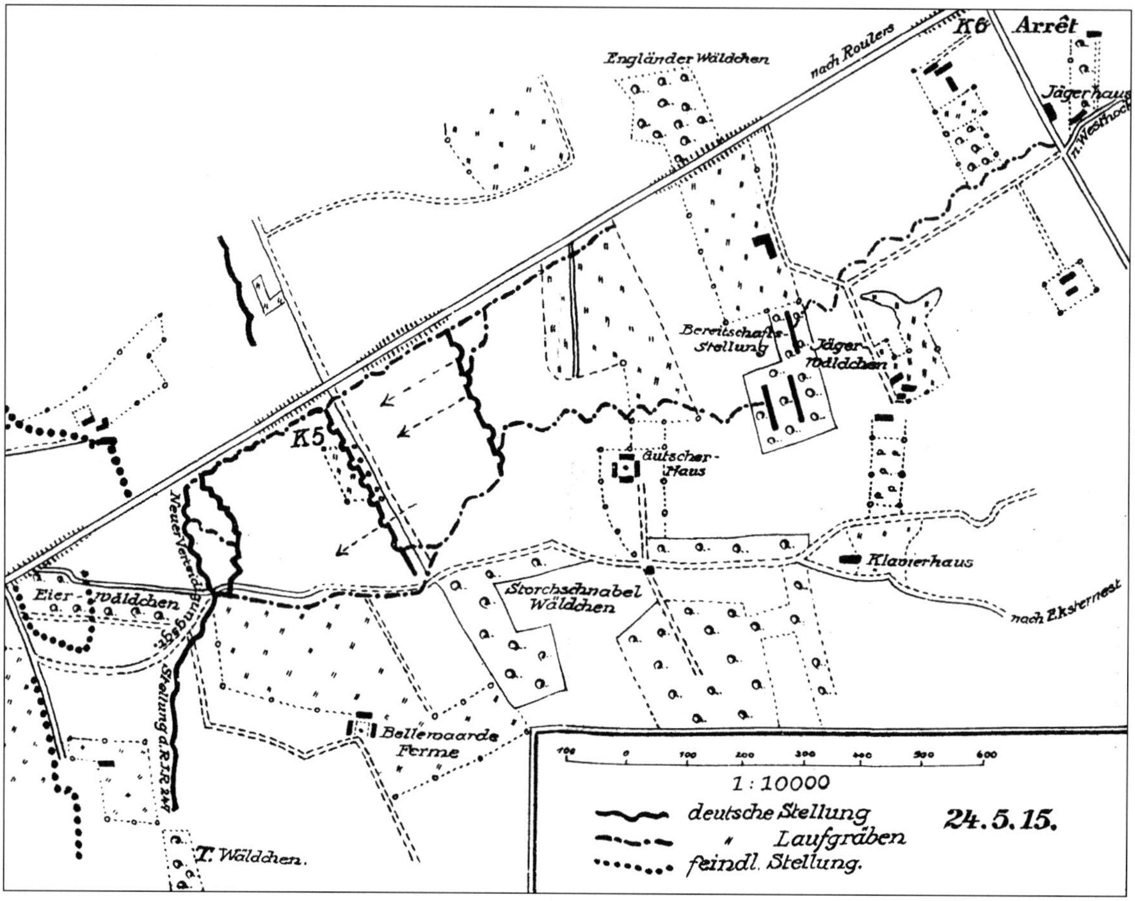

The sector left of the Ypres–Roulers railway, showing the attack of RIR 245 and the attached RJB 26 on 13 May (the dotted arrows) as well as the trenches established after the battle. On 18 May the regiment took over the adjoining sector right of the railway from 53. RD.

Map extract showing the rear area of this sector as far back as the northwest corner of Polygon Wood, including the regimental HQ in Westhoek and Major von Heygendorff's later 'home' at Villa Haanebeke (here spelled 'Haanebeek').

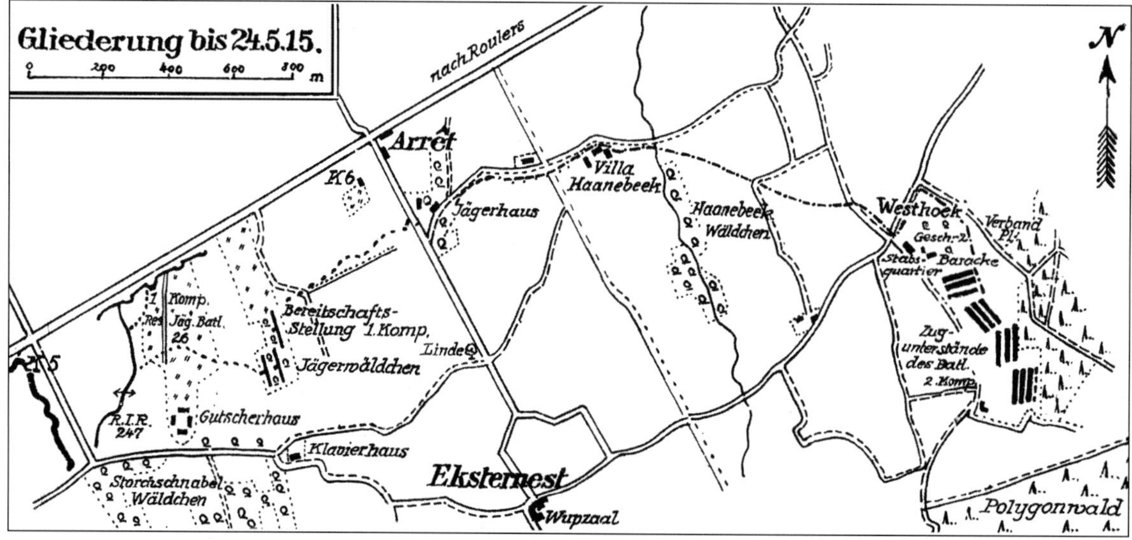

15 May

Rode early to see the *regimentszahlmeister*[10] at Rolleghem-capelle with v. Vahl. The ride through the long disputed Polygon Wood and Molenarelsthoek was curious. The presumption that we had a fortress in front of us was mistaken – simple trenches, bad dugouts, bulky [wire] obstacles and many flank defences. If we had only had more artillery we could have taken the position sooner. Ate like a prince at our old home in Waterdamhoek: a change of dishes! What a luxury! At the *kasino*, the costs of which are already covered, I drank a glass of wine. Worked [until?] ½6 in the evening 'at home' in Westhoek. Ate in the evening with Bachmann, the regimental clerk and telephonist Feldwebel Fischer-Brill. The latter is well travelled and speaks very enjoyably about it.

16 May

Slept for a long time, cold wind; worked on two judicial cases, regimental files, as not everything is running smoothly yet etc. In the evening I throw a party for Bachmann, who has received the EK1. Alert about 10 pm, as the English are attacking to our left. They were quickly greased.

17 May

Exzellenz v. Schäfer comes to visit me early, while I was still asleep. Spent the whole day writing. Outside there is rain, inside heavenly peace as Bachmann is on duty in Waterdamhoek. In the evening a cosy meal in the dugout with a few gentlemen of the III. Bataillon.

18 May

Caught a bad cold, so sleep as long as some Belgian rats permit. In the afternoon I receive a new sector, to the right of my former one. It is like in December: mud, mud and yet more mud. My poor lads sleep in the rain without protection. I take over the sector and see to finding shelters for my 2nd line, which is very difficult among the shot-up houses. It will take many days' work to make a difference here.

19 May

Early council of war with the divisional commander, to organise the planned cylinder attack. Afternoon in the line. To our front it is hopeless, all just swamp. We must build a sandbag wall and that takes thousands of sandbags, there are already 700 out there. In the centre 4 platoons can already be accomodated.

20 May

Visit from von Exzellenz v. Schäfer; much work, as I am moving into the 'Villa Haanebeke'. I get a room for myself and put Bachmann with the blower far away, as his constant

Major von Heygendorff on the telephone at his HQ in Westhoek, with Leutnant Bachmann on his left and Leutnant von Vahl on his right.

telephone calls drive me mad. The little house is still in good shape. The commanders of the centre line were securely housed here. There is still a lot of English rubbish to be removed, but it will soon be very habitable. In the evening Major Ingenbrand of II. / RFAR53 eats with me along with his adjutant Donner, who sang and accompanied himself on the lute.[11]

---

21 to 25 May

Here there is a gap in Major von Heygendorff's published diary entries, probably due to the abortive gas attack on 24 May. The regimental history records that batteries of chlorine cylinders were installed in the front line on the 22nd, and the depleted regiment brought up to strength with replacements. The next day the regiment took up fighting positions north of the railway line, with advance warning for a probable attack early on 24 May. Since the wind appeared favourable the cylinders were opened at 3:45 am all along the fronts of XXVI. and XXVII. RK in the largest gas attack yet attempted. Though not as disastrous as in the sectors of RIR241 and 242 (see pp. 111–112), the deficiencies of the inexperienced and ill-equipped 'stinkpioniere' *conducting the operation also affected RIR245. Many of the pipes did not fit the cylinders, many of which were opened late or not at all, while the wind blew some of the gas up in the air and reduced its effectiveness. Many cylinders were still venting when the infantry went over the top into the gas cloud at 4:00 am as ordered, where they immediately came under murderous machine-gun fire. Each time the men lay down between forward bounds they were exposed to the densest concentration of gas. Although the* 'riechpäckchen' *offered some protection, the men soon discovered that it greatly impeded their breathing. Paralysed with horror in this ghastly situation, the newly arrived recruits were cut down in droves while they were struggling out of the trenches. The enemy had seemingly pulled most of his men back from his trenches and put down a heavy defensive barrage on and in front of his own line. Notified too late of the attack, von Heygendorff's reserves were cut to pieces by the British artillery as they tried to move up in support. Having advanced 400 metres and taken the British front line, RIR245 was forced to halt there under concentrated fire from three sides due to the delayed advance of RIR242 and RJB26 on their flanks. In total the day cost the regiment*

A well-earned rest at Westhoek in late May 1915. From front to back (Leutnant?) Flinsch, Prof. Dr. Fredenhagen (with *Pickelhaube*; a 37 year old war volunteer from the University of Leipzig), Leutnant von Vahl, Major von Heygendorff, Leutnant Bachmann.

The regimental staff at Villa Haanebeke after Major von Heygendorff took up residence there on 20 May 1915.

325 casualties. Its attacking I. Bataillon suffered 40% losses, with many of the survivors suffering from the effects of the gas. This disaster marked the end of the offensive, and the regiment consolidated on its new front line. It is readily apparent from the following entry that Major von Heygendorff made his outrage at the conduct of this final attack abundantly clear to his superiors.

---

26 May

My wedding anniversary – my poor wife! I go into the battle HQ, do some shooting and organise the 2nd line. In the afternoon go to see General von Erpff and report how the attack on the 24th went. I am most energetic in asking him not to demand the impossible, and urge him to work to ensure that no attacks are being ordered which will worsen the position of the regiment even further due to the terrain. He soothes me and tells me to get some rest, because the Western Front is now to go on the defensive and await further developments. It's about time; six attacks since 24 April is no joke. Yesterday Leutnant Weber's nerves gave out, today Major von Aspern, three officers in the past three weeks. The men are worn out and the new replacements too hastily trained.

Writing to a friend the same day in a significantly more up-beat and bellicose tone, von Heygendorff summarises his regiment's involvement in the Second Battle of Ypres.

Written 26.5.1915, Villa Haanebeke

Dear Herr v. d. Gabelentz![12]

Many thanks for your greetings. We've had a proper tussle here. I've been through a lot: from 24 April to today six attacks, laurels earned twice as corps reserve, two earthworks stormed and our English cousins caught in the flank. We have gained a really beautiful amount of ground; I've left Westhoek and lived for ten days in a cellar or else in dugouts. For four days now I've been living in a farmhouse which was plastered with filth when the English handed it over to me. The English have had colossal losses, but they are resilient. Their heavy artillery is already on the far side of the canal. The 'gentle Heinrich' still sends shrapnel pots over our heads every day. The regiment has many casualties, but relatively few dead and many lightly wounded. Fourteen officers lost in fourteen days, three of them dead. There are plenty of mosquitoes and flies here, plenty of sun, little water, plenty of work and aggravation. What do you think about Italy?[13] Such bitches. I'd love to travel to the 'boot' and give it a good thrashing from leg to toe with fire and sword.

Best wishes

Your Heygendorff

Hauptmann John (right) in conversation with Major von Heygendorff (seated with Leutnant von Vahl on the ex-civilian carriage).

A HUNDRED YEARS LATER

The von Heygendorff family tomb at the *Trinitatisfriedhof* in Dresden. The left-hand panel commemorates Major (later Oberstleutnant) Alfred von Heygendorff and his widow Elsa. On the right can be seen the name of his son Egon, killed two days before his father at Rancourt on the Somme while serving under him as regimental orderly officer. Below Egon's name is that of Alfred von Heygendorff's daughter Wera, who died in Dresden in 1993.

Chapter 6

The Second Battle of Ypres | XXVII. Reservekorps

Members of Reserve-Infanterie-Regiment 242 pose triumphantly in a captured British trench near the Broodseinde crossroads. Since October 1914 thousands of British, French and German soldiers had given their lives for control of the Broodseinde Ridge, and many of them still lay there in April 1915. After the fall of Zonnebeke on 4 May and the subsequent advance, these old trenches were systematically stripped of all reuseable materials and two large cemeteries established at the crossroads (see pp. 232–233).

THE SECOND BATTLE OF YPRES | XXVII. RESERVEKORPS

The Saxon-Württemberg corps on the attack from Zonnebeke to Bellewaarde 22 April–28 May 1915

(s.) 53. Reserve-Division	**(w.) 54. Reserve-Division**
(s.) 105. Reserve-Infanterie-Brigade	(w.) 107. Reserve-Infanterie-Brigade
(s.) Reserve-Infanterie-Regiment 241	(s.) Reserve-Infanterie-Regiment 245
(s.) Reserve-Infanterie-Regiment 243	(w.) Reserve-Infanterie-Regiment 247
	(s.) Reserve-Jäger-Bataillon 26
(s.) 106. Reserve-Infanterie-Brigade	(w.) 108. Reserve-Infanterie-Brigade
(s.) Reserve-Infanterie-Regiment 242	(w.) Reserve-Infanterie-Regiment 246
(s.) Reserve-Infanterie-Regiment 244	(w.) Reserve-Infanterie-Regiment 248
(s.) Reserve-Jäger-Bataillon 25	
(s.) Reserve-Kavallerie-Abteilung 53	(w.) Reserve-Kavallerie-Abteilung 54
(s.) Reserve-Feldartillerie-Regiment 53	(s. / w.) Reserve-Feldartillerie-Regiment 54
(s.) Reserve-Pionier-Kompanie 53	(s.) Reserve-Pionier-Kompanie 54
(s.) Reserve-Divisions-Brückentrain 53	(w.) Reserve-Divisions-Brückentrain 54
(s.) Reserve-Sanitätskompanie 53	(w.) Reserve-Sanitätskompanie 54

The following plus a varying number of heavy batteries were attached in April–May 1915

(p.) Feldartillerie-Ersatz-Abteilung 59	(p.) 2. Festungs-Pionier-Kompanie / Pionier-Regiment 24

(p.) 38. Landwehr-Infanterie-Brigade

(p.) Landwehr-Infanterie-Regiment 77	(p.) Landwehr-Infanterie-Regiment 78

(s.) = Saxon units (w.) = Württemberg units (p.) = Prussian units

General der Artillerie Richard von Schubert (19 April 1850–13 May 1933)

After the former Saxon war minister Genltn. von Carlowitz had left the post with a 'heart condition' amid bitter recriminations, General von Schubert became the only Prussian officer to lead a Saxon corps in battle on 27 October 1914. Having fallen out with von Hindenburg due to his 'overcautious' command of 8. Armee on the Eastern Front, his new command might well be considered a poisoned chalice.

Nicknamed 'General Hintendurch'[1] by his men and accused by his subordinates of senseless attacks and front-line micromanagement of their units, this highly experienced Prussian commander was nevertheless renowned for his indifference to personal danger and apparent indestructibility. On 21 May 1915 he inspected the recently captured *Klavierhaus* in the RIR 248 sector. The next day Oltn. d. R. Fischer of RIR 241 received a visit: *"On the morning of 22 May Excellenz von Schubert came into the trenches. So I put on my tall hat* [Pickelhaube] *and led him through my company's sector. We had just come to the most dangerous spot, and I informed him that if anyone showed so much as the tip of his nose here the machine-guns would instantly start blazing away. The next moment he stood up on the fire-step to study the landscape. So there was nothing for it but for me to join him up there, in order to provide the necessary commentary. In doing so Exc. von Schubert with his beautiful red general's collar stood out above the parapet about as far as his waist, while I in my tall hat and being a head taller than him was accordingly even more exposed. We stood up there for nearly five minutes, and not a single shot was fired. After all it was always so. When Exc. von Schubert showed up anywhere and exposed himself quite carelessly to fire he was never shot at. At the storming of Frezenberg on 8 May he sat there on horseback right in the target area for the enemy artillery, and nothing happened to him."*[2]

Situation on the corps front in early 1915

The front held by XXVII. RK in early 1915 lay in a wide irregular arc around the eastern end of the Ypres salient, where its advance on the city had ground to a bloody halt the previous autumn. By late January unit sectors were well established, and the trench system extensively developed. On the left flank RIR 248 held Polderhoek park, facing Polygon Wood to the north with RIR 246 at Reutel on their right (see map p. 69). The line of RIR 247 crossed open ground east of the wood in a series of sharp angles known as the *Zickzack* (zigzag). At the boundary with RIR 245 was the *Hexenkessel* (witches' cauldron), a flashpoint where the lines lay only fifteen metres apart amid ruined buildings and both sides had put up mesh screens against hand grenades. The RIR 245 sector extended across the Becelaere–Broodseinde road near In de Ster Cabaret, with RJB 26 on the right at *Calvairewald* (Justice Wood; see map p. 79), scene of terrible carnage in November 1914. The inter-divisional boundary was the *Gutscherweg* (Keibergmolen road), beyond which lay RIR 243 and then RIR 241 as far as Broodseinde.

The vital higher ground at this crossing of the Zonnebeke–Moorslede and Passchendaele–Becelaere roads had always been hotly disputed. On the morning of 25 January, units of 106. Res. Inf. Brig. made a meticulously planned assault on the crossroads after a brief artillery and *minenwerfer* barrage. This failed disastrously, and attacking elements of RIR 242, RIR 244 and RJB 25 were mown down by French rifles and machine-guns. By nightfall, 53. RD had lost sixty-eight confirmed dead, 211 wounded, 208 missing and eight confirmed captured. Having barely rebuilt its shattered units from near-destruction in 1914, this was a grave blow to divisional morale. Many of the dead were left rotting in No Man's Land and only retrieved in May. Several minor raids on the crossroads by 105. Res. Inf. Brig. in late February and early March also failed, but at a far smaller cost. RIR 241 then beat off a French attack on 10 April, presumably intended to cover their relief by British 28th Division.

RJB 25 held a small sector north of the crossroads until 17 February, when it was relieved by the adjacent RIR 244. Until April the northernmost organic unit of the corps was usually RIR 242, with its flank at the Ypres–Roulers railway. Beyond this point on the front west of Passchendaele was the Prussian 38. Landwehr-Brigade, attached to XXVII. RK since December. From 9 April, the southern end of their line was held by RJB 25.

NCOs and men of 4. Kompanie / Reserve-Infanterie-Regiment 241 in front of their billets in the weeks before the battle. Writing on the back to a friend on 23 April 1915, the wildly optimistic Gefreiter Erdmann (second from left) hints at the ongoing offensive: *"I have some expectations of peace. It will come soon. We still have some tidying up to do first. [This] has already started."*

The former trenches of RIR 245 after the advance of 4 May. In the distance on the left are the houses of Molenaarelsthoek, behind the old British front line. On the right is the infamous Calvairewald.

Preparations for the offensive

The offensive which became known as the *Zweite Flandernschlacht* (Second Battle of Ypres) was essentially a large-scale field trial for weaponised chlorine gas, discharged from massed 'batteries' of pressurised cylinders (*F-batterien*). While tear gases had already been tried to little effect by French and Germans alike, this would be the first modern military use of a lethal chemical agent. Although regarded with widespread scepticism and distaste at all levels, gas offered the hope of gaining ground without the ruinous losses of 1914. With Germany's strategic focus on the Eastern front however the cautious von Falkenhayn was unwilling to gamble any of his reserves, and 4. Armee would receive no extra troops for the operation.

On 25 January, General von Deimling of XV. Armeekorps learned that his sector (see map p. 109) had been chosen for the gas attack. General von Schubert was probably notified at the same time, since preparations were complete slightly earlier opposite Polygon Wood than on von Deimling's front at Hill 60. By mid-February a volunteer company of what would become Pionier-Regiment 36 was surveying and excavating positions for *F-batterien*, and by 8 March, a thousand cylinders in batches of ten were in place in the trenches of RIR 246 and 247. The infantry now received the so-called *schutzpäckchen* or *riechpäckchen* (a rubberised bag attached to the tunic, containing a chemically impregnated cotton pad to tie over the mouth; see photo p. 81) and all arms made exhaustive preparations for the storming of Polygon Wood. All that was missing was the right wind, for which front line weather stations continually checked speed and direction with burning rags – to the uncomprehending amusement of the French. On 22 and again on 29 March the troops 'stood to' for the attack, but each time the wind changed. On 5 April the frustrated *'stinkpioniere'* began installing cylinders on the northern face of the Ypres salient, which now became the focus of the planned offensive. Although disrupted by the British attack on 17 April, the *F-batterien* at Hill 60 would finally be used on 1 May. Meanwhile 54. RD was alerted on 22 and 25 April in the fruitless hope of discharging its cylinders in conjunction with gas attacks further north. The unused *F-batterien* at Polygon Wood were finally dismantled after the British withdrawal.

While 54. RD focused on the gas operation, 53. RD was preoccupied with securing the Broodseinde Ridge. After a systematic week-long siege operation, RIR 241 took successive sections of British sap near the crossroads on 14 and 15 April with the aid of *minenwerfers* and bombing parties from Pi. Regt. 24. The *minenwerfers* tore a large gap in the British parapet on the 16th, allowing raiders to occupy part of the line after nightfall. Although driven out the next day, the Saxons returned the following night and dug in firmly enough to repel all counterattacks on the 18th. After another trench section was taken on the 20th, the new line was connected to the main position. Finally on 21 April a surveyor from Pi. Regt. 24 verified that RIR 241 was now holding the crossroads. The expected attempt to retake it did not occur before the opening of the offensive, during which it proved its value for artillery observation.

From 22 April both divisions strove to 'pin' the enemy on their front by incessant fire, patrolling and mock attacks – which also served to test the prospects for real attacks. One of our featured diarists in *Fighting the Kaiser's War*, Ersatz-Reservist Hans Brückner of RIR 242, describes a typical operation on 22 or 23 April: *"We set up dummies… by hanging greatcoats on scaling ladders with helmets tied on the top. At 9pm precisely we held them up a little above the parapet – as if we intended to launch an assault – and when the whistle sounded the entire battalion occupying the regimental positions began to bellow 'Hurra!'"*[3]

This immediately provoked half an hour of frenzied small arms and artillery fire, leading to the cancellation of both a second mock attack that day and a real one the next morning.

The battle begins

So far as the enemy could see, all regiments of XXVII. RK remained in their usual sectors. However on 23 April an ad-hoc mixed *Sturmbrigade* was assembled at Moorslede under Genmaj. von Schmieden and his staff from 105. Res. Inf. Brig., comprising six reserve battalions of 53. RD and 38. Landwehr-Brigade. Oberst Wilhelmi of LIR 78 led one ad-hoc regiment (II. and III./78 plus II./244), while Oberstltn. Reußner of RIR 241 led another (II. and III./241 plus II./242). A battalion of RFAR 53, two heavy batteries and a platoon of *pioniere* were also attached. Initially in corps reserve was a third regiment formed by 54. RD under Major von Heygendorff of RIR 245 (III./245, composite *Bataillon Kölle* of RIR 246 and II./247). Meanwhile the regimental staff of RIR 243 took command of the rump of 105. Res. Inf. Brig. holding the trenches.

At 4 am on 24 April the *Sturmbrigade* deployed south of Poelkapelle with *Regiment Reußner* right and *Wilhelmi* left. Its orders were to join the advance of 51. RD on its right, and secure Hill 32 (between St. Julien and s'Gravenstafel). At 5 am chlorine was discharged from the trenches of 2. Reserve-Ersatz-Brigade, to devastating effect on 8th and 15th Battalion

NCOs of RJB 25 and (with the horse) RFAR 53 relax in reserve at Calvairewald after the advance.

CEF. By 6 am the Saxons could see wounded and gassed Canadians falling back. Without waiting for 51. RD or the end of the bombardment, II. and III. / 241 surged through the ground-holding unit in front of them and overran the enemy front line, taking about 300 prisoners. With its flank exposed, 13th Btn. was butchered by German artillery while retiring over Hill 32. However 8th Btn. and the British artillery held off *Regt. Wilhelmi* all day, despite flank attacks by III. / 241. After a fresh bombardment, *Regt. Reußner* advanced and dug in on the hill, where it was later reinforced by naval infantry of Matrosen-Regt. 5.

A heavy but uncoordinated Anglo-Canadian counterattack early on 25 April ran into 51. RD at St. Julien and the Saxons advancing down Hill 32. Although this soon collapsed under withering fire, the German advance had been delayed. The offensive resumed after 3pm, with *Regt. von Heygendorff* attacking west of Wallemolen alongside *Regt. Wilhelmi*, while *Regt. Reußner* pushed south-eastward. Hundreds of prisoners were taken, and the enemy forced to abandon the old Canadian front line after dark. 3. / 246 (plus parts of 8. / 244 and 4. / 246) got within 400m of the s'Gravenstafel crossroads and spent the night in a protracted firefight.

Meanwhile 53. RD had made a diversionary thrust toward Zonnebeke. British 28th Division was shelled steadily from 6 am, with copious use of *T-Granaten* (tear gas shells). However there were not enough heavy guns to do serious damage, and British losses were light. Despite doubts that the target was *sturmreif* (ripe for storming), an attack was ordered for 2.15 pm. On the right the trenches of RJB 25 had been hit by five 21cm *T-Granaten* and flooded with gas, and their officers judged it 'insane' to advance through the thick mud into the furious hail of rifle and machine-gun fire. Nevertheless RIR 242 and 244 attacked in force, supported by RIR 243, and reached the British line in three places. In the centre of RIR 242's attack front was 10. / 242 under Oltn. Harry Linck, a New Yorker by birth who had travelled from South America while ill in 1914 to report for duty; later in the war he was to serve as a storm troop leader with the Sturmabteilung der 53. RD and Prussian Sturm-Bataillon 8. Together with elements of 4. and 9. / 242, Linck's company broke into the centre of Trench 25 and held it against stubborn resistance despite the death of Ltn. d. R. Scholze (4. / 242) and severe wounding of Oltn. Scheube (9. / 242). This position was connected to the old front line that night, and repeated attempts to retake it over the next few days would cost the British dearly. On the regiment's left flank, 12. / 242 under Hptm. d. L. a. D. Dr. Oskar Dähnhardt (rector of the *Nikolai-Gymnasium* in Leipzig and a distinguished classical scholar) took part of Trench 24 together with several prisoners and machine-guns, but were driven out in a bayonet charge by 8th Btn. Middlesex Regi-

French dead still lying in former No Man's Land where they fell in 1914, prior to their burial by the Germans in May 1915.

Crude trenches and shelters in Polygon Wood, abandoned by British 28th Division on the night of 3–4 May.

ment and Hptm. Dähnhardt killed (see photo p. 236). Further left Hptm. Krause of 10./244 and about fifty men broke into Trench 23, but were cut off there by 2nd Btn. East Surrey Regiment and overwhelmed. The other attacking platoons of RIR 244 were pinned down in No Man's Land, where they dug a crude trench which was connected to the main position that night. This operation had cost RIR 242 and 244 alone a combined total of 111 dead, 261 wounded and thirty-three captured.

The focus of the wider battle on 26 April was west of St. Julien, where the Lahore Division launched a major counterattack against XXVI. RK. Lacking flank support, the progress of *Sturmbrigade von Schmieden* was therefore limited. On the right *Regt. Reußner*, Matrosen-Regt. 5 and part of *Regt. Wilhelmi* pushed into the valley of the Paddebeek in protracted fighting with British and Canadian rearguards. 5./244 were the first to reach the Bombarded Crossroads, where they seized a British telephone station and brought a captured Vickers into action to defend their foothold. On the left, II./247 and more of the sailors surprised and overran the defenders of the s'Gravenstafel crossroads. As the regimental history of RIR 247 relates, the north-western end of the Gravenstafel Ridge offered an amazing view of the salient: *"About 9 o'clock the fog lifted, and an astonishing sight met our eyes: there below lay Zonnebeke, the shot-up windmill on the hill in front of it was 'de kleine Molen'. And there in the distance, two spectral and leaden towers – that was Ypres, which we now saw for the first time! Ypres, the object of so much fighting, around which the ring of steel was now tightening. And with our binoculars we could see right into the enemy dugouts near Broodseinde. They were facing the same way as us! And now something came howling over through the air, and a black cloud of smoke erupted from the ground to our front. Our own artillery opposite was firing and hitting the enemy in front of us."*[4]

Regt. Reußner was withdrawn over the next two days, the *Sturmbrigade* dissolved on 29 April and its elements returned to their donor units, though *Regt. von Heygendorff* remained in place. That night RIR 244 and half of RJB 25 extended the front of 106. Res. Inf. Brig. up to the inter-divisional boundary, while 105. Res. Inf. Brig. took over north of the railway. On 2 May a fresh concentration of reserves was assembled near Wallemolen, including *Regt. von Heygendorff*, I. and II./241, the other half of RJB 25, a composite battalion of RIR 243 and a mixed battalion from RIR 242 and 244. The assault on the 'nose' of the salient would be made by I./243 (left) and III./241 (right), the objective being *Höhe 38* (Abraham Heights).

The Saxons reach Zonnebeke

At 6 am on 3 May the massed artillery opened up on Berlin Wood and the British strongpoint known as the *Erdwerk* ('Berlin') near s'Gravenstafel. The first attack at 8.30 am gained only a few hundred metres due to intense machine-gun crossfire. *Regt. von Heygendorff* was called on, and II./247 committed in the centre. After a devastating bombardment the wood and *Erdwerk* were stormed with fixed bayonets sometime after 4 pm and the defenders wiped out. However their machine-guns had taken a dreadful toll, and RIR 241 finally dug in fifty metres short of *Höhe 38*. That night the enemy retreated to the Frezenberg heights under cover of darkness, rain and dense fog, while rearguards kept up a lively rifle fire until the last possible minute. Although a British retirement from the increasingly untenable salient had long been predicted and forward patrols were out all night, they did not detect the withdrawal before about 4 am. RIR 241 and 243 were already 'standing to' for a fresh attack, and advanced immediately. Arthur Kühne of 1./241 describes the scene in the regimental history: *"The assault was to be launched on the morning of 4 May. All night long it had rained in torrents. As we clambered out of the trenches to hurl ourselves at the enemy with shouts of 'hurra', not a single shot was fired. Cautiously and distrustfully we approached the first trench, where to our amazement we realised that the enemy had retreated ahead of our attack. Plenty of bodies and pieces of kit lay scattered about – backpacks, belt equipment and rifles – evidence of the mad rush in which the enemy had fled, driven by a single-minded urge to save themselves. On both sides of our sector, regiment after regiment now emerged from the trenches, und as if on manoeuvres we went forward in extended order with our rifles under our arms. A magnificent spectacle unfolded. The artillery had been informed at once and now drove forward, unlimbered on open ground and sent the first shells hurtling after the fleeing enemy. Forward patrols reported that the enemy was in full retreat toward Ypres. Without a fight we occupied Zonnebeke, which had been disputed for seven months. On the Frezenberg heights the English halted and brought our impetuous advance to a temporary end. The 1. Kompagnie remained as reserve in Zonnebeke, and we now began searching the shot-up houses. Gradually we pulled out into the sunlight a total of twenty Englishmen who had slept through the retreat. Suddenly a cry rang out: 'watch out, clear the way!' A battery came racing by along the street despite the fierce small-arms fire. The gunners kept their heads down, a horse that had been hit was cut free of its harness in a flash, and within moments of the artillery battalion driving out into the open field the first shots were already banging out of the barrels. All day long there were forward thrusts to hinder the*

The ruins of 'Grote Molen' after the battle. This mill stood at the corner of Grote Molenstraat and Kleine Molenstraat in Zonnebeke.

The main street of Zonnebeke, looking south-westward toward the church tower (later demolished on 20 June 1915).

enemy from consolidating their line. In a shot-up windmill on high ground a senior staff set up its observation post, and aircraft came hovering overhead to drop messages in sacks weighted with lead shot.

In Zonnebeke we captured large numbers of rifles and entrenching tools – and, to our particular delight, hundreds of cans of corned beef. There was butter and jam too in abundance, as well as white English bread and biscuits. Everyone found something worth picking up as a souvenir of this day. A great hubbub arose when a herd of cows approached from the direction of the front line. The milking got underway right there on the street, and this milk we had (in a sense) captured tasted especially good. In the evening we retired to the completely wrecked church of Zonnebeke and slept like gods, even though we could have been called forward at any moment and the walls were shaking at every shot from the 21 cm Mörser *which stood right alongside us. What a day that was!"*[5]

Regt. von Heygendorff had also joined the advance, but was soon withdrawn to Broodseinde where it was personally commended by General von Schubert and the army commander, Duke Albrecht of Württemberg. The corps commander then proceeded to Zonnebeke, where his HQ flag was flying by 10am. South of the railway, RIR 244 had been the first to move. One of their patrols under Uffz. Süß may have been the first into Zonnebeke and brought back three prisoners. By about 7 am their brigade commander Genmaj. von der Decken appeared in the front line to order a general advance. Further south, RIR 248 had noticed as early as 3 am that dugouts opposite were on fire. By 4 am the British front line was known to be empty, and patrols from all forward units of 54. RD probed cautiously into Polygon Wood, which was suspected to be full of booby traps. For the most part they merely found unspeakable squalor and the litter of retreat. Where a concrete fortress studded with machine-gun nests had long been imagined, there was only a primitive and ill-maintained trench system devoid of the most basic sanitation. The Württembergers were shocked by the wretched dugouts and alarmed by mine galleries near Reutel and under the *Hexenkessel*. But most of all they were sickened by the countless partly and wholly unburied French dead. Uffz. Ingelfinger of 5./246 later recalled: *"A few metres behind the enemy trench, near the so-called 'Tabakhaus', lay three dead cows which gave off such a stench that it was impossible to remain nearby. A drainage ditch had been dug alongside (indeed, right alongside) the cows, proof that the French could have buried or covered them. The position in question was always occupied in strength. Very close by, likewise behind the trenches and easily reachable, lay an unburied Frenchman. In three places where water had broken into the enemy trench, I observed three corpses simply floating unburied in the water. At another point a Frenchman was buried in the wall with his knee sticking out into the trench; on the well-trodden ground it was possible to see how the French had habitually swerved right or left around this knee. In one stretch of about twelve metres divided by a traverse lay seven dead Frenchmen right inside the position, just as they had fallen. By the look of the corpses they must have been there for months. About three metres in front of the enemy trench I found a French sapper, apparently killed while putting up a wire obstacle; he could quite comfortably have been hauled into the trench by night. In places where there was plenty of cover, graves with a stray arm or foot sticking out were no rarity. I need scarcely add that we immediately buried the dead where they lay."*[6]

Amid the debris RJB 26 found a single living Tommy, evidently wounded while on rearguard duty. Over the following weeks, units in reserve would spend hours in the old trenches of both sides salvaging everything of any further use – including duckboards, corrugated iron, loophole plates, wire and thousands of sandbags. Meanwhile many shots were traded as the Germans probed the new British line. Upon approaching the Frezenberg–Eksternest road south of Arrêt, II./244 found itself unsupported and under attack. After I./244 had arrived to stabilise the situation, both sides went to ground and the firefight continued until dusk. Having lost twelve dead and thirty-five wounded, RIR 244 was then withdrawn to Zonnebeke along with RJB 25. The day's advance had dramatically narrowed the corps front, and many units now got a well-earned rest – RIR 246 saw no action for the rest of the month, serving instead as a labour force for less fortunate regiments. By morning on 5 May the front was held as follows. North of the Zonnebeke–Frezenberg road was 105. Res. Inf. Brig., with 106. Res. Inf. Brig. from that road to the railway line. Each had one battalion in line, initially from RIR 243 and 242 respectively. 54. RD chose to group all its front elements under Genmaj. von Erpf's 107. Res. Inf. Brig., with RIR 245, 247 and 248 from the railway line to the small road junction between Eksternest and the Menin Road. At first no room could be found for all of the artillery, so that a third of RFAR 54 went into reserve.

The offensive continues

53. RD made its first assault on Frezenberg early on 5 May, under cover of a perfunctory barrage. While the right flank of III./243 got to within 200 metres of the enemy, the re-

The ruins of Frezenberg (captured on 8 May) seen from the main Zonnebeke–Ypres road.

Leutnant Lorenz of RIR 245 examines a 9.14 cm Behelfsminenwerfer *System Mauser* (a simple smoothbore trench mortar) in his regiment's trenches, watched by his men and the weapon's probable operator from Reserve-Pionier-Kompanie 54 (left).

mainder of both attacking battalions was soon pinned down under heavy fire. After a fresh bombardment the advance resumed at 4 pm. Each bound brought further losses, but when the attack was called off III./243 dug in within eighty metres of the British lines. RIR 244 was 'stood to' early the next day, but soon learned that the next attack had been postponed until 8 May. During this pause Major von Heygendorff's ad-hoc regiment was finally dissolved and its elements returned to their parent units. The British artillery was now targeting Zonnebeke, but this did little to dampen the mood. Part of RJB 25 was billeted in the bullet-riddled chateau, and the more daring among them took to skinny-dipping in the nearby lake. This caused great hilarity when a sudden hail of shrapnel forced them to run for cover in the nude. Beside the road to the west of the town a piano had been set up, which was played constantly by musicians of varying ability.

Over the next two days the artillery was busy studying new targets, establishing forward observation posts and bringing all available guns into action. This even included an ad-hoc battery of obsolete (1873 vintage) 9cm pieces with scratch crews from RFAR 54. In the RIR 245 sector heavy *minenwerfers* were emplaced to destroy the enemy wire. The British artillery however was also increasingly active, with RIR 247 reporting fire from a super-heavy naval gun – mercifully, many of its massive shells were duds. On the morning of the 7th, enemy fire reached such intensity that a counter-attack was briefly expected. That night all units drove their lines further forward by sapping. 105. Res. Inf. Brig. was to attack with I./241 in the lead and the rest of the regiment in support. 106. Res. Inf. Brig. had RJB 25 on the right and II./242 on the left in two waves of two companies each, with I./242 behind. This would be the first time RJB 25 had attacked since January, and the *jägers* were full of nervous excitement. From left to right, 54. RD had I.//248, III./247, I./247 and I./245 in the line.

The shelling began at 7 am. At first the guns registered, finding the range as casually as possible to avoid alerting the enemy. The British sandbag lines on the forward slope north of Frezenberg proved excellent targets. At 8 am the *wirkungsschiessen* (fire for effect) began, with sporadic pauses to lure the enemy out of cover. The British trenches were systematically pulverised, while most of their own artillery fire fell behind the German lines. RFAR 54 alone fired off 6,500 rounds, and Hptm. von Legl of I./248 treated their forward observers in his sector to champagne that evening. By 9.30 am white rags were seen waving above the British parapet opposite I./241, but a few men who broke cover to take prisoners were driven back by small arms fire. Sources differ on when the attack began, but it clearly did so ahead of schedule. The published history of RIR 241 claims that on seeing the enemy start to retire, *"at 10.30 we broke forth and no other regiment came with us."*[7] The momentum of the assault was irresistible, and soon all units were advancing. RIR 241 (with some elements of RIR 243 and LIR 78) stormed through Frezenberg into Verlorenhoek, where the RAMC dressing station was nearly overrun. Hundreds of prisoners were taken, and the wake of the assault was strewn with British dead and wounded. On the left RJB 25 and RIR 242 were also successful; an eyewitness account appears in *Fighting the Kaiser's War* (p. 216). By about midday II./242 had cleared the British dugouts in *Engländerwäldchen* (Wilde Wood), but 53. RD was then forced to dig in under intense artillery fire due to slower progress on its right. I./245 and III./247 had both overrun the British front line, and 1./245 on the right flank of 54. RD had reached the 5km mark on the railway. However enemy machine-gun fire was intense, and I./247 was pinned down in No Man's Land. On the division's left flank I./248 had driven Princess Patricia's Canadian Light Infantry back to their support line, inflicting grievous losses. II./247 was now sent forward to aid I./247, but went too far to the left and entered the lines of IR 132 (39. ID / XV. AK).

About 2 pm the rest of RIR 243 was committed to the right of RIR 241, and LIR 77 subordinated to 105. Res. Inf. Brig. However the renewed advance soon stalled under a hail of shrapnel, and Genmaj. von Schmieden was among the wounded. Later that afternoon LIR 78 finally made progress on the right, and III./244 was inserted between RIR 241 and RJB 25 near Verlorenhoek. This battalion found the position full of enemy casualties, and its stretcher bearers struggled to cope. South of the railway, a counterattack forced the depleted I./245 to cede 200 metres. That evening most of RIR 243 was withdrawn, while I./247 finally advanced and the 54. RD line stabilised. At Verlorenhoek, 1./241 ambushed a British officer's patrol, killing 'a corporal and a major' and wounding a third man; later a lost British artillery despatch rider was captured. After midnight a counterattack was attempted south of the village. Lacking flares, 106. Res. Inf. Brig. blazed away blindly while RIR 245 saw their targets silhouetted against the burning houses; dawn revealed about forty British dead and wounded.

Due to slower progress by its neighbours, XXVII. RK did not attack that morning. RIR 241 and the attached 10./243

This Tommy was supposedly killed when a lucky German shot caused his rifle ammunition to explode.

The approximate lines and sectors held by XXVII. RK and its neighbours at the beginning and end of the offensive. The dotted line indicates the gains up to 26 April (including the contribution of *Sturmbrigade von Schmieden*).

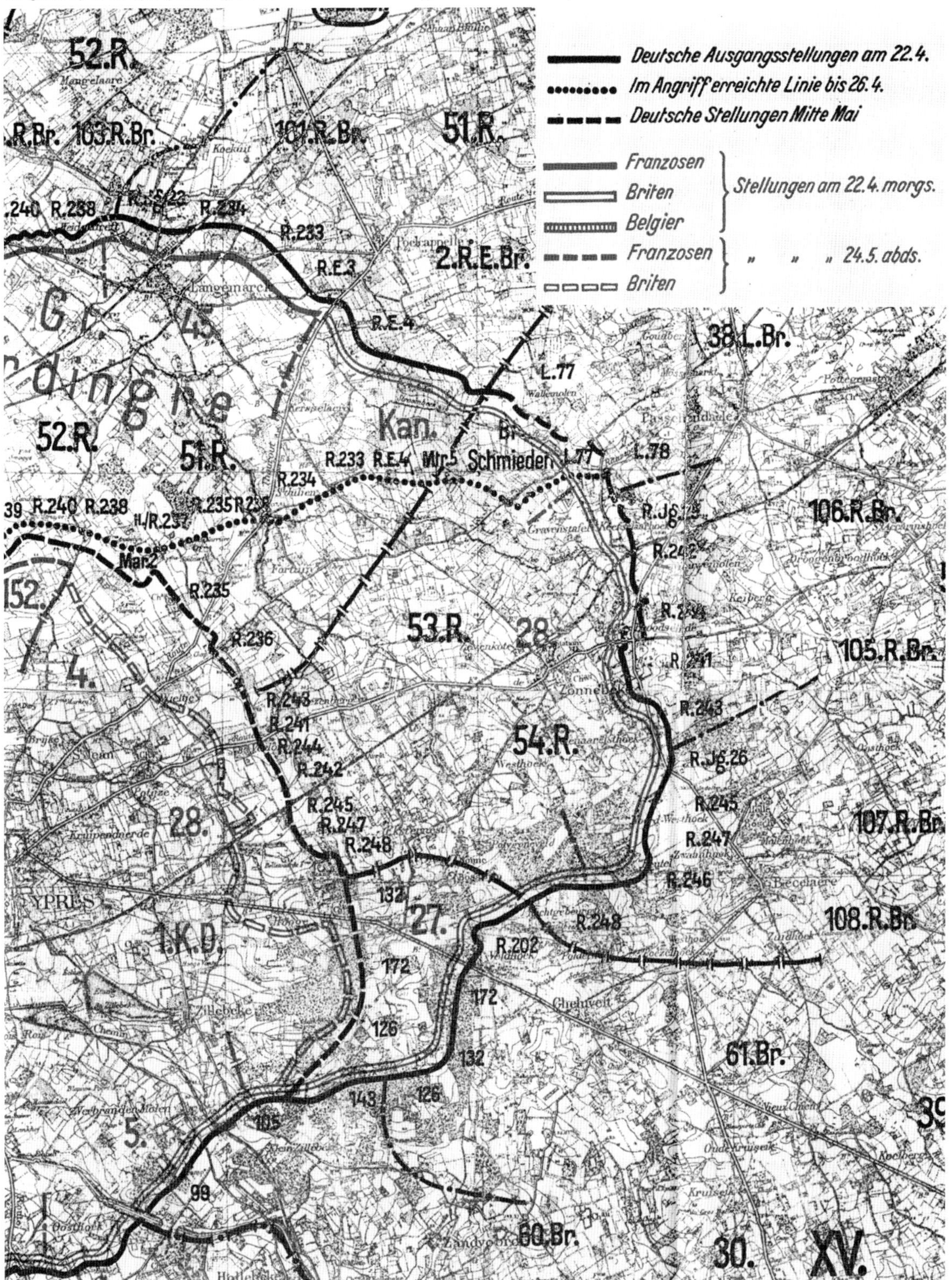

found that it was safe to walk above ground, and several hundred demoralised Tommies surrendered to them during the day. RJB 25 however reported heavy shelling. RIR 247 occupied the *Klavierhaus* (see photo p. 112), where a piano (*Klavier*) and a live pig were 'captured' and taken to the rear. After a relatively light barrage 106. Res. Inf. Brig. and 54. RD made a hasty attack at 5pm. There was little progress north of the railway and heavy losses, but 54. RD reached the western edge of *Storchschnabelwäldchen* (Dead Man's Bottom) before machine-gun fire from across Bellewaarde Lake stalled the advance. Next day RIR 248 made another small advance on the left.

Over the nights of 11–13 May, Pi. Regt. 35 installed *F-batterien* along the corps front, now reduced on the right with the inter-brigade boundary of 53. RD some 300 metres southwest of Verlorenhoek. RJB 25 was withdrawn and each brigade sector held by a battalion each from two regiments (left to right RIR 242, 244, 241 and 243). The newly formed Pi. Regt. 36 had now departed for the Eastern Front, taking with it most of the experienced gas engineers and leaving Pi. Regt. 35 to conduct gas operations in Flanders with their freshly trained replacements (including a Württemberg company of volunteers from 54. RD).

13 May was *Christi Himmelfahrt* (Ascension Day). As RIR 247 grimly noted *"we celebrated in our own manner"*.[9] The wind was unsuitable for gas, but heavy conventional shelling began at 5 am. Despite pre-registration RIR 247 and 248 suffered severely from 15cm and 21cm drop-shorts, while their opponents were untouched; after frantic appeals, the shells fell behind the British line. The bombardment lifted about 7.45, by which time heavy rain was turning the battlefield into a swamp and the men struggled to keep their rifles

Overview of the advance achieved, showing the dramatic shortening of the corps front.

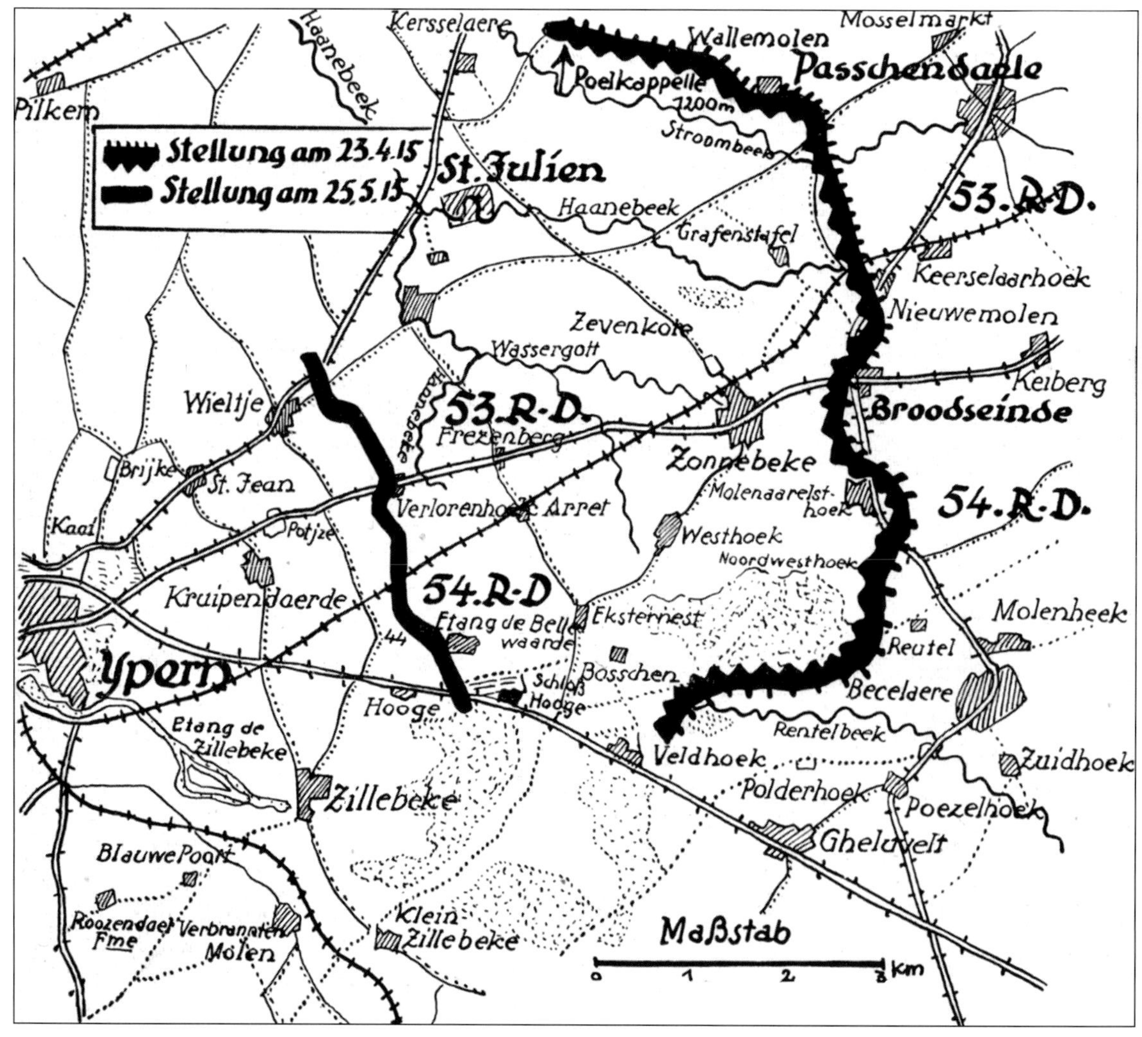

clean. Somehow RIR 241, 242 and 244 took the British front line, and one group even reached the Wieltje road. However there was no cohesive line, flanking fire was murderous and from midday enemy artillery took a dreadful toll. At 3.20 pm British dismounted cavalry counterattacked, driving the Saxons back to their start line. Losses were appalling, with 600 killed or wounded from RIR 244 alone. The next day brought a lull and further heavy rain, during which officers of III. / 241 met British medical personnel in No Man's Land and arranged an hour's truce for the recovery of the dead and wounded.

All brigade sectors were now enlarged and 38. Landwehr-Brigade withdrawn. RIR 245 shifted north of the railway, while the new inter-brigade boundary of 53. RD was north of Verlorenhoek and its right flank near Wieltje. Each of its brigade sectors was held by two battalions of one regiment, rotated every three days. During their battalion's shift Gefr. Illing and Sold. Protze of 10. / 243 discovered that a British trench 200 metres to their front was empty, gaining RIR 243 a bloodless advance. At Eksternest, RIR 247 found an elderly couple still living in one of the houses. Sadly the husband was later killed by a shell, and the wife then evacuated under protest in a wheelbarrow. RIR 241 was equally amazed on the 23rd at the discovery of an emaciated Tommy who had lain gravely wounded in a dugout since the 8th.

On 24 May *Pfingsten* (Whit Monday) was marked at home while XXVI. and XXVII. RK made a final onslaught on Ypres, preceded at 3.45 am by the largest chlorine attack to date. In the RIR 241 sector the cylinders were in the second line. Appallingly, advance notice of the discharge only reached regimental HQ at 3.20. The first the men in the front line heard of it was at 3.35 from the gas engineers manning the *F-batterien*. The infantry had barely left their dugouts when the gas was released. As they tried to flee over the top or down crowded communication trenches, the inexperienced engineers tried in vain to close the cylinders and were themselves gassed. Incredibly at 4 am the regiment still advanced a few hundred metres through the gas cloud before digging in. Everyone was gassed to some degree, and 126 men hospitalised. In the RIR 242 sector, due to ill-fitting pipes and inexperienced engineers many cylinders vented into the front line or not at all. Partly gassed and enfiladed from the right, the regiment nevertheless gained ground with the aid of the artillery and reinforcement by 5. / 244. The British foothold in Verlorenhoek was reduced to a small group of houses on the western edge, and about 200 prisoners were taken. On their left the gas actually worked as intended and RIR 245 soon took the British front line. While awaiting support however they came under withering fire, while their advancing

Officers' quarters of 3. Battr. / RFAR 54 at Zevenkote in summer 1915; the battery position was about 1 km to the west.

Left to right: Vfw. Zickler from Dresden (KIA as a *leutnant* on the Somme on 12 September 1916), Oltn. d. R. Aulhorn from Dresden, Stabsveterinär (senior veterinary officer) d. L. Uhlemann from Burgstädt, Ltn. Schneider from Zeitz and (with the horses) Gefr. Neef.

reserves were shattered by artillery. South of the railway doubts about the wind prevented discharge of all the cylinders in the RJB 26 sector and many of those in the neighbouring RIR 247 sector, while others had their pipes shot off by machine-gun fire with predictable results. RIR 248 was luckier and did attack at 4 am, but the gas failed to subdue its opponents and the advance soon stalled. Having brought up its reserves, RJB 26 attacked at 6 am together with 2./247. The enemy appeared to panic, so that despite heavy artillery fire the *jägers* reached the edge of *Eierwäldchen* (Railway Wood). Meanwhile RIR 247 worked forward carefully with support from two field guns of RFAR 54 in the *Klavierhaus* and *Storchschnabelwäldchen*, knocking out the British machine-guns one by one and gradually breaking into their line. On their left, Ltn. d. L. Wegenast (adjutant of II./248) led the storming of Bellewaarde Farm, which was then occupied at once by artillery observers. By 9.30 am a general assault developed south of the railway, leading to the collapse and rout of the British line. One group of Württembergers reached *T-Wäldchen* (Y Wood) and shot up British reserves at Witte Poort Farm, while a few dug in on the Menin Road behind Hooge and fired into the British rear. From 11 am the new positions came under intense shrapnel fire (some of it 'friendly'), making it near impossible to bring forward reserves or supplies and breaking every telephone line laid by RFAR 54. The gap between the two woods proved too dangerous to hold, and 10./247 was shot to pieces attempting it. Although there were no machine-guns in the front line the counterattack of 84th Brigade at 3.45 pm failed bloodily, but did force the group on the Menin Road to retire.

Furious British artillery fire continued well into the night, before repeated counterattacks in the small hours and morning of the 25th. Now reinforced with machine-guns, the Württembergers and *jägers* mowed the Tommies down in heaps. Although hammered by heavy guns for the rest of the day, 54. RD consolidated its position. This victory came at a fearful price, especially for RIR 247 with 1,468 killed or wounded between 24 and 28 May. With both sides completely exhausted and no reserves to press the offensive, the battle was over. On the night of 6–7 June 54. RD took over the entire corps front, which would henceforth be held by the two divisions alternately until 1916. A week later, home leave was at last offered – for the first time since XXVII. RK left Germany in 1914.

British dead near Bellewaarde Farm. The pig at top left may be the one found by RIR 247 at the *Klavierhaus*.

Gathering point for the dead of RIR 247 after the attack of 24 May at the chapel in Eksternest.

RIR 247 was relieved by RIR 246 on 28 May and held a mass funeral service at Molenhoek the next day.

One of the divisional chaplains (*divisionspfarrer*) conducts a mass funeral for RIR 242 at Passchendaele-Moorslede railway station.

Offiziersstellvertreter Paul Hauweide of RIR 244 in the new second position built behind the corps front in summer 1915. On the back he tells his wife how he took a bullet a little forward and left of this spot in May; according to the casualty lists he was wounded twice.

Radio station in the *Klavierhaus* with mixed Saxons and Württembergers of 54. RD in summer 1915.

Three photos and what they tell us

These group photos from 11. Kompanie / Reserve-Infanterie-Regiment 242 were all taken in rest quarters at Moorslede prior to the offensive. Thanks to the extensive annotation we have identified many of these men with reasonable certainty; in most cases, those marked with a cross have been confirmed killed in spring or summer 1915. Note that names in the photo captions read from left to right. Birthplaces are given in brackets below.

Ers.-Res. August BERNHARD (Großopitz), lightly wounded in head ca. 11.–20.5.1915 • Sold.? Otto DABERKOW (Großröhrsdorf), lightly wounded in head 7.1915 • 'Flemming' may be Uffz. Oskar FLEMMING of 12./242 (Klingenberg), KIA Kerselaerhoek 25.4.1915 • Gefr. Paul FRENZEL (Pulsnitz), KIA Frezenberg 25.4.1915 • Ers.-Res. Heinrich Albin GERSDORF (Neukirch), severely wounded ca. 11.–20.5.1915 • Ers.-Res. Max Hugo GRAHL (Reinhardtsgrimma), fatally wounded in stomach ca. 11.–20.5.1915 • Ers.-Res. Max Martin HANTSCH (Porschdorf), lightly wounded in head ca. 11–20.5.1915 • Ers.-Res. Erwin HEINRICH (Bretnig), KIA St. Eloi 10.7.1915 • Ers.-Res. Gustav Alfred HERMANN (Dresden), wounded ca. 1.–8.5.1915 • Sold.? Gustav KEUL (Steinigtwolmsdorf), KIA St. Eloi 10.7.1915 • Ers.-Res. Emil Arthur KLUGE (Döbeln), severely wounded in r. hand ca. 24.–25.5.1915 • Ers.-Res. Otto Alfred KRANICH (Zwickau-Marienthal), lightly wounded ca. 11.–20.5.1915 • Ers.-Res. Michael KRAUTSCHICK (Räckelwitz), lightly wounded ca. 11.–20.5.1915 • Ers.-Res. Ernst KRETSCHEL (Mittelbach), KIA Kerselaerhoek 25.4.1915 • Sold.? Richard KUNZE (Kamenz), lightly wounded in head and lower r. arm ca. 10.–15.7.1915 • Ers.-Res. Max LEUSCHNER (Obergrüna), died in hospital at Moorslede 12.8.1915 • Sold. Arthur MEIßNER (Deuben), KIA Kerselaerhoek 25.4.1915 • 'Oehmigen' may be Uffz. d. L. Friedrich Oswald OEHMICHEN (Seehausen), severely wounded in l. leg ca. 11.–20.5.1915 • Ers.-Res. Hermann SCHNEIDER (Dresden), KIA Frezenberg 13.5.1915 • Ltn. d. R. Fritz SCHÖNFELDER (Bautzen), lightly wounded (not killed) ca. 11.–20.5.1915 • Vfw. d. L. Paul TODTERMUSCHKE (Bischheim), KIA Kerselaerhoek 25.4.1915 • Uffz. Oswin UHLMANN (Großenhain), KIA Kerselaerhoek 25.4.1915 • Ltn. d. L. Bruno WAGNER (Grünhainichen), KIA Kerselaerhoek 25.4.1915 • Uffz. Paul ZIMMERMANN (Friedersdorf), KIA Frezenberg 13.5.1915

2. Korporalschaft, 20 April 1915. Standing: Leuschner, Kluge, Grahl, Bernhard, Sauermann, Kunze, Krautschick, Körner, Griebner, Daberkow, Hantsch. Seated: Keul, Heinrich (Erwin), Uffz. Zimmermann, Gefr. Frenzel, Heinrich (Ernst), Mikolni (?)

15 April 1915. Lying: Uffz. Müller, Uffz. Zimmermann. Seated: Vfw. Meißner, Fw. Hörnig, Ltn. Schönfelder, Offz. Stv. Wagner, Vfw. Todtermuschke, Uffz. Uhlmann. first row standing: Uffz. Oehmigen, Uffz. Flemming, Uffz. Gruhl, Uffz. Wilkat, Uffz. Skalf(?), Gefr. Salersky, Gefr. Schulze, Uffz. Tauchert.

---

1. Korporalschaft, 22 March 1915. Standing: Schneider, Koch, Meißner, Wünsche, Uffz. Müller, Uffz. Wilkat, Mahlisch, Schaafe, Kretschel, Gefr. Burger, Gersdorf. Unclear (more men than names): Zimmermann, Müller, Hermann, unknown, Kranich.

Chapter 7
In the rear of XXVII. Reservekorps

Five members of the 5. Kompanie/Reserve-Infanterie-Regiment 241 pictured at a local photographic studio during their battalion's rest period in Izegem (from 26 January to 29 February 1916). Unusually they have chosen to simulate the routine task of cleaning their Mauser Gewehr 98 rifles for the camera.

In the rear of XXVII. Reservekorps

Between the trenches and the German border – accommodation, supply, training and medical services

Behind the German trenches lay a vast area of even greater mystery for Tommies at the time and for British readers today. Here the fighting troops spent much of their time, co-existing with the civilian population and the thousands of officers and men permanently based there on command, communications, transport, administrative and security duties. Life here for soldiers and civilians alike was dominated by the demands of the front for men and materiel, and the demands of German war industry for raw materials and labour.

German-occupied Belgium and France were divided into three zones, popularly likened to hell, purgatory and heaven. In front lay the *operationsgebiet* (operational area) under the direct control of the field armies – in this case **Armee-oberkommando 4** (AOK 4) in Tielt – and their subordinate corps. The Belgian coast was similarly under direct naval administration. The exact boundaries and depth of this zone varied substantially, but reached back to include the areas where corps reserves were billeted and the corps HQ and supply units were based. Each habitable town or village here had an *ortskommandant* (town major) responsible for billeting, maintenance of order and traffic control. This officer, usually older and unfit for frontline service, could be likened comically to a mayor (like Ltn. d. L. Prof. Ramshorn on p. 146–148) or a petty king (as depicted in Ernst Jünger's *In Stahlgewittern*). Nevertheless in his little domain he wielded the power of military law, and could call on the *feldgendarmerie* or even the *geheime feldpolizei* (plainclothes field police). Soldiers would need to report at the *ortskommandantur* on arrival, as might civilians e.g. when travelling outside their place of residence. Public orders and proclamations were posted here and travel documents issued.

East of the line Bruges–Kortrijk–Tournai lay the *etappengebiet* or *etappe* (lines of communication), governed by **Etappen-Inspektion 4** in Gent. This 'rear-area inspectorate' was a huge military bureaucracy responsible for the supply lines of 4. Armee, represented in each town and village by an *etappenkommandant*. The etappe was home to numerous transport, labour and administrative formations, derided by visiting *frontschweine* ('front pigs', equivalent to 'poor bloody infantry') as *etappenschweine* or *etappenhengste*. These terms had the same connotations as 'REMF' and could be applied facetiously to anyone based further back than the speaker. Entire divisions spent extended periods in the etappe when 'resting' and rebuilding and/or in army reserve.

From the rear of the *etappe* to the Dutch and French borders lay the domain of **Generalgouvernement Belgien**. This German military and civil administration in Brussels ruled via the existing systems of the Belgian state, economically exploiting its territory for the war effort with an increasingly heavy hand. This zone had a less conspicuously military character than the *etappe*, and leave here was considered the next best thing to home leave in Germany.

Given the importance of the railways for long-distance transport of troops and supplies from Germany right up to the rearward *operationsgebiet*, each station in occupied territory was supervised by a *bahnhofskommandantur*.

During the 1914 campaign the Flemish civilian population was regarded with suspicion, albeit far less so than their Francophone compatriots. 53. RD reported combat with armed civilians at Rollegem-Kapelle and Ledegem on 19 October, and RIR 241 summarily executed six alleged *franc-tireurs*. Paranoia about possible spies persisted throughout the battle just as it did on the British side. The XXVII. RK order of the day for 6 February 1915 reports the arrest of a self-confessed Belgian spy, but also hints at increasing fraternisation by reiterating the ban on the common practice of soldiers using their names and unit stamps to send mail through the *feldpost* system on behalf of Belgian civilians (for whom no postal service existed in the *operationsgebiet*).[1]

Saxon unit histories and personal accounts often stress their good relationship with their Flemish hosts, and assert that they were better liked than other German contingents. Whatever the truth of this, it is clear that a tolerable *modus vivendi* often existed, aided by the ease of mutual comprehension between Flemish and many German dialects. Outside the official requisition system, soldiers and civilians traded by barter on the black market (inevitably including un-regulated prostitution). Official restrictions on every facet of civilian life, most especially the movements of men of military age and resident enemy aliens, grew increasingly onerous as the war ground on. Under the pressure of the British blockade, destitution and starvation were kept at bay only by international relief efforts.

Command and control

The corps staff (**Generalkommando XXVII. Reserve-Korps**) was based at Dadizele from October 1914 until its departure from this front. From here the entire 30,000–40,000 man corps was directed and the territory under its occupation administered. In total the *generalkommando* numbered around 300 officers and men. Its core was a team of four staff officers with accompanying adjutants and orderlies, under the *stabschef* (chief of staff) – the commanding general's right-hand man. It also included legal officials, corps chief medical and veterinary officers, the chiefs of the corps *pioniere, fussartillerie* and *trains* (see p. 125) and a postmaster. The *korpsintendant* (chief of the commissariat) was responsible for accounting and supply administration, including the paychest and the *korpsproviantamt* (corps food supply depot) in Ledegem. All of these officers were served by batmen, grooms and cooks, and protected by a *stabswache* (sentry detail) led by a commandant. In December 1914 Dadizele gained a permanent *ortswache* (of two NCOs and seventy men on weekly rotation).

Due to the presence of the corps HQ, Dadizele also housed the **Feldgendarmerietrupp des XXVII. RK** (military police) and **Reserve-Fernsprech-Abteilung 27** (the corps telephone detachment). Its church was frequently used for Christian services by divisional chaplains, as well as all the occasional services for the Jewish personnel of the corps given by the visiting *feldrabbiner* (field rabbi) of 4. Armee. Other facilities in the village included baths (established by Reserve-Pionier-Kompanie 54), a regular *ortskommandantur* and main collecting points for salvaged weapons and equipment. By June 1915 Dadizele lay at the intersection of the Becelaere–Kortrijk, Becelaere–Izegem und Ledegem–Geluwe narrow-gauge field railway lines.

Divisional HQs were established nearby at Chateau Koekuithoek east of Moorslede (53. Reserve-Division, from 1 December 1914 onwards) and in Terhand (54. Reserve-Division). Besides its commander each *divisionskommando* had a single staff officer, an orderly officer / translator, two adjutants, legal officials, a *divisionsintendant* (controlling the *divisionsproviantamt*), chief medical officer, *führer der großen bagage* (chief of the divisional baggage), guard commandant and at least two chaplains (see Chapter 4 Note 21). Accompanying each *divisionskommando* was its *feldpostexpedition*, a mobile field post office with personnel seconded from the *Deutsche Reichspost* (the empire's unified civilian postal service).

The staff of Generalkommando XXVII. Reservekorps await a royal visit at Dadizele chateau. The corps was visited by H.M. the King of Saxony in December 1914 and June 1915, and by the King of Württemberg on 15 April 1915. The chateau and grounds still survive largely unchanged.

Gefr. Hans Hertrich of the Feldgendarmerietrupp des XXVII. RK. About a third of its around sixty military policemen were seconded civilian gendarmerie NCOs, and the rest cavalry NCOs or *gefreiters*. The individually numbered gorget (*ringkragen*) was their badge of office.

Baggage personnel of RIR 243 in the rear in January 1915. Second right is Oltn. Franke, *führer der großen bagage* (regimental baggage train commander); fourth right is Ltn. Keller, *verpflegungsoffizier* (battalion supply officer) of I. / 243 throughout the regiment's existence.

Oberst z.D. Kurt von Holleben (1862–1941), commander of RIR 243, in Roulers ca. January 1915. Commander of Landwehr-Bezirk Zwickau in peacetime, he was awarded the MStHO on 7 December 1914 after personally leading the final assault on the Calvairewald on 14 November.

The cumbersome non-standard *packwagen* (baggage wagon) of 3./RIR 241 and crew. Each company had a field kitchen and ammunition wagon which followed it as *gefechtsbagage* (combat baggage) and a baggage wagon and provision wagon with the regiment's *große bagage* in the rear.

Butchers and slaughtermen of the Feldschlachterei der 53. Reserve-Division in Beitem (its 54. RD counterpart was in Ledegem). Butchery units had originally existed only in the *etappe*, but were soon improvised by divisions and corps as an adaptation to static trench warfare.

Reserve-Bäckerei-Kolonne 33, the divisional bakery column of 53. RD, before departure from Dresden; note 'Reserve Train 12' helmet covers.

Shoeing horses at the *feldschmiede* (field smithy) of 3. Battr. / RFAR 54 in Strooiboomhoek, midway between Dadizele and Waterdamhoek.

Reserve-Kavallerie-Abteilung 53 was the divisional cavalry squadron, raised from reservists of various regiments and uniformed as uhlans. It scouted ahead of the division in October 1914, but was soon relegated to escorting prisoners, carrying messages and rear-area guard duty.

Officers and NCOs of Feldluftschiffer-Abteilung 12, a Prussian observation balloon unit attached to XXVII. RK until the beginning of 1916.

Traditional climbing exercises in light equipment for new arrivals (and convalescents) at the Feldrekrutendepot des XXVII. RK in Oudenaarde.

The supply chain

Like most published orders of battle, the one on p. 98 omits the corps ammunition train (*munitionskolonnen-abteilung*) and supply train (*train-abteilung*) which kept the fighting troops operational. Although their losses were few and their deeds seldom celebrated, these units had their own share of hardship. Operating in the open on muddy and shell-holed roads, in all weathers and often at night, supply drivers risked shelling, air attack and lethal accidents. The corps trains and the *bagage* of the fighting units of XXVII. RK were manned by older reservists and used many non-standard (often civilian) vehicles. Until late 1914 even the infantry used a heavy four-wheeled substitute for the company field kitchen (see p. 138), and thus could not get hot food far enough forward to reach the combatants.

Munitionskolonnen-Abteilung des XXVII. RK brought munitions up to replenish the regimental ammunition wagons of the fighting units. It had four artillery ammunition columns (**Reserve-Artillerie-Munitionskolonne 71–73** (Saxon) and **74** (Württemberg), two per field artillery regiment as in an active corps. As was the norm, even its two infantry small arms ammunition columns (**Reserve-Infanterie-Munitionskolonne 54** and **55**) consisted of artillerymen. The corps also had an organic heavy artillery ammunition column (**leichte Reserve-Fussartillerie-Munitionskolonne 27**).

While the regimental baggage could carry a few days worth of provisions, fodder, construction materials and dressings, longer-term supply depended on the **Train-Abteilung des XXVII. RK**. This was around half the size of its counterpart in an active corps, with five supply park columns (**Reserve- Fuhrpark-Kolonne 86–90**), two bakery columns with massive mobile bread ovens (**Reserve-Bäckerei-Kolonne 33** and **34**) and a remount depot (**Württemberg Reserve-Pferdedepot 27**). It also organisationally included the field hospitals (see p. 129) and a horse hospital (**Pferdelazarett des XXVII. RK**). All were units of the *train*, the traditional horse-drawn supply transport arm. The two divisional bridging columns (**Reserve-Divisions-Brückentrain 53** and **54**) were also drawn mainly from the *train* but under direct command of the divisional *pioniere*.

Unlike Britain's Army Service Corps, the *train* had no motor vehicles. These were at least officially the preserve of the *kraftfahrtruppen* (motor transport troops), part of the *verkehrstruppen* (communication troops). On 1 July 1915 the corps gained a motorised transport column (**Korps-Kraftwagen-Kolonne des XXVII. RK**).

An artilleryman's sketch from November 1914 of the Flemish farm which housed his battalion's organic *leichte munitionskolonne* (light ammunition column) in the 54. Reserve-Division sector between Terhand and Geluwe. In the background is the Arcemolen mill. Since this card was posted to an address in Leipzig, this column was presumably that of the I. (sächs.) Abteilung / Reserve-Feldartillerie-Regiment 54.

Artillerymen of Reserve-Feldartillerie-Regiment 53 with a 7.7cm ammunition wagon of Reserve-Artillerie-Munitions-Kolonne 71 in late 1914.

Reserve-(Feldhaubitzen-)Artillerie-Munitions-Kolonne 73, one of the corps' four field artillery ammunition columns (three of them Saxon).

The corps' two infantry ammunition columns (here Reserve-Infanterie-Munitionskolonne 55) also consisted – as was the norm – of artillerymen.

Drivers of leichte Fußartillerie-Munitionskolonne des XXVII. RK, which supplied schwere Reserve-Feldhaubitze-Batterie 27 (see p.146).

Personnel of Reserve-Fuhrpark-Kolonne 86, one of the five corps supply vehicle parks (numbered 86–90, all Saxon).

The 'permanent' *bautrupp* (installation team) of Reserve-Fernsprech-Abteilung 27 under Uffz. Benedict was dissolved again early in 1916. Half of these corps telephonists wear the climbing harness used by linemen of the *Reichspost* (which ran German's civilian telephone system).

Medical services

One of the most serious inadequacies of the XXVII. Reservekorps at formation was in medical provision. The Saxon active corps were mobilised with as many as fourteen field hospitals (*feldlazarette*) and three medical companies (*sanitäts-kompanien*) each, and the XII. Reserve-Korps eight hospitals and two companies. In October 1914, the XXVII. Reservekorps had only four field hospitals (**Saxon Reserve-Feldlazarett 91** and **92**, **Württemberg Reserve-Feldlazarett 93** and **94**) and two medical companies (**Saxon Reserve-Sanitäts-Kompanie 53** and **Württemberg Reserve-Sanitäts-Kompanie 54**). Like every corps it also had a small war hospital detachment (**Kriegslazarettabteilung 127**) to set up additional hospitals in the field using local personnel and facilities; these soon passed to the control of Etappen-Inspektion 4. At the head of corps medical services was the staff of the *korpsarzt* (chief medical officer) Oberstabsarzt Dr. Arno Thalmann, including a pharmacist, hygienist and consulting surgeon.

In October a *truppenverbandsplatz* (forward aid post) was established in Becelaere church, and divisional *hauptverbandsplätze* (casualty clearing stations) by 53. RD at Strooiboomhoek and 54. RD at Dadizele. The latter treated around 4,700 casualties in October alone, before Res. San. Komp. 54 moved to Geluveld and Geluwe in November.

Res.-Feldlaz. 91 was based at Moorslede, apparently moving to Moorsele in December and returning in May 1915. Res.-Feldlaz. 92 was briefly at Dadizele and Moorsele, moving to Lendelede (29 October) and Oekene (6 December). Res.-Feldlaz. 93 was at Dadizele, then Slijpskapelle (17 November) and Beitem (5 December). Res.-Feldlaz. 94 used the hospital, church and school in Ledegem. In early November they were reinforced by Saxon Feldlazarett 3 des XII. Armeekorps at St.-Eloois-Winkel and Prussian Feldlazarett 8 des X. Armeekorps at Lendelede. After delays en route, Kriegslazarettabteilung 127 reached Kortrijk on 29 October 1914 and set up several *kriegslazarette*. After handing these over to the Kriegslazarettabteilung des Gardekorps in November, it moved to Izegem.

With the end of the immediate crisis in November 1914, the corps medical services extended their remit to disease prevention, dentistry and the recovery, identification and interment of the dead (see Chapter 12). Cases of infectious diseases and of mental illness were sent to specialist facilities in the *etappe*, the latter to the Kriegslazarett Neue Justizpalast Gent.

Krankenträger (stretcher bearers) of Reserve-Sanitäts-Kompanie 53, the dedicated divisional medical company of 53. RD, before its departure from Saxony in October 1914; the corresponding formation of 54. RD was Württemberg Reserve-Sanitäts-Kompanie 54. Units of all the fighting arms also had their own regimental and battalion medical officers, with orderlies and bandsmen doubling as additional stretcher bearers.

Medical personnel and vehicles at the *'Schrapnellhaus'* west of Keibergmolen, ruined by British artillery on 20 October 1914. The building served in November 1914 as a brigade observation post, and the forward dressing station of RIR 243 operated in the basement.

The first stop for casualties in the front line – a first aid post *(sanitätsunterstand)* manned by regimental *sanitäter* of RIR 243.

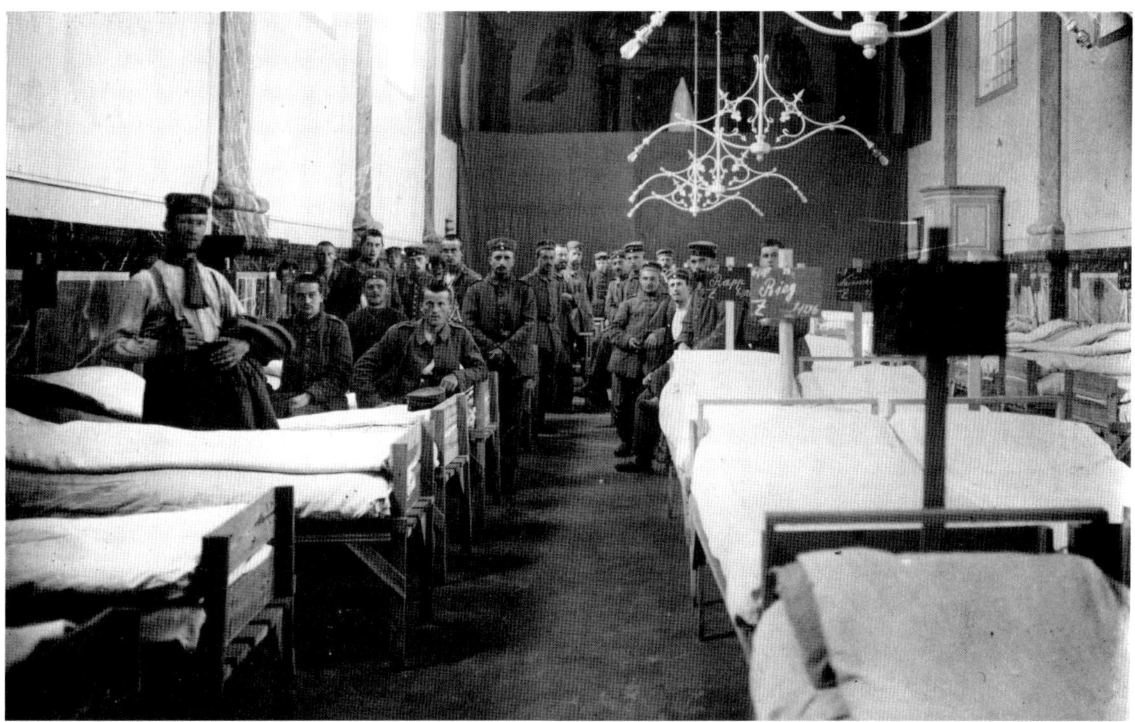

As a major communications hub behind the front Izegem soon became a major hospital town. In addition to a newly erected storage depot and a local nursing home, the Capuchin friary was also requisitioned as a hospital on 11 November 1914.

Krankenträger of Reserve-Feldlazarett 92 stand by to load casualties into an ambulance for transport to Izegem station in late March 1915.

Kommandos

The word *kommando* denoted either a higher staff (division upwards) or a party detached from its parent unit(s) to perform a task. A *kommando* in the latter sense could be anything from an ad-hoc working party to a specialised unit which likewise relied on 'borrowed' manpower. A *kommando* was not always a desirable posting, but did at least offer a break from military routine. Under the unprecedented labour demands of trench warfare, the number, variety and duration of *kommandos* dramatically increased.

By the end of 1914 demand for the skills of the *pioniere* had clearly exceeded supply. The only solution was for the *pioniere* to instruct *kommandos* (ideally of men with relevant skills) in one aspect of their role. Each infantry regiment formed *handgranatentrupps* and *infanterie-pionier-kommandos* (*later infanterie-pionier-kompanien*) to take over grenade throwing and construction of field works, and contributed miners to what would become divisional *mineur-kompanien*. Other skilled *kommandos* tackled tasks without *pionier* precedent like concreting, electrical engineering and drainage. Manpower was also required for the manufacture of trench construction materials, which reached the front via the *kleinbahn* (narrow-gauge railways built and operated by the *pioniere*) and on the backs of *trägerkommandos* (carrying parties).

In the rear of the *operationsgebiet*, numerous small *wachen* and *wachkommandos* were needed to guard the various *kommandanturen*, supply dumps and base facilities. By June 1915 a training cadre of officers and men was serving at Oudenaarde in the *etappe* with the **Feldrekrutendepot des XXVII. RK**, a training formation up to nine companies strong to which new recruits and convalescents were assigned on arrival.

The published history of Reserve-Jäger-Bataillon 26 gives some idea of the manpower demands of *kommandos* in autumn 1915: *The battalion soon dissolves into a plethora of* kommandos. *To be provided are: the* korpswache *[corps HQ guard] in Dadizeele, the* ortswache *[town guard] in Molenhoek, a permanent* arbeitskommando *[working party] under Oberjäger Wolf,* friedhofs- *[cemetery management],* hürdenbau- *[hurdle making],* wasserbau- *[water engineering],* entwässerungs- *[drainage],* strassenbau- *[road building] and* fliegerabwehrkommando *[anti-aircraft defense]. There is not much left for service with the battalion.*[2]

By 1916 increased provision of *pioniere* and unarmed labour units eased both skilled and unskilled labour shortages, while many once-specialist skills such as grenade throwing and trench construction were now universal. *Kommandos* nevertheless remained a fact of life.

This *kommando* from RIR 245 in November 1915 is serving as *fliegerwache* (anti-aircraft sentries), surely a welcome break from the trenches.

A working party from RIR 243 directed by an *unteroffizier*, engaged in the common task of making wickerwork for use in construction. This was widely used to prevent muddy trench walls from collapsing inward, as seen e.g. in chapter 8.

Korpswache (corps HQ sentries) seconded from 2. Kompanie / Reserve-Jäger-Bataillon 25 at Chateau Dadizele in spring 1915.

Workshop of the *zimmerlingsgruppe* (carpentry section) of Infanterie-Pionier-Kompanie / RIR 244 in 1915. The regiment formed this 120-strong company while at *Bayernwald* in summer 1915 to establish *"a cadre of men trained and experienced in trench construction"*.[3]

Infanterie-pioniere of RIR 243 in a freshly constructed rear-area training trench (complete with dugout) at Moorslede in 1915.

Gunners from RFAR 53 working on a 7.7cm FK 96 n.A. at the Roulers branch of Artillerie-Werkstatt 4, which maintained the guns of 4. Armee.

After the British mine explosion in the RIR 248 sector on 25 September 1915, the Infanterie-Mineur-Kompanie der 54. RD was formed under Ltn. d. L. Wagner to relieve the 53. RD tunnellers seen here. The new unit became Württemberg Pionier-Mineur-Kompanie 314 on 20 May 1916.

Rest and rebuilding

In October 1914 the troops of XXVII. RK faced weeks of relentless fighting with only rudimentary relief, holding rough positions in increasingly grim conditions. Attempts were made to give each infantry company a weekly respite from the line to clean themselves and get adequate sleep, but the dwindling manpower of the much-bloodied corps made it ever harder to spare them.

Meaningful relief first became possible in late November, as the battle devolved into localised attempts to improve the line and replacements began to arrive from Germany. For example, the remnants of RIR 242 (only three composite companies strong) and of RIR 244 now relieved each other every 48 hours, with the resting 'regiment' at Waterdamhoek. RIR 242 received 1000 replacements on 19 November (now forming three battalions with two companies each) and was briefly withdrawn to Waterdamhoek on 2 December (where it again formed a full twelve companies). From the night of 3–4 December it held the line between the Moorslede–Zonnebeke road and the Ypres–Roulers railway with all three battalions abreast. After repelling a French attack on the 14th, its sector was reduced on 18 December and henceforth held by only six companies at a time. The six 'resting' companies were often employed that winter in efforts to render the forward positions habitable and establish support positions in the rear. It was not until 5 April 1915 that RIR 242 introduced a more conventional relief cycle, rotating its three battalions every three days through the roles of *kampfbataillon* (trench holding), *bereitschaftsbataillon* (support) and *ruhebataillon* (rest). After the advance of May 1915, the XXVII. RK frontage was then so dramatically reduced that it could be held by one division at a time with the other 'resting' or in reserve.

Resting elements of a regiment in the line were by necessity billeted in villages close behind the front, inevitably at risk of artillery fire. Here they had a solid roof over their heads and were able to clean themselves and their equipment. At the battalion canteen (see pp. 140 and 149) they could purchase small luxuries such as beer, tobacco and postcards for writing home. Units in reserve further back had access to shower baths, mass delousing and the leisure facilities of the *etappe* including field bookshops, theatres, cinemas, estaminets and medically inspected brothels. For battle-weary troops, simply being in an undevastated town with visible civilian life provided a vital psychological respite from the stress of the front.

The men were seldom left to their own devices for long while at 'rest'. Besides the inevitable labour and transport kommandos, there was the constant round of drill, instruction, marches and tactical exercises in the extensive training facilities established at divisional, corps and army level.

As our books demonstrate, photos were wildly popular as keepsakes for families at home, as future souvenirs of the war and as a way to memorialise dear friends who could perish at any moment. The demand both for professional studio portraits and also for development of shots taken by hobbyist soldiers was met by a combination of local businesses and semi-official unit photographers. This is the 'photographic workshop' of Soldat Gustav Mühlfriedel (2./RIR 243), peacetime owner-operator of a studio in Zwickau and currently running its 'branch' (*zweiggeschäft*) in Moorslede. He proudly boasts the 'sovereign recognition' of the King of Saxony.

Hauptmann d. L. Paul Wilski (third from right), commander of 3. Kompanie / Reserve-Jäger-Bataillon 26, with his HQ personnel and hostess at their billets in winter 1914–15. Even for Saxons, the casual attitude and dress (including clogs and warm civilian clothing) is exceptional.

The Saxon I. Abteilung *(Abteilung Reimer)* of Württemberg Reserve-Feldartillerie-Regiment 54 celebrates the King of Saxony's birthday at Rollegem-Kapelle on 25 May 1915. The artillery battalion's medical and administrative personnel are gathered around the flag on the right.

At least two miners of Infanterie-Mineur-Kompanie der 54. RD here wear Saxon cockades, although it was later officially a Württemberg unit.

Feldküche or (colloquially) *'gulaschkanone'* of 2. Battr. / RFAR 53; each company or battery possessed one of these mobile field kitchens.

Civilian rest billets of RJB 26 with a typical Flemish pigeon cot. All remaining pigeons were requisitioned by the Germans in May 1915.

The newly formed *regimentsmusik* of RIR 241 at Bousbecque in 1915. All regiments of XXVII. RK lacked bands when mobilised in 1914.

Battalion canteen of III./RIR 244 in Quesnoy-sur-Deûle during the regiment's deployment at Ploegsteert Wood in autumn 1915 (see p. 48).

Reserve-Pionier-Kompanie 54 gave their quarters in Terhand the grandiose name *'König Friedrich August Kaserne'* (King Friedrich August barracks). Construction material for their work was stockpiled in front of this building.

This pub's name *'Zum Maschinengewehr'* refers to the *Maschinengewehrschule* (divisional MG school) established in Swevezele in early 1916 under Oltn. von Tschammer und Osten of MGK/RIR 244. This school aimed to give all regiments of 53. RD a reserve of trained machine-gunners.

Members of RIR 244 and civilians at another small establishment, *'Die Krone'* (The Crown) in neighbouring Coolscamp in early 1916.

Saxon soldiers in Izegem fooling with a mock anti-aircraft gun. Such devices were constructed to mislead enemy aerial observers.

Infantrymen of RIR 241 relaxing in rest billets at Izegem, before they were committed to the Champagne fighting in October 1915.

The *Straubeplatz* near the mill in Vierkavenhoek (between Moorslede and Roulers) was the regular parade ground of RIR 244.

Men of RIR 245 training at Meulebeke in summer 1915 with hand grenades, a former *pionier* weapon introduced to the infantry that year.

Assistenzarzt (junior medical officer) Uhlmann and friend relax at the so-called *Bismarckpark* near the *Jägerheim* (see map p. 69). This was a support position held by the reserve company of RJB 26 prior to the Second Battle of Ypres, and later became the battalion's rest quarters.

Artillerymen of RFAR 53 on a 'seaside holiday' in Ostend, photographed with sailors of Marinekorps Flandern.

4. Kompanie / Reserve-Jäger-Bataillon 26 bathing in the Roeselare-Leie Canal, while resting at Emelgem in summer 1915. The battalion history states: *For almost 8 weeks, the battalion and with it the division retired from the fighting. They were able to enjoy the rest period undisturbed. Unheard-of pleasures of existence were restored to us. One slept in a bed, was able to undress at night, was not alerted, was able to bathe in the canal and swim. As everyone knows, Belgium abounds with countless small pubs. All ranks could get their money's worth. In Isegem, one could even dance. And there were people who weren't soldiers, women and young girls among them!* [4]

Private soldiers of RJB 26 posing for the camera with Flemish children. Note the holstered wire-cutters (right) and early use of puttees.

Sentry on duty with a locally acquired sentry box.

Geschäftszimmer (orderly room) of 2./25 in Pittem; note the postbox.

Street view of the *geschäftszimmer* on Schulferskapellestraat in Pittem with the church visible in the background (see p.156).

A platoon of 2./25 'standing to' with a bugler at their head outside the *geschäftszimmer* prior to a training exercise.

A welcome issue of hot soup or goulash from the company field kitchen of 2./25, temporarily parked on Schulferskapellestraat. .

Schlachtfest (traditional German communal feast of a freshly slaughtered pig) at the Lauwers family's home in Pittem on 12 February 1916.

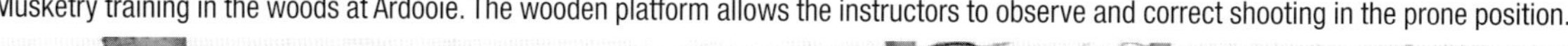

Musketry training in the woods at Ardooie. The wooden platform allows the instructors to observe and correct shooting in the prone position.

Seemingly cheerful Flemish civilians cleaning mud from the boots of their Saxon 'guests'.

Lace-making was a traditional Flemish cottage industry, the products of which were much admired and purchased as souvenirs by both sides.

A HUNDRED YEARS LATER

The Café Waterdam at Waterdamhoek crossroads in summer 2017; we were unable to establish whether it is currently in operation. This building rose in the 1920s from the ruins of the inn shown on p.149, which had successively served RIR 245 and RIR 244.

A view from 2017 of the Schulferskapellestraat in Pittem, where RJB 25 had its rest billets in winter 1915–1916 (see for comparison the lower photo on page 152). The building housing the *geschäftszimmer* of 2./25 was to the left of the still recognisable house in the foreground.

Chapter 8

In the Wytschaete Salient 1915–1916 | Infanterie-Regiment 182

A subsector boundary in the front or immediate support line at Croonaert Wood, named *Bayernwald* by the Germans in honour of the Bavarians who captured it. From October 1915 to March 1916 the eastern and western halves of the wood were usually defended by Infanterie-Regiment 178 and 182 respectively of the Saxon 123. Infanterie-Division. The name *Bayernwald* survives today thanks to the reconstructed German trench system on this site (see p.176)

In the Wytschaete Salient 1915–1916 | Infanterie-Regiment 182

Letters home from Leutnant d. R. Pache, commander of the 8. Kompagnie

Alfred Pache (born 31 December 1878 in Steinigtwolmsdorf near Bautzen) was a senior secondary school teacher. Like many such professionals he was also a reserve officer, and at mobilisation became a platoon commander in *Kgl. Sächs. 16. Infanterie-Regiment Nr. 182,* Germany's youngest peacetime infantry regiment. Formed in October 1912 and garrisoned at Freiberg, it fought in 1914 with 23. Infanterie-Division / XII. Armeekorps on the Marne and subsequently held the line north of Reims. When 23. ID was reduced to one infantry brigade of three regiments in March 1915, IR 182 joined the likewise 'surplus' IR 178 (from 32. ID) and RIR 106 (from 24. RD) as part of the new 123. Infanterie-Division. Initially deployed with XII. AK on the Aisne, 123. ID soon moved to the Lille area in OHL reserve. After briefly holding sectors near Lens and in the *Wytschaetebogen* (Wytschaete Salient) in June and July it was committed in August to the murderous Souchez sector facing Notre Dame de Lorette and bore the brunt of the French offensive there on 25 September. Within four days IR 182 alone lost 39 officers and 1,250 NCOs and men killed, wounded or missing. Although himself wounded, Pache remained in action and became a company commander on 29 September as replacement for the slain Oltn. von Mücke of 8. / 182. From 30 September to 14 October his regiment was in *bereitschaft* (immediate reserve) at Wingles, where it received large replacement drafts and began rebuilding. It then returned to Wytschaete, initially (like IR 178 and RIR 106) holding exactly the same sector as in July.

Leutnant der Reserve Alfred Pache.

The small wood north of Wytschaete known to Pache as *Bayernwald* had many names. To the Flemish it was *Kroonaard-* or *Croonaertbos*, and accordingly Croonaert Wood to the British. They also knew it as Wood 40, referring like the French *Bois Quarante* to the height above sea level from which it dominated the terrain to the north and west. The French only ceded this vital ground to 6. Kgl. Bayer. Reserve-Division on 16 November 1914 after many days of hard fighting. In honour of the Bavarians the former *Beilwald* (Axe Wood) became *Bayernwald* on German maps. In 1915 it extended much further than today, not only towards St. Eloi but also into part of the field opposite the current entrance. Here lay the front line, plagued from the outset by sloping ground, high groundwater and flanking artillery fire directed from the *Kemmelberg.* It was supported on either flank by German positions at Hollandsche Schuur Farm and St. Eloi, both already targeted by British tunnelers and destined for destruction on 7 June 1917 (see p. 174). In the winter of 1915–1916 however the greatest concern for the Saxons was the rising water level which collapsed trenches and rendered parts of *Bayernwald* uninhabitable. As a result the Prussians who followed them began work in summer 1916 on a new, deeper trench system behind and uphill of the old line – which it then replaced as the main position from February 1917. The reconstructed *Bayernwald* trenches which can be visited today represent only a small part of this newer trench line.

After leaving Flanders in summer 1916 the 123. ID was committed to the Somme, where Pache earned the Saxon *Ritterkreuz des Militär-St.-Heinrichs-Ordens: "Together with his company Ltn. Pache distinguished himself in the battle of the Somme by outstanding courage in the fierce, bloody fighting for the possession of Trônes Wood in the sector of 12. Reserve-Division during the days 10 to 16 July 1916. After II. Batl. / Inf.-Regt. 182 had taken the wood in a magnificent assault on 9 July, it had to repel an extremely strong English counterattack which was pressed home following the strongest drumfire. The Englishmen who broke into the wood were thrown out again by Ltn. Pache after heavy, dogged single combat. Numerous prisoners were taken and the entire position held. It is only thanks to the valiant conduct of him and his men, his vigilance and initiative, that this attack too – driven home by the English northwest of Combles with superior forces – entirely failed."*

The energetic and articulate Pache was highly active in the IR 182 veterans' association, and his letters from the Somme appeared in its published history in 1924. The following letters from the Wytschaete salient were serialised in the 1930s by the Saxon veterans' newsletter *Der Feldkamerad.*

At Bayernwald

In the line near Wytschaete, *Bußtag*[1] [19 November] 1915
After so many brief cards I am jumping once again into a letter, even if I am continually disturbed from it by orderlies, reports, the telephone, arrivals, papers to sign, shrapnel and shells. Today we are in the line for the third day. After two days of light frost and sunny weather it is once again raining in torrents. Under the floorboards of my dugout the water squelches, and must be pumped out with an hour's work every day and night. On top of that a tough struggle is being waged with the latrine – previously the pride of the sector in its snug and cosy comfort, but now that it lies in our immediate vicinity the problem child, which constantly threatens to overflow and – like Joffre – constantly tries to break through.
Further forward in the trenches it looks appalling. The moisture makes the tough clay of the slopes and swampy meadows, through which our line extends, start moving and sliding – everywhere it presses on the trench walls, many sections are submerged and collapse, in addition to which in many places the water is up to our knees and, if it weren't continually pumped out, would soon be up to our nostrils. It's truly a Danaidic labour which our poor, but ever willing and hardworking men must perform.
The communication trenches from the ruined town of Wytschaete to the forward positions (still almost three quarters of an hour's march!) – true marvels of solid construction, built with an abundance of materials and diligence – are likewise in several places collapsed or swamped to such an extent that one wades for ten to twenty paces up to the knee in thick, ice-cold mud. Hence at our last relief we needed over an hour to cross a trench section we could otherwise cover in ten minutes. Nevertheless the old warriors are tough and hardened too.
With all this work the days pass very quickly here in the front line. The way back to Comines is always a bit of a slap in the face, as the streets – although continually worked on – are full of mud and treacherous shellholes, so that one has to be painstakingly careful on horseback as well. The food out here is good; in Comines it used to be very nice, still it's beginning to become unpleasant now. When we relieved the Bavarians here, the position was very calm and peaceful as far as artillery is concerned, only a couple of harmless shrapnels now and then. But then the idyll was disturbed. The English shoot a lot into our trenches and the rearward lines of communication in the towns behind the front. A few days ago they also bombarded Comines with heavies, especially the railway line, the station and the area around the church. During the second barrage one soldier was killed and two wounded. During the third (the day before yesterday), in which they set an empty barracks behind the hospital ablaze with forty or fifty incendiary bombs, there were – besides

A deep and well-drained communication trench in Wytschaete, still featuring multi-coloured sandbags made of civilian fabric.

numerous backpacks burned – seventeen civilians killed and five wounded, but no soldiers were hit. Prior to this they had thrown letters to the population from aircraft, with advance notice of the shelling and a request to flee beforehand. At the fourth shell the street was already filled with outbound baggage wagons, pioneer carts, field kitchens etc., as well as fleeing civilians in great mobs, all 'withdrawing' to use the technical term.

The day before yesterday our artillery put down heavy retaliatory fire on the English in their trenches and the villages behind their front. Nevertheless they have shot at Comines again every day. Today we had our revenge again. Behind the so-called *Kemmelberg*, which unfortunately offers the English first-rate observation of our trenches, there is – as had become known to us – a big English fuel dump. Tonight uncannily dense pillars of smoke suddenly erupted from there, the dump was on fire! Vengeance for Comines! But now one asks oneself nervously, what will the English do after this?

On the 14th during our approach march we once again had a little experience with aircraft. In front of the village of Houthem four English fliers suddenly appeared over the marching battalion – in itself, nothing unusual. However they were not scared off by the wild shrapnel fire of the anti-aircraft guns, but rather kept circling back and dropped three incendiaries and two conventional aerial bombs. Nothing came of it, but we nevertheless grew quite worried, waited half an hour and anticipated, when the aircraft disappeared, a shelling of the approach route by enemy artillery. However this luckily did not occur.

I am just now back again from my nightly rounds. The rainy weather mixed with snow showers which persisted throughout the morning and afternoon, has fortunately given way again to a strong frost. Maybe we can go along the trenches tomorrow on ice skates. Over the trenches, scrub bushes, corpses, shot-up woods and spectrally towering ruins lies a wonderful clear moonlit night, and countless stars twinkle – and encourage thoughts of the approaching Christmas. Is it not *Bußtag* today back at home? Here one loses all sense of the individual weekdays. Often while writing the war diary, which has now already expanded to its seventh volume, one suddenly feels a slight shock and wistfulness that once again a Sunday has gone by. A Sunday without any of the beautiful, solemn and sedate things that each Sunday stands for in peacetime life. When will there be Sundays for us again?

Due to groundwater the forward trenches at *Bayernwald* were dug no more than a metre below ground level and built up with sandbags.

The layered sandbag and plank roof of this machine-gun post offer little protection against anything heavier than rainfall.

Although this officer is dressed for muddy conditions, the dry trench floor suggests these photos date back as far as October 1915.

Soon after arriving in the salient the 123. ID replaced its crude cloth pads soaked in anti-gas solution with the modern *Gummimaske.*

Comines, 6 December 1915
... since a few days ago we have been withdrawn from our position at Wytschaete and are sapping in the neighbouring sector with the 178ers, but still have our quarters in Comines. All the houses here which have a bomb-proof cellar are now marked with a little red flag, so that everyone can hide themselves at the start of a barrage – if there is enough time – and gigantic concrete dugouts are being built everywhere. My hosts have heavily reinforced their cellar too, and even covered the floors of the ground-floor rooms with sandbags. We have really strenuous work. I have already spent seven nights sapping with my company and had only two rest days. Marched out at six o'clock in the evening, back again about seven in the morning. The weather is unspeakably bad, just rain all the time. The fields are partially flooded; the streets, despite fresh gravel, full of mud; the trenches are morasses. When one comes back, one resembles a lump of clay; the greatcoat can scarcely be dried out again. What my brave lads still achieve despite these adverse conditions is astounding...

In the trenches at Wytschaete, 28 January 1916
For a long time I've only been able to fob you off with cards. During the six days in the line I have a great deal to do, as at present the reconstruction of the trenches demands constant supervision. So one is either out and about or crouched in the dugout, and has a lot of documents and arrivals to deal with. If after that one is tired out from clambering about and writing, sketching and reporting, discussions with one's superiors – then there is no longer much time left for the more pleasant duties, such as mealtimes, reading, receiving 'visits' (which have more to do with the full food container than its carrier!) and sleeping or rather trying to sleep, as the nights here at the front are for the most part devoted to work. The couple of hours during which one tries to sleep in the dugout are then delightfully interrupted at half- or quarter-hourly intervals – by the checking in and out of the leaders of the carrying parties, who haul materiel up here by night for hours on end; by the continual racket of the telephone, which must be tested for serviceability every couple of minutes; by the coming and going of patrol leaders, who pass on their observations, platoon leaders, who proffer their wishes and complaints, and orderlies, who request ammunition, signal flares, rifle grenades, sandbags etc.
At 1 am at night sappers arrive from a Prussian regiment, who are helping to develop our positions; our men are at work until about 2 or 3 am; then, panting and cursing,

The *Schweinlesteig* led from Wytschaete to the front (see p.167).

Telephone station at 245. Inf. Brig. battle HQ in Oosttaverne.

there lumbers and shuffles by an assortment of *pioniere* and working parties, who are working on the systematic drainage of the position. One tries to dose off and succeeds too, even though outside with brief pauses our and the Englishmen's machine-guns clatter and chatter, and occasionally with a sharp crack explosive projectiles strike the brick walls of the ruined house outside, in the shadow of which we have established ourselves. For remarkably enough the thunder of the guns, the racket of machine-guns and rifle shots don't disturb one at all – but the squawking of the telephone, which whines like an unruly baby, is exasperating! And the snoring of an orderly is a more abominable noise than the bursting of a heavy shell! So – despite it all one has now finally fallen asleep; then it's already 4 am again, the telephonist wakes up, and one must gather one's sleep-drunk thoughts to cobble together the early morning telephone report to the battalion. Finally – and one is well aware, that the telephone can be the most insidious and for the user the most distressing invention of the human spirit – one has brought one's report to the fellow and curled up again shivering in one's blankets. Then yet again the telephone squawks. "What's going on?" It punctually conveys the latest army order of the day to every company, unfortunately at an unpleasant hour of the night. But it could be the high point of the whole day and night, if for example it were to announce the conclusion of a general peace agreement.

One prepares oneself for it, despite one's exhaustion, with a pleasant straining of all the senses; the telephonist listens for a while intently at the apparatus, queries, nods, writes, queries again, queries once more and then reads out: "in all theatres of war nothing of significance!" Now however one gets to sleep properly. Maybe a full, precious hour, maybe more. Then the clerk comes and brings the reports of the platoon leaders on the night and their work. Now for better or worse one must get up, check, compile and expand the reports of the platoon leaders, add the work of the past 24 hours to a pictorial sketch and many other tasks. With a sigh of relief one hands over the sketch and report to the orderly, impresses on the telephonist to allow only highly important and official matters to reach the bed, suffers another ten minutes of infernal racket made by the telephonist in his struggle with the stubborn stove which has long been reluctant to resume its daily duty, swaddles oneself in the blankets and firmly decides not to relinquish the dugout for anything short of drumfire. For how long? That depends on the favourability of the circumstances.

Thus passes the normal night here. A 'delightful Nocturne', is it not? All that's missing still as accompaniment are the nightly bursts of intense fire from the companies, which we now take pains to carry out repeatedly, in order to disturb the English. That is for ten minutes then a tremendous concert of machine-guns and hundreds of rifles. We had previously only used these here a little. Then about a week ago the English began to bother us intensely and more impudently every night with such things. One can hear and see such rifle grenades coming – but then in most cases it is already too late to take cover. On the first night five men were wounded straight away by a single rifle grenade. They usually inflict numerous and very painful, though for the most part also not life-threatening wounds. For three days we have had two sets of rifle grenade apparatus at our disposal and it is a joy to behold how our men exert themselves at the eager work of revenge. Since we now put thirty to forty of this kind into the enemy trenches every night, they have become a bit more cautious and restrained over there. Each company also works on improving and smartening up the accommodation in their section (although there are some companies which settle themselves like the cuckoo in a warm, prepared nest and let others toil for themselves). And should a dugout become the pride and joy of the whole sector, fate comes and derisively drops a shell on it! Sadly there was a tragic case yesterday too. In the afternoon the enemy artillery suddenly opened a half-hour's drumfire on the second trench in our reserve line. We hadn't heard such a racket since Souchez. Luckily my detachment was spared. Only a couple of heavy shells und shrapnel pots went onto the second line of our position. However they did drive us out of the dugout, which rang in all its brand-new joints at every distant or close impact. Outside we observed how the howling masses of iron went over us toward Wytschaete, the *Rote Villa*, the *Zahnstocherwald* and the *Sachsengraben*. Then suddenly a huge flame arose among the shot-denuded spruce trunks of the so-called *Zahnstocherwald*[2] (the name very aptly describes the state of the remaining trees) and dense smoke welled skyward. A dugout was burning. It was the company commander's dugout in the so-called *bereitstellung*. Every two weeks I too am there for six days together with batmen and orderlies. When the artillery duel had died down somewhat, I sent my orderlies up there and allowed myself to make enquiries. Meanwhile the commander of the company there, Rittmeister C[3], was already being sought after by telephone throughout the regimental sector. He had first been transferred to our regiment after Souchez. Around evening it became a tragic certainty, that along with his batman and orderly he had been burned and buried in the dugout. It was only today that the three bodies could be excavated.

Before the world war 'death on the field of battle' was for every man surely an occurrence more or less enveloped in poetry – but in reality it is for the most part so heavily accompanied by terrible, even sickening details, that one understands why poetry must subsequently exert its mitigating, transfiguring effect, if man is at least to be able to bear it in memory. Nothing is so unpoetic, so gruesomely prosaic as such a death – therefore poetry must come and elevate it into the sphere of the high and the beautiful, out of the realms of filth, stench and loathsome hardship!

You wouldn't believe what an effect the sight of the first snowdrop has after such an experience! I found it blooming in the ruined and overgrown garden of the so-called *Einödhof*, which lies in the meadow right behind our trench. And the day before I had heard the first starling singing on the barren, shattered stumps of the *Zahnstocherwald*! A starling, a snowdrop! When one sees dear and diligent men die in such a terrible and needlessly gruesome way, one may doubt God's goodness – but the first twittering of birds, the first shy bloom of the coming spring lets us fervently believe in it again!

In the trenches at Wytschaete, 11 March 1916

The past three rest days in Comines were once again agreeable. Because of the persistently bad weather, which has flooded the huge pastures for far and wide around the twin town on the Lys, it wasn't possible to do much drill. On the first day 'bathing and delousing' is scheduled for the men (who for the most part only came out of the line around 3 o'clock in the morning). Naturally on this morning there will first be a long and extensive sleep. That day's afternoon is devoted to 'domesticity' and usually full of visitors. You'd hardly believe what and who I have visiting me! Besides regimental comrades who are thirsty for coffee, and men stating their requests, there are a bunch of old acquaintances who are based nearby or passing through Comines with their unit – where there are always a lot of troop movements, because it lies at the junction of the 6. and 4. Armee. You should see the constantly changing military scenes by day and night on the streets of Comines. Prussians, Saxons, Württembergers, Belgians and French and Flemings – to name the nations and tribes for starters. Marching columns of all arms of service, often with their bands and followed by numerous baggage wagons, rattling artillery pieces, speeding staff cars and roaring *pionier* lorries. Swift requisitioned calèches[4] and little trailers (with small captured Russian horses brought from the East); donkey carts and field kitchens; despatch riders, *feldgendarmes* and dashing cavalry officers on charming beasts; comrades out on a pleasure ride. Columns of *schippers*[5]; bearded *landsturm* men and the youngest recruits; labour units of the male inhabitants under military escort; great swarms of Russian prisoners who work in the surrounding area, and wake from their stupor and lethargy to start grinning amiably when they see that you want to photograph them. Numerous locals, both elegant and ragged, well-fed and screaming children and doddering old fellows, fat devoutly smiling nuns and dainty little 'nun-lets'; stout, portly priests and gaunt, skinny parsons, who greet everyone with great politeness. And now and then – routinely – day in, day out – funeral processions with two, three or four modest, ivy-draped coffins; the funeral orchestra in the lead, and in the rear comrades who will perhaps be carried like this tomorrow too. For such coffins slowly swaying along through the hubbub all stand still – the soldiers salute, the civilians take off their hats and cross themselves. – And when the serious throng has passed, a scene which has repeated itself here daily for months now, the colourful, restless bustle of the narrow alleys begins anew. It is at its most colourful at the pretty Grande Place in French Comines with its beautiful belfry on the ancient town hall.

On the afternoon of the first rest day we had a merry *Fastnachtsfeier*[6] for the NCOs of the battalion in the *soldatenheim.* Free beer, a rousing speech by the battalion commander, the regimental band and a huge program of singers, company comedians, conjurers, poetry recitals – not exactly suitable for the daughters of the gentry, but rather coarse soldier's fare – but the chief aim was achieved: for a few hours everyone forgot the dreadful seriousness of our time and recuperated from the unutterable exertions of the preceding weeks, in which the regiment had an especially great deal to put up with from the enemy artillery and hostile elements. When we [officers] absented ourselves about 10 o'clock to go to the *kasino* for an hour or so, spirits were already quite high and I had just seen the tables being cleared to permit dancing with each other – for lack of fair womanhood, which was represented there only by a couple of fat, elderly nuns.

Resting at Ruddervoorde

Ruddervoorde Chateau, 21 March 1916

For ten days I wrote in a wet, musty, poorly lit dugout with shrapnel and shells whizzing by – now I sit at an elegant mahogany writing desk in a stylish room, with a marble chimney which glitters back from the high mirrors, in a regular stately home, and if I look up from this letter, my gaze wanders – not as usual over clay and dirty boards, rotting sandbags and vile scampering rats, but rather over a wide lawn with laurel trees clipped into balls, rhododendron bushes in the first flower, and a wide double avenue, in the far background of which the red rooves of a little hermitage chuckle. This change is truly magical! One can still barely believe in the reality of it!

The last days in the line were especially unpleasant and exhausting too. My sector had been badly shot up in the front line shortly before, and in the so-called 1b line about 150m behind the first, in which my dugout lies, the enemy had destroyed the concrete bunker for the machine-gun, the painstakingly constructed drainage and runoff ditches were blocked up by shell impacts, enormous masses of water had built up in the trenches, in places 1 to 1.5 metres deep [and] the trench walls were collapsing and squeezing together, on top of which it rained and snowed incessantly – in short by way of farewell the position once again demonstrated its total malevolence. There was absolutely no possibility of getting through to the advanced sap during the day; everything was deeply mired and collapsing, and the defensive fitness of the entire sector seriously brought into question. And how much labour and effort had already been sunk there! How much exertion and drudgery still lay before us, before it could all be dug back into a tolerably navigable condition! I was really beside myself on the first night as I returned from my rounds soaked through and befouled like a sewer dredger; the following day I made a long report, which was one long urgent appeal for support – and received 75 *pioniere* that same night to work in the front line.

From the 10th it was already rumoured that we were to be relieved. But at first there only came an order for the battalion to go into *bereitschaft* (in the second position) and sap at the front at night. I was the only company commander who had the good fortune of going with two platoons to Comines, otherwise I would have gazed upon it for the last time with quite different eyes. What a lot of severe and sorrowful experiences we had there over the last five months. The carefree and cheerful hours had been thinner on the ground here than in previous positions (e.g. in our beautiful position near Reims in the early spring of 1915!). And yet, with all the worry and hardship, all the filth and ugliness, that we had seen and experienced, one still felt a certain attachment too, almost so to speak some 'sense of home' for these dank, swampy trenches, which had cost our regiment so much sweat and blood.

The final days in Comines from the 12th to the 15th were still very nice and refreshing. Gradually it trickled through that we would be going to rest [further] behind the front. Soon the troops who were to relieve us arrived. On the 15th we set out by foot march, initially to Halluin – a big French factory town, ugly, but in a pretty location on the Lys – where our *rekrutendepot* was billeted. Right beside it lies the Belgian town of Menen (Meenen [sic.] in Flemish), where we spent the next afternoon; a still very populous, picturesque place with beautiful old towers, monasteries, old fortified walls and a tiny harbour on the canal. The streets were

Aerial view from 1915 of IR 105 (the sole Saxon regiment of 30. ID / XV. AK) 'standing to' on both sides of the marketplace in Menen.

teeming with the Württemberg military, and everywhere one heard the pleasant sound of the Swabian dialect.

Besides the good eating the 'main attraction' was a visit to the military cinema. What things our soldiers, the big children, can still laugh at and how warmly and uproariously too! In the evening we were loaded up in Menen and got out after a relatively short journey in Thourout. About midnight we then proceeded on a longer march to our destination, Ruddervoorde. Here we have stayed for a week now already, and it is one of the most carefree and beautiful places we have been allowed to enjoy in the whole war.

The battalion is by itself in this large village full of good billets, which still today despite the war gives the impression of prosperity and well-kept neatness, and the generally red-brown houses of which peek out so picturesquely from the alder bushes, poplar rows and willows. The landscape is splendid – *"the country is like a garden to behold"*[7]. Everywhere are rich fields and lush meadows, paddocks, little woods, perfectly surfaced highways often with convenient bridleways alongside; the area is overabundant in chateaus both small and large, and then mostly in a sober mass style, brick buildings with obligatory corner towers – but the parks with their gigantic azalea shrubberies, ivy-covered old elms and plane trees, stately groups of conifers and bright dainty birchwoods always make up the most beautiful part of it. Above it all then are the swiftly changing cloud pictures of the sky near the North Sea, in an ever new and ever more appealing illumination of the landscape scenes.

The people are uniformly Flemings, with whom one can make oneself well understood, and who are obliging and friendly. In almost every house one sees women and girls engaged in lace-making, and everywhere in the little shops hang masterworks of this cottage industry. I've struck it especially lucky with my billet – I am in Chateau Ruddervoorde, which belonged to the Baron de Peksteen[8]. Other chateaus in the area were hastily abandoned by their residents at the approach of the Germans. The Peksteens have sensibly remained. It is a splendid estate, which they have preserved in this manner from the dilapidation and gradual demolition, which naturally tends to affect the houses that were found empty and used for months on end for the constantly changing billeting of troops. How long will our village and chateau idyll last? The Gods and the General Staff know! Here one forgets the whole rotten world war! Only sometimes the sound of the grumbling guns reaches us, from the coast in the vicinity of Dixmuide – like an admonitory greeting from a worse world, to which we fundamentally belong and which only allowed us to slip away for a little while, to one 'fine' day suck (us) back up in its vengeance – but one doesn't think about that! *"The hours are ours, and the living are in the right!"*[9]

Platoon or company HQ dugout behind *Hessenwald* in front of Kapelleriemolen. *Rote Villa* (left) held the forward battalion battle HQ..

Divisional *pioniere* of Pionier-Kompagnie 245 in their billets behind the front.

Here we must briefly interrupt Leutnant Pache's letters. While his account of the dilapidation of the trench system by rain and artillery fire sounds quite plausible, the Flanders veterans of Prussian RIR 213 (46. RD / XXIII. RK) showed little sympathy when relieving Infanterie-Regiment 182 on 14 March 1916. The published history of Reserve-Infanterie-Regiment 213 is exceedingly critical:

The Verdict of Reserve-Infanterie-Regiment 213

For RIR 213 the I. / 213 came under consideration as the first battalion to be deployed. Hptm. Plange, his four company commanders and one officer each from the MGK and MWA drove to Werwick [sic.] on 13 March, proceeded from there to Comines and on the morning of the 14th to the front, to inspect and take over the position there. The approach route via Houthem and Osttaverne [sic.] to Wytschaete could well have pleased them, especially as it was possible to drive right up to Wytschaete under cover of the ridge. All the worse then was the impression made by the trench system, of which a report of the 92. RIB tellingly states: *"it is conspicuous how the strength and development of the defensive works declines from the rear to the front. Shot-proof accommodation is provided for the staffs, reserves and artillery in the most extensive manner. Thus far the infantry in the front line has received no such protection."* The 91. RIB begins its report with the sentence: *"the position made a disagreeable impression at the time of the handover"*. To be sure the relieved 123. ID admitted in its report of 9 March 1916 that *"the trench system of the 123. ID is not in good condition."* However their excuse – that the deficiencies which had been recognised from the outset could not have been remedied owing to the water conditions – found no credence whatsoever with the 46. RD and its regiments, since the water conditions in their old sector [RIR 213 was previously on the Yser near Het Sas] had been much worse than in the Wytschaete sector. And nevertheless through tireless, diligent labour our regiments had created a good position there with many shot-proof concrete dugouts in the front line. The report of the *General der Pioniere* on the staff of 4. Armee, which labelled the state of the position as *"deficient"*, was scathing for the 123. ID. On the subject of drainage, this report noted it was *"easily possible everywhere"*, and yet the relieved division had sought to excuse themselves with the water conditions.

As a result the feeling within the 46. RD toward the troops they had relieved was very soon anything but rosy, as the neglect of the front line – one cannot describe its state in any other way – became apparent to the men, and many deeply felt curses were sent after them… In *Abschnitt IV* (IR 182) the so-called *Schweinlesteg* led as communication trench and approach to the front line. This began at the main Armentières–Ypres road. Around 150m north of the crossroads east of Wytschaete one climbed into the communication trench, the good condition of which initially deceived the newcomer regarding the state of the position as a whole. Thereafter the *Schweinlesteg* led in a northwesterly direction past Wytschaete, veered left via the *Sachsengraben*, reached the Wytschaete–Groote Vierstraat road and led along this close by the hospice and about 800m further to the fork in the road at the so-called *Rote Villa*, in the rubble of which the battle HQ of the front-line battalion was situated. Here to the right there branched the *Claus-Weg*, which led in a northward direction through the *Hessenwald*, while on the left a trench system, the second line, extended through the *Zahnstocherwald*. On the slopes west of the *Hessenwald* and the *Zahnstocherwald* is the majority of the front line of *Abschnitt IV*, on either side of the road to Groote Vierstraat, with its most advanced point at Hollandsche Schuur Farm. The width of the [regimental] sector is over 1500m. The front line trench had suffered severely from artillery and rain, and was in many places even without continuous connection, at others so low that by day it was only passable hunched over or crawling. At still other places it was so narrow that e.g. the evacuation of the wounded appeared impossible. The few dugouts available were not even splinter-proof. Traverses were hardly present at all, but were somewhat substituted for by the winding course of the line. The wire obstacles were modest. The MG posts were especially unsatisfactory, and were divided into day and night posts. The day posts lay in the rearward area, from which an elevated effect was possible. However the whole system of MG distribution was awkward and thus impractical. The support trench dug behind the front line was similar in its condition to the latter. For its utilisation it also lacked above all sufficient connecting trenches to the front line. Here too the dugouts were few and bad. The second line ran through the *Zahnstocherwald*, beginning at *Dingelreiter-Hof*, and around the *Hessenwald*. For the most part it was flooded, or in places levelled by the heavy fire which lay upon it. The third line ran close to the west of Wytschaete around that town, then north running through the *Sachsengraben*, reaching the Armentieres–Ypres road at the so-called *Novemberfeste* and thereupon led along the [edge of the] *Grenzwald*. It was not complete, but possessed a good wire obstacle line.

Minenwerfers had thus far not been deployed in the sector, as the 123. ID had no autonomous *minenwerfer* company yet and its infantry regiments no MWA. For the leader of this [MWA] in 213 entirely new tasks consequently arose, for which he first had to receive new materiel, as the mortars had been left in fixed positions in the old sector and handed over to his successors.

The impressions of their new position which the first 213ers received on their inspection visit were similar to these. Now too it was clear why the XXIII. RK remained with 4. Armee and was deployed in this place. Not for nothing had Herzog Albrecht bestowed such high praise on the working efficiency of the corps in its old sector. Surely it was expected of the corps to do a similarly thorough job in the Wytschaete sector and rebuild the position, and above all in the first instance to make it defensible. For it was clear to all involved, that the position would not stand up to a serious attack with some degree of artillery preparation, and that the accommodation of so many precious human lives in it was not justifiable in its current state. It was a good thing that the soldier did not think much about such things, but rather was content if things were going tolerably for him at the moment.

Trench map from the regimental history of RIR 213, showing the former subsectors of both IR 182 (left) and IR 178 (right).

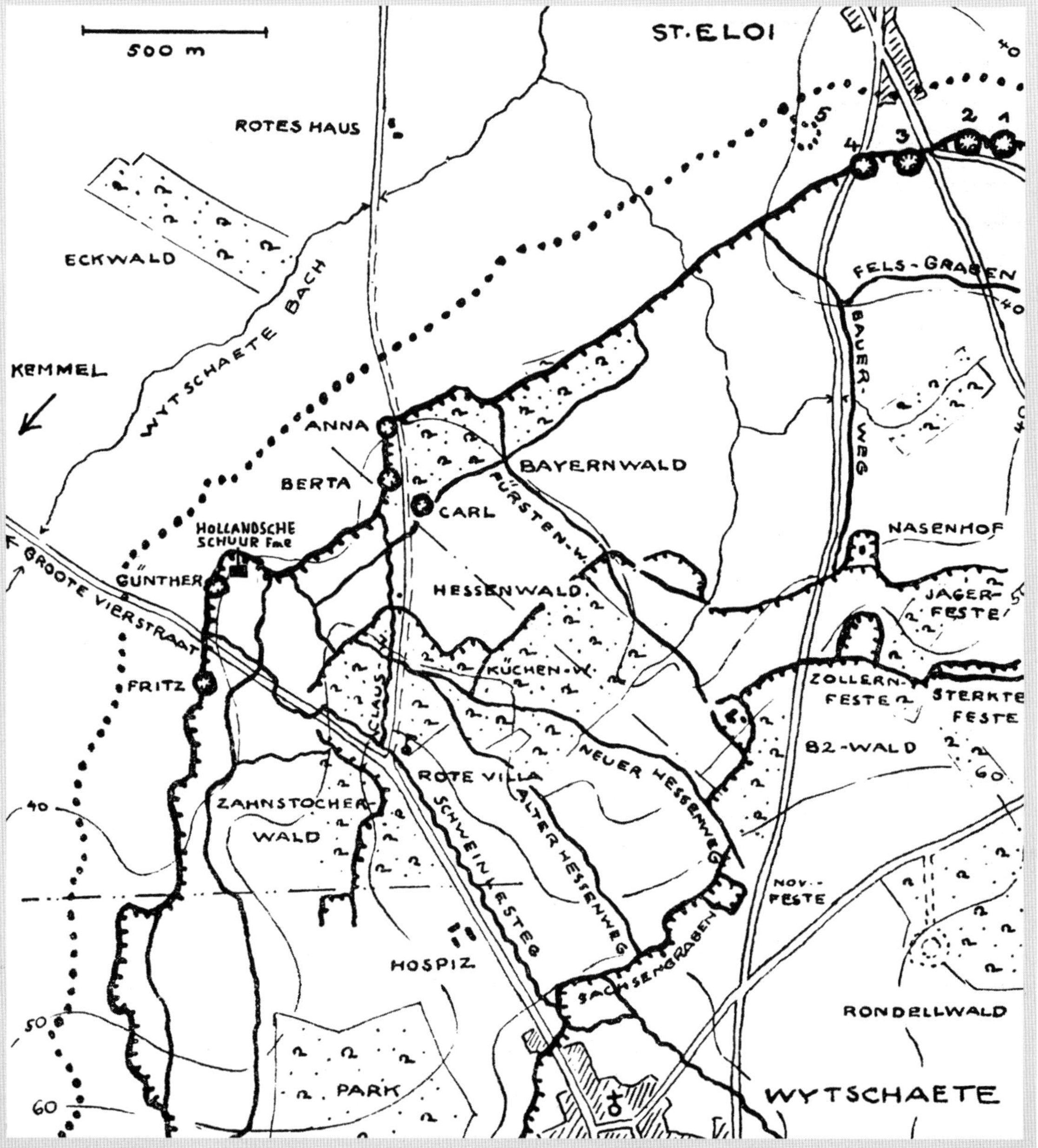

From this harsh Prussian critique of 123.ID we now rejoin Pache in the right sub-sector, between St. Eloi and the canal bank.

St. Eloi and Halluin

Dammwegstellung near St. Eloi, 4. April 1916

On Sunday our chateau idyll at Ruddervoorde suddenly burst like a gay soap-bubble. While we were sat snugly at dinner in the *kasino*, suddenly there came an alert and marching orders. That night we entrained at Thourout. At first we were going to be sapping, but our task was changed en route and the next morning we came into the line here, somewhat to the north of our old Wytschaete position, to relieve troops who have been in heavy fighting since 27 March. You've probably read the official report of the mine explosion which the enemy successfully pulled off here at St. Eloi on the 27th. Five enormous craters, one of which was still held by our side until early yesterday. Since we've been here, the fighting has somewhat subsided. The English too are evidently exhausted and seem to be content with occupation of the craters. Our line has been pulled back a bit. It must have been a gruesomely hard week for our predecessors here. I'm still the best off with my company, we are only deployed forward at night and are in a well-hidden wooded gulley by day. The trenches in front are wickedly wrecked by drumfire. This filth! This destruction! Our peaceful dream is well and truly over. Once again we are flung from one extreme into another. *"C'est la gare!"* [sic] as our regimental adjutant is wont to say. Many of us were off on leave in the surrounding area, at the seaside, in Brussels etc. and didn't arrive until later, straight into the filth of the trenches in elegant, long trousers and greatcoats!

Halluin, 6 June 1916

Once again my suitcases are packed and waiting on the baggage wagon. Once again one mentally puts a full stop under one small chapter of the war diary and begins a new heading, somewhat thoughtfully and hesitantly, as one longs all too keenly to know in advance all that this new chapter will contain.

Today the company was lucky. We had a night without sapping, and were able to sleep in and pack our 'bits and pieces' in peace. Outside it rains in torrents. The other companies were soaked through when they arrived, and had to spend the train journey to our new rest area in sodden clothing.

Until 19 May we stayed in our pretty, rustic hamlet of Zedelghem, drilled vigorously and went on route marches,

The solidly concreted *gefechtsstand* (battle HQ) on *Dammstraße* for the regiment in the division's right subsector (initially RIR 106).

HQ dugout used by the reserves in the *Raabgrund* (Ravine Wood), the "well-hidden wooded gulley" mentioned by Pache, in summer 1916.

rode a lot, strolled in the woods, and indulged in cheap eggs, 9 Pfennigs a piece. On 20 May we entrained at Halluin, which lies three stations away from our old winter billet of Comines. We had to build a new line (the so-called *Sehnenstellung*, it was occupied and held by the Germans on 7 June 1917 after the great mine detonations in the *Wytschaetebogen*) behind the front right across the so-called *Ypernbogen*, in the area where the German battery positions are located; at first just laying wire obstacles (which is a much more unpleasant task for the men than digging) and concreting machine-gun posts. Three companies were sent out each time, so there was rest every fourth day. In the first week it was especially tiring, as it was already midnight when we set out, then after a train journey – which was short in itself but often interspersed with long delays – we had about two hours' approach march, began work between 3 and 4 o'clock in the morning and were back in H[alluin] at 1 in the afternoon.

For weeks in Ruddervoorde and Zedelghem with only 14 days' interruption at St. Eloi we had got our regular night's sleep, had become used to it and so at first found it doubly hard, especially the unpleasant nightly approach march. Later the sapping procession set out at 4 am, so that one got a couple of valuable hours of night's rest. Apart from the meagre sleep (as there was inherently little peace and quiet in the afternoon) it was a carefree existence. The weather, not counting a few bad rainy days, was wonderful for the most part. There were magnificent sunrises and wonderful morning hours outside in the shrub-rich Flemish countryside with its gay meadows and its hedges twittering with birds. These areas looked so ugly and dreary in winter, in the gloomy grey of endless rainy days, with their ground often flooded for weeks and their quagmires, their bare poplars and ungainly willow stumps – now they laugh so beautifully and gracefully in the dewy freshness of the May morning. Even the many wretched ruins of shot-up houses no longer look so sad and depressing, and hide themselves everywhere behind the richly scented elder bushes. The men were in the best of spirits and worked with love and enthusiasm, even though it cost the state many pairs of trousers on the barbed wire. They go about this work with ten times more enthusiasm than they drill, and at night on the way back to the station sing like woodlarks – whereas on the march to the parade ground in Zedelghem they always need to be cajoled into doing so.

While sapping we were generally only slightly disturbed by the enemy. On some days the aerial harassment was quite great, mostly though the morning fog favoured us and we made our way back in small groups where it was necessary to reach – if possible before the other companies – one of the numerous primitive narrow-gauge railways which take materiel to the front, and frequently offered us a much-desired shortcut to our march with a jolly, rather breakneck journey on the crowded railcar. Now and then a couple of shells came near us – especially where the new line passes battery positions – or a couple of 'blue beans' whistled sharply into the trees, and brought it home to us that we are actually at war. Twice however the situation for my company grew more ticklish. We were working in one of the larger woods, where the dense undergrowth interspersed with swamp and water-filled shellholes made the wiring especially difficult. Behind the rear end of the wood, 100 paces away from us, was a howitzer battery. We had barely arrived, when a couple of British shells flew that way. Then it was quiet again, so I allowed the work to be resumed. Suddenly a fire flared up at the edge of the wood. One of the shells had exploded and set something ablaze. At first it looked like only the dry broom-trees or an old dugout were burning. We returned to work, as no calls for help came over to us, and the gunners would already be managing by themselves if it was just a trivial fire. All at once, after almost quarter of an hour, there was a tremendous explosion. A towering burst of flame crackled out, and the lush ground where we were working was littered with splinters and clods of earth. I had heard many bangs already in this noisy world war, but none like this beauty! My landsers scattered like a barrelful of fleas, I stumbled into the nearest shellhole and ducked down under the rain of splinters and earth-clods. No-one was wounded – miraculously! Later once it had got light and the source of the fire over there had been extinguished, we were able to clear up what the bang was and take a look at the whole mess. One of the English shells had struck the battery's ammunition dump, as an artillery officer described it to me 300 rounds of 15cm shell went up in the air! No-one from the artillery was injured either, as the crews of the guns were further back at the time in their dugouts. The guns were undamaged, but a couple of nearby dugouts were demolished and an enormous blast crater blown out of the ground.

On Ascension Day – we had just had our night off from sapping – we were able to observe from the kasino garden a rare and exciting spectacle… the shooting down of a huge enemy captive balloon, which had torn loose from its moorings and drifted over our lines. The anti-balloon guns shot like crazy at the monstrosity, but without success. It flew through a myriad of bursting white and grey shrapnel clouds, but at first remained unscathed and approached the town at high speed. Once it had passed out of the defensive

The *Raabschloss* (Delbske Farm) lay about 500m behind the *Dammstraße*, near the *pionierlager* at the northern end of the *Raabgrund*.

zone of the anti-balloon artillery, six aircraft rose in rapid succession from *Flugplatz Halluin*, which lies right in front of the town. Like swift sharks swarming around a plump whale these soon circled around it and attacked with machine-guns, so that bullets flew into our courtyard. It was brought down right over our garden. An aircraft flew over it repeatedly and ever louder we heard the rat-tat-tat of the machine-guns. Suddenly the colossus began to sink increasingly quickly and capsized, so that the steel framework finally stood vertically upright, folded together in the middle and went limp like a crumpled pig's bladder. Down the street the motor cars of the flying officers already came racing to apprehend their prey out in the fields.

On our last night of sapping, due to the abortive English counterattack at Zillebeke and Hooge there was a lot of severe artillery fire, which occasionally spread into our vicinity. As we marched out to go sapping in the third hour of the morning on 3 June, the imposing and thrilling spectacle of such a counterattack again played out in front of us. From a distance and at night, where one can only see the flares and the muzzle flashes of the guns and hear their roaring thunder, this is a great deal more exciting than by day. Something of this kind always plays itself out 'by the program' so to speak: through the previously intermittent artillery shots there suddenly rings out the increasingly furious rattle of rifles and machine-guns. Then all of a sudden countless white flares soar aloft in a long line; the enemy is attacking! He will be seen, wherever he approaches from and in whatever strength. Gradually red double flares start to gleam among the numerous gold and silver ones; that is the urgent distress signal of our men to the German artillery: the enemy is attacking! Help us! Put down defensive fire! And now in a few seconds there promptly ensues a terrific, deafening cannonade from numerous batteries all around us. It doesn't last long, as already green flares are mixed among the white and red ones. That again is an anxious and even more urgent appeal from the fighters: our own artillery is firing too short. Move fire further forward! Then as a nocturnal spectator one is doubly apprehensive for the brave men there at the front, because one knows what that means and what a paralysing effect it has on ones courage and trust. But soon the sinister greens are gone; the artillery comes crashing down again like mad, so heavily that its fury completely drowns out the fainter and more distant sounds of close combat – rifles, machine-guns and hand grenades. Once a gigantic glittering burst of countless silver flares soars towering upwards, spits and blossoms like a monstrous bouquet of stars and sinks again into the lightning-seared darkness – apparently a shell set off a signal rocket store. On that night we had to sap on the right flank, right next to the area under attack, in a wood near the oft-mentioned Chateau Hollebeke (this means, that there was

H.M. the King of Saxony (second from left in the group of officers) inspects the 123. ID at Wervik on 13 November 1915.

once a chateau there!). We had barely got there, when the English put the wood and the adjacent meadows under heavy fire. Under such conditions it was impossible to think of sapping. I was lucky enough to extricate the company from this tight corner, und miraculously we had only one wounded, although our whole half-hour's way back lay under steadily increasing fire from heavy calibres.

That was however not to be the last war experience of this 3 June. Once we had detrained again that afternoon in Halluin, right while the three companies were still standing in close order in the vicinity of the railway station, a squadron of enemy aircraft suddenly appeared over the city and came under heavy fire from our anti-balloon guns. I was going with a comrade, the commander of 6. Kompagnie, over to the big hospital right by the station. One scarcely looks up anymore at the all too frequent spectacle of such anti-aircraft shooting. I was just saying to a comrade: "these flying visits are highly superfluous if they don't drop anything, taking photos won't be much use to them here!" "Don't tempt fate!" he replied, "they could still throw something!" "Do you believe that?" I rejoined. "That only happens quite rarely though!" But I'd scarcely uttered this word and already the aerial bombs were banging, 15 to 20 of them. The aircraft were already over the station area. After the first muffled detonations the previously lively streets were quite suddenly empty and abandoned, all that can be seen were a couple of crying, scurrying women and a pack of children, weeping and falling down in fear. The last bang was not at all far from us, then all of a sudden the whole, long street was enveloped in dust, smoke and fumes. In the expectation of further greetings from on high I hurried into the arched entrance of the hospital. It was full of wounded soldiers, who had fallen out of their rooms and beds. From the skies the buzz of the propeller and the bursting of shrapnel rounds could be heard. Then German defensive fliers also took to the air. For a couple of minute we were still in a state of feverish uncertainty whether more bombs would be dropped, but the aircraft disappeared into the blue. Now the whole great courtyard teemed with soldiers, patients, doctors and civilians. Three wounded Belgians were brought in; a loudly wailing woman with bleeding hands and two severely wounded men. The last bomb had hit and torn apart the courtyard wall of the hospital, and in addition had badly mauled and demolished a little house with a small garden which stood there. The windowpanes of the whole long block of houses were shattered. The companies at the station had only three lightly wounded. Shortly before the same squadron of aircraft had dropped bombs on Menen, the neighbouring Belgian town, and killed or wounded a number of the inhabitants there – so that the German *heeresbericht* of 4 June could truthfully report that *"no military damage was incurred."*

THE OTHER SIDE OF NO MAN'S LAND

Around 8th October the Canadian 4th Brigade (18th, 19th, 20th and 21st Battalions) relieved the British between the Vierstraat road and the Bois Confluent *(Raabwald)*, with brigade reserve at Ridge Wood *(Seewald)*. Together with 5th Brigade (22nd, 24th, 25th and 26th Battalions) west of Wytschaete and 6th Brigade further south it formed 2nd Canadian Division of the recently formed Canadian Corps. While the 1st Canadian Division now opposite the 40. ID at Ploegsteert Wood had fought in the Second Battle of Ypres, the Canadians facing IR 182 and the left flank of IR 178 had only reached the front in mid-September after four months of tactical training in south-east England. Each Canadian brigade held its sector with two regularly rotated battalions abreast throughout the residence of 123. ID.

Their British neighbour-sector at St. Eloi opposite IR 178 and RIR 106 was however held successively by three different divisions. The 123. ID arrived almost simultaneously with British 24th Division, a New Army ('Kitchener') formation raised overwhelmingly from volunteers in September 1914. It had lost over 4,000 officers and men killed or wounded in its first day at the front, on 26 September 1915 during the Battle of Loos. After this ordeal, it exchanged a brigade with the regular 6th Division as 'stiffening' and went to Flanders to 'rest' and rebuild – much like the Saxons opposite, some of whom had actually helped to repulse the 24th Division's attack at Loos.

Both the Canadians and the British found the sector uncomfortable from the start. Much of their line was overlooked from higher ground, impeding construction and worsening drainage problems. Its dugouts were damp, rat-infested and offered little protection from artillery. Opposite *Bayernwald* on the Canadian flank, medical officer Capt. K E Cook CAMC of 21st Battalion repeatedly damned the trenches as *"very poor"* in the war diary, noting on 17 October how *"bullets came right through the parapet"* to wound a man. 2nd Lt. F.C. Hitchcock of 'C' Coy., 2nd Btn. The Leinster Regiment first saw the British flank at the Bois Confluent on 18 October. His battalion of tough Irish regulars had just joined 24th Division but were no strangers to the Saxon Army, having spent a winter at L'Epinette facing IR 139. Hitchcock judged St. Eloi an *"uninteresting area. Enemy trenches on a commanding ridge looking down into ours which run through a small wood. We hold several unhealthy-looking advanced posts, approximate breadth of No-Man's Land, 100 yards."* He considered the Canadians on his right a *"redeeming feature"*, clearly placing more trust in them than in the New Army battalions of 24th Division. The British support line was connected to the rear by field railway and included a *"redoubt"* in the wood – this featured an *"excellent"* parapet but *"the rest consisted of wood, corrugated iron, and sandbags only!"* The Diependaalbeek (*Tiefentalbach* to the Germans) ran downhill from *Bayernwald* through the British lines at *Raabwald*, where the Leinsters posted sentries to prevent anyone drinking water potentially poisoned by the enemy. According to the regimental history of IR 178, a British dam here would later cause flooding in the *Bayernwald I* trenches.

The focus of the underground war on the front held by 123. ID was at St. Eloi, where the energetic 172nd Tunneling Company R.E. had blown five large mines under the German line on 10 July. By the autumn they were digging the first true deep gallery through the blue clay stratum beneath the infamous *Kemmel-Schwimmsand*, while still waging the smaller war of mines and countermines nearer the surface. This project resulted in the detonation described by Pache on 27 March 1916, when five charges totalling 82,300 pounds (37,331kg) of high explosive inflicted horrific losses mainly on Reserve-Jäger-Bataillon 17 (45. RD / XXIII. RK). However the only noteworthy detonation while IR 178 held the sector was a German counter-mine blown on 25 October, which led to a week of brutal hand grenade fighting for possession of the crater.

Five of the great mines blown in the Messines offensive of 7 June 1917 were begun while IR 182 held the target areas, wholly oblivious to the scale of the underground threat. In November 1915 the 250th Tunnelling Company R.E. started the main gallery for the three deep mines which would obliterate Hollandsche Schuur Farm. In December they began a second deep gallery for the pair of mines which would cut off the protruding 'nose' of the German line at Petit Bois *(Markwald)*. The opposing *pioniere* had blown a large mine

Approximate sector boundaries for both sides down to brigade (British / Canadian) or regimental (German) level in autumn 1915.

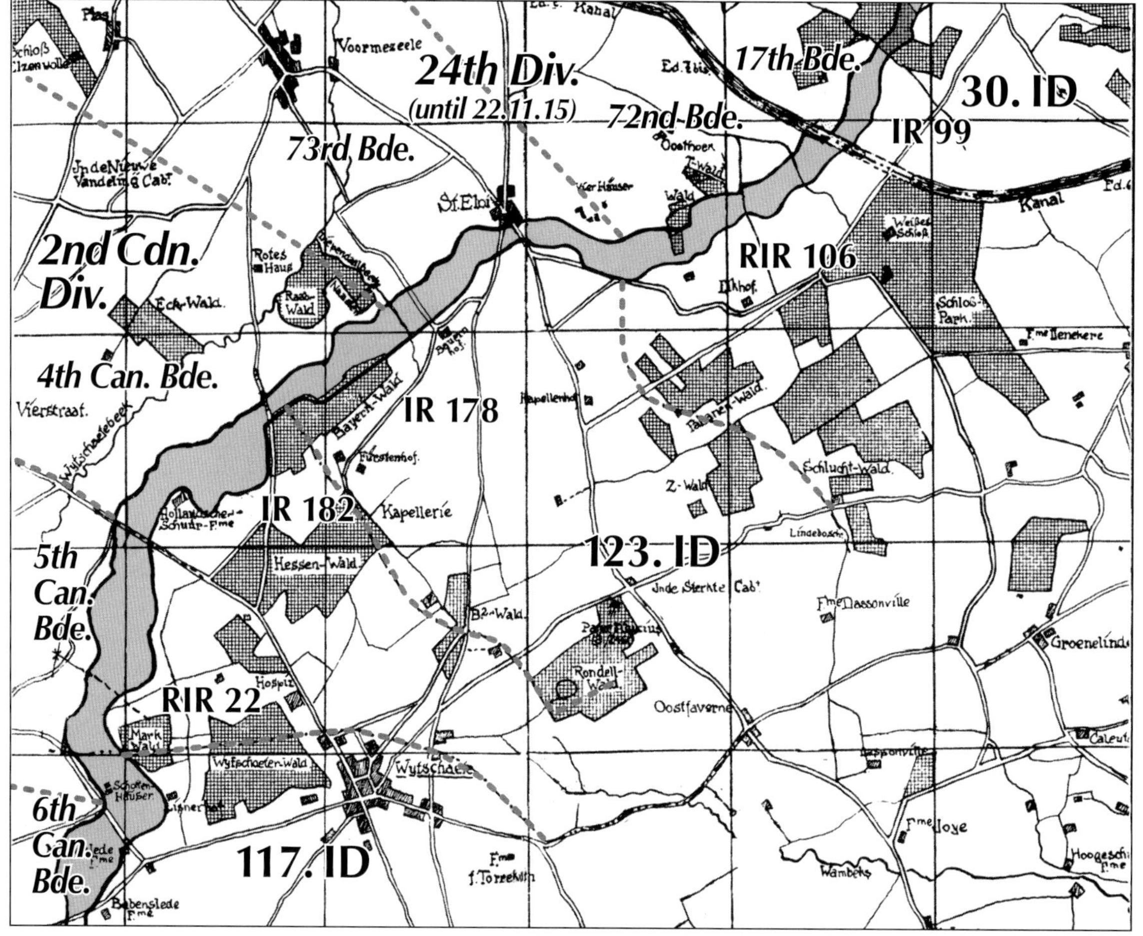

immediately to the south of this wood on 8 October, killing a dozen Canadians of 25th Battalion and wounding twenty more; two more detonations simultaneously hit 6th Brigade further south. By the time the Saxons arrived, a divisional Tunnelling Section of Canadian volunteers bent on revenge were aiding the British mining effort.

The arrival of the tired Saxon division did not bring peace to the sector – in fact 21st Battalion reported increased artillery activity, numerous rifle grenades and even a grenade battle with a forward patrol on the 20th. By the end of October however the autumn rains had begun to overwhelm drainage systems, collapse trenches and dampen spirits. As the weather worsened in November, even the artillery was hampered by flooded gunpits and poor visibility.

On 28 October Capt. Cook of 21st Btn. noted *"parapet fell in in two places. Men's dugouts fell in on top of them"* (no injuries resulted). On 8 November their war diary recorded that *"Germans were observed pumping water over their front line trenches. Our trenches are very wet being over knee deep in water in many places, making a diving suit more serviceable than the ordinary issue of clothing"*. The next day it noted *"the Huns were observed bailing water over front line parapet opposite N5 & N6 thus proving they could also benefit by diving suits instead of their ordinary suits"*.

Unlike the Germans, the Canadians were at least equipped with up to 4,000 pairs of rubber waders per division. Hitchcock's Irish battalion received rubber 'gum boots' on 3 November. *"However, as they only came up to one's knees, and in most places the water came well up the thighs, they welled water at every step. The result was that the owners often preferred to pull their feet out of them by the aid of the suction of the mud, and carry on in their socks!"* These were familiar problems for Germans wearing jackboots in the Flanders swamp.

At the St. Eloi craters, the Leinsters found *"one continuous nightmare of mud"* and waist-deep water on 2 November. Within days, the incessant hand grenade fighting had ended and both sides were working in the open. An implicit localised truce and fraternisation followed, continuing even after relief of 24th Division by the regular 3rd Division on about the 20th. On the German right, RIR 106 enjoyed only a couple of days of working above ground unmolested. On the left, the Canadians sniped anyone trying to do so and dispersed working parties with hand grenades. Although suffering from depleted morale and many cases of respiratory illness, they did not let their guard down. On 29 November the French-speaking 22nd Battalion (known as the 'Van Doos') west of Wytschaete recorded that *"a patrol was out last night and a message in German language sent to the German lines inviting them to surrender in small parties & that we will take good care of them but the message remained without an answer [sic.] and our invitation does not seem to have been accepted."*

British High Command was emphatic that there would be no 1915 Christmas Truce. Opposite 3rd Division, IR 178 was shelled on Christmas Day. The Canadian Corps was less concerned. 26th Battalion reported *"Christmas Day very quiet with practically no shooting. A few Germans showed themselves in the afternoon but there was no fraternizing on our Battn. front."* In other places on the corps front greetings were certainly exchanged between the opposing lines.

Hostilities rapidly escalated in the New Year. After six days out of the line, 26th Battalion reported on 6 January *"enemy aggressive – especially their artillery and snipers. Lieut. Chadwick killed by German sniper."* The Canadians increasingly complained of German rifle grenades, one of which killed Major Charles Sale of 18th Battalion on 17 January. It is tempting to connect Pache's description of his platoon's use of this weapon (p. 163) with a note in the War Diary of 21st Battalion on 26 January: *"at 8.30 pm enemy sent over 18 Rifle Grenades to which we effectively replied with 31. Casualties nil."* By the end of the month patrol activity was also underway again; in foggy conditions on 31 January 26th Battalion reported *"for first time in months hostile patrol seen near our trenches"*.

A HUNDRED YEARS LATER

The *Bayernwald* trench system in 2015. This section was rebuilt in 2003 and has been open to visitors (upon request at the Tourist Office in Kemmel) since 2004. It includes two original mineshafts and four concrete dugouts. Since this line was too exposed to enemy observation for concrete casting on site, the latter were constructed from prefabricated blocks brought up by working parties. Due to the popularity of such blocks as a post-war building material, this type of bunker is now a great rarity.

The British Croonaert Chapel Cemetery to the west of *Bayernwald*, with the *Kemmelberg* in the background. In 1915–1916 this was No Man's Land. At the left edge of the photo is the site of Hollandsche Schuur Farm (see map p. 167), the advanced strongpoint which anchored the German line here. Already targeted by tunnelers in 1915, it was obliterated by three huge mines on 7 June 1917.

German grave at Houtem church with the inscription „INF. F. MELZER, I.R. 182, † 14.2.1916". The erroneous Bavarian rank 'Infanterist' suggests later (re-)burial by another regiment. We believe this to be the grave of Soldat Kurt Melzer (2. / 182), killed in the trenches near Wytschaete on 12 November 1915 – the same day that I. Batl. / IR 182 relieved II. Batl. / RIR 64 in the sector.

Chapter 9

A Summer in Flanders: 1917 | 23. Reserve-Division

A seemingly idyllic sunny day with pets in *Abschnitt Pilckem* in early summer 1917. This fortified building has clearly survived major battles, as have these decorated veterans of Grenadier-Reserve-Regiment 100. Only a drab pair of *litzen* on the collar of the 1915 economy *feldbluse* is left of the uniform tradition of the Saxon grenadiers.

A Summer in Flanders: 1917 | 23. Reserve-Division

Man and landscape under drumfire

While we usually focus on the actions and experiences of individuals and units, in this chapter we will try to convey an impression of the horrifying transformation of the landscape around Ypres in the latter half of 1917 and its impact on the men who were forced to live and fight in it. We have therefore placed less emphasis on individual deeds and on the precise details of troop movements and reliefs, beyond what is necessary to give some idea of how long the units and sub-units we mention were subjected to the conditions described.

It was and is scarcely imaginable how huge swathes of green and fruitful farmland around Ypres, albeit already scarred by major battles and years of trench warfare, could be transformed within weeks that summer into a near-featureless muddy wasteland extending for kilometres in every direction. Plant life was erased as both sides took chemical warfare to new heights with a terrible exterminatory zeal. The Germans introduced mustard gas (known by its codename as *Lost* or by its shell marking as *Gelbkreuz* – 'Yellow Cross') in July for area denial, while the British used massed Livens Projectors to drop gas in unprecedented volumes directly into the German lines. The colour green vanished from a landscape painted in tones of brown, grey and yellow with occasional splashes of blood red and glimpses of blue through the clouds overhead. The old soldier's saw that artillery would not strike twice in the same spot was rendered wholly absurd as the German defensive zone was hammered into a single continuous expanse of craters. Yet human life still existed here. Scarcely distinguishable from the mud that covered them, men crouched for days on end in shellholes with – at best – the rudimentary protection of a piece of corrugated iron or a *zeltbahn* against the elements and that of a helmet and gasmask against the merciless bombardment. Others crammed like sardines into the quaking concrete bunkers which attracted the attention of the biggest enemy guns. Even on days without infantry attacks the shelling could persist for hours at the intensity of drumfire (*trommelfeuer*), where individual detonations merged into a continuous roll of earth-shaking thunder.

Personal accounts from the Third Battle of Ypres (*Dritte Flandernschlacht*) can only hint at the extremity of such an ordeal – trapped for days under the omnipresent, obtrusive threat of death with every sense overloaded with horror by the hellish environment. Human minds and bodies were pushed to, and beyond their limits. The effect at unit level is clear in what remains of reports and war diaries, where we can discern a desperate struggle for a relief cycle short enough to have enough men alive and fit to fight if the enemy attacked on the last day. Even divisions well outside the direct focus of the offensive (see Chapter 10) suffered horrifying losses. Bodies torn *en masse* into anonymous fragments, sunk forever in the mud and devoured by rats swelled the numbers of the missing, while lovingly tended military cemeteries were obliterated by shells and the mass-interred dead expiring in the overcrowded field hospitals became so numerous that coffins ran short even before the offensive began.

The orderly and fruitful farmland found in the once-devastated area today is a tribute to the generation of Flemings who returned to obliterated villages and farms after 1918. Setting up home at first in old bunkers and crude huts with no clean water or electricity, they slowly recreated the shattered drainage system and worked the deeply polluted earth back to a state where crops could grow again over the countless unexploded shells and the missing of both sides. Although the towns are now swollen well beyond their 1914 boundaries with later buildings alongside the traditional red-brick reconstruction of the 1920s, a visitor to the Ypres Salient in spring can readily understand the pleasant impression the largely unspoiled rear areas still made in April 1917.

The Saxon 23. Reserve-Division had spent almost two years on the infamously barren and bloody Champagne front before two tours on the Somme in 1916, interspersed with a 'quiet' period at Vimy Ridge. It had spent the winter of 1916–17 rebuilding on the bleak Arras front. By the time the men of 23. RD saw the area of Langemarck (a name already synonymous with slaughter in Germany) it was already criss-crossed with trenches, its ruined villages visibly scarred by two major battles and its woods systematically pillaged for construction material and fuel. Nevertheless the accounts of those early days in the regimental histories describe the Flanders of spring 1917 in fondly nostalgic and almost idyllic terms. That autumn the division would be bled white a few kilometres further east in the apocalyptic fighting for Passchendaele, a similarly ill-omened name for the British which finally signified only a shell-ravaged crossroads where brickdust hinted at the past existence of buildings. By the time the shattered 23. RD was finally withdrawn at the end of September, both it and the area it had defended had become virtually unrecognisable as what they had been only half a year earlier.

At Het Sas and Bikschote

The men of 23. Reserve-Division arrived in Flanders at the end of March 1917, accompanied by their sister 24. Reserve-Division. They were still united as they had been in August 1914 under the command of General der Artillerie Hans von Kirchbach as XII. Reserve-Korps, which was now designated *Gruppe Ypern*. Upon arrival the 23. RD was billetted in Bruges – its first stay in a wholly undamaged town since the outbreak of war. Sadly its officers and men had little time to enjoy the novelty before packing and preparations began anew for both divisions to go into the line. Beginning on 10 April, 23. RD took over *Abschnitt Langemarck* (holding the ruins of Pilkem) with 24. RD alongside in *Abschnitt Passchendaele*. An account given in the regimental history of Grenadier-Reserve-Regiment 100 looks back on this period as follows:

The wide Flemish plain stretched out before us in all its spring finery. Handsome farms, enclosed by thick hedges among bright green meadows. Streets as straight as a die, edged with skewed poplars. Islands of bushes and trees, fenced pastures. Countless drainage ditches, overshadowed by clumps of willows. It was the battle zone whose names the whole German homeland had spoken with a mute shudder since autumn 1914: Ypres, Langemarck. The Yser Canal divided the opposing lines. The high groundwater level had forced the trenches to be established mostly above ground. Between walls of fascines lay the trench floor covered with duckboards. Beams and boards bridged the drainage ditches. In dense woodland concrete strongpoints had been built, whose fields of fire complemented each other so they formed the belt of a blocking fortress within the sector. The garrisons of these strongpoints were to maintain significant iron supplies of food and ammunition, in order to hold out for as long as possible. A series of well-developed streets and approach routes led right up to the rear of the sector. In general the shelling was very moderate. Only in the canal line did the Belgians employ cylinder, chain, finned and ball mines.[1]

In order to train the regiments in the latest tactics of elastic defense and organised counterattack, their reserve battalions took part in major training exercises incorporating telephones, signal lamps, mutually-supporting machine-guns, *minenwerfers*, grenade launchers and aircraft. With retrospective irony a training area at Houthulst Forest had to be cratered deliberately, so as to have a large enough area to practice defense in depth under battlefield conditions.

On 17 April the division also took over the quiet Het Sas and Bikschote subsectors on its right, relieving 19. Landwehr-

Grenadiers of GRR 100 practice crawling forward in light assault order, at one of the numerous barracks hutments (possibly the so-called *Jägerlager*) constructed to meet the ever-increasing demand for troop accommodation behind the Flanders front.

Trench sentry post of GRR 100 in the Bikschote sector, built up above ground level due to the high water table near the Yser Canal.

The dignified individual funeral of Sanitäts-Unteroffizier Eduard Herrmann of IR 392 (killed 20 April 1917) at Manneken Farm on the southern edge of Houthulst Forest. By October this entire area would become a flooded wasteland of anonymous mass death.

An infantry *kommando* from 23. Reserve-Division under *pionier* supervision takes a break from logging for construction in May 1917.

Division. This purely ground-holding formation temporarily left the Saxon Landwehr-Infanterie-Regiment 388 behind, where it was temporarily attached to 23. RD. Composed mainly of older men in the lower fitness grades, LIR 388 was never intended to serve on an active front but would nevertheless do so with 19. LD west of Houthulst Forest that October.

In the Third Battle of Ypres – Pilkem und Langemarck

At the end of May the 23. RD was relieved and assigned to *Gruppe Gent* for training and border garrison duty. Its sister 24. RD had already been withdrawn at the end of April and sent to the Eastern Front, separating the two for the rest of the war. 23. RD was alerted again on 12 June as reserve to *Gruppe Dixmuide* and billeted in the Mangelaare–Zarren–Staden area. From 23 June it held the Pilkem sector again with two regiments abreast, within which the battalions rotated through the roles of *kampfbataillon* (front line), *bereitschaftsbataillon* (immediate support) and *reservebataillon*. The third regiment was wholly in reserve. Directly opposite, the French 1ère Armee took over the front from Boesinge northwards on 7 July so that 23. RD now faced both the French and British simultaneously. This sign of the impending offensive was less obvious than the increasingly aggressive artillery preparation throughout the Ypres salient. As the regimental history of GRR 100 records:

The heavy fire of all calibres directed by enemy aircraft relentlessly smashed the lightly constructed trenches. The wooded parts of the trench sectors collapsed under the firestorm of shells. Soon the colossal grey bulks of the concrete bunkers protruded visibly from the tangle of trunks, roots and crowns, and were shattered or overturned by the hammer blows of super-heavy artillery. High-angle fire directed from the air reached out for approach routes, for rearward observation and command posts, for batteries, ammunition and equipment dumps as well as rearward troop accommodation. … Due to the heavy shelling the appearance of our positions was constantly changing. The heavy impacts fell ever closer around the still standing concrete strongpoints, ripping up mighty fountains of earth which came clattering down in clumps, until with an eerie rising howl and a shrieking bang the first direct hit landed. The cratered wasteland grew ever more desolate.[2]

The troops were increasingly plagued by artillery not only in the trenches but also in reserve behind the line. The numerous *barackenlager* (camps of accommodation huts) built to house them became the focus of long-range shelling, and replacements constantly needed to be constructed. Under such conditions 'rest' was out of the question. Eventually accommodation had to be more widely dispersed in order to minimise losses. By mid-July the entire sector from the front line to deep in the rear was permanently under fire. While the forward area was relentlessly hammered into

Two games of *skat* in the infantry's rest billets. Left: RIR 102; right: IR 392 (taken in Schaap Balie on 3 July 1917)..

Two pictures from the album of Ltn. Schaffer of Minenwerfer-Kompanie 223 (the divisional trench mortar company), showing the unit's arrival at Vijfwegen between Langemarck and Staden on 28 June 1917. The second photo is labelled *"Flemish forced labour girls thinning out turnips near Vijfwege. They don't overly exert themselves, sing a great deal but don't run away when our camp is shelled."*.

GRR 100 maintains a rough approximation of cosy domesticity in battered concrete bunkers amid the ruins of the Pilkem-Langemarck area in early summer 1917. The bunker below was 'signed' by the Bavarian *pionier* company which constructed it (bayerische Pionier-Kompagnie 13).

one continual field of craters, every exit from Langemarck and every approach to the front was under continual harassing fire from heavy guns. Low-flying enemy aircraft, largely unopposed, directed fire onto any visible movement in the devastated landscape.

Since relieving GRR 100 in *Abschnitt Pilckem* on the 11th, RIR 102 had been shelled every day with increasing severity. On the night of 14–15 July it endured a gas attack from massed Livens Projectors on such a scale that gas could be smelled far into the rear. Upon relief by I./102 on the 18th, II./102 (*bereitschaftsbataillon* since 11 July and *kampfbataillon* since 15 July) reported as follows on its week-long ordeal:

The troops are physically and mentally exhausted by the heavy and super-heavy calibre annihilation fire, which has steadily increased without interruption since 9.45pm on 14 July, to such an extent that holding out after a five-day tour seems very risky. The constant evasive movements of the men and lying in shell-holes robs the individual man of any rest whatsoever. The fighting spirit which needs to be present in a high degree in order to withstand fresh enemy forces, is naturally no longer present since the battalion in the front line has been exposed to attritional fire since 14 July. As a result of the gas and the powder smoke the trench garrison suffers terribly from thirst, and sleep is impossible. In view of the situation the battalion requests that the fighting troops be relieved after three days' deployment. Issue of alcohol in small quantities is advisable.[3]

British aggression escalated to small probing attacks on 18 and 20 July, which were then repeated daily from 26 July, often gaining surprise by using no obvious pre-attack barrage and attacking late in the day with the sun at their backs. Each time they were ejected by local counter-attacks, but it was clear that 23. RD would not have the numbers to withstand a full-scale assault. With grim practicality on 25 July the *divisions-kommando* had ordered that the dead could be buried in their *zeltbahnen* due to the critical shortage of coffins. Losses, especially of officers, had reached the point where the division could no longer even man the cratered ruins of the second line in sufficient strength. Most of the exhausted survivors were relieved in the last days of July; only the luckless III./392 was still in the battle zone on 31 July when the British offensive opened, and saw terrible fighting alongside the Lehr-Infanterie-Regiment which had come to relieve them. After this narrow escape the division spent the whole of August resting at Bruges, where it received large numbers of replacements (GRR 100 for instance receiving 429 men from the *feldrekrutendepot*). When not occupied with drill or with coastal and border guard duties, the troops had opportunities to sunbathe and swim at the Belgian seaside resorts.

Front line of IR 392 in the thoroughly devastated area of the *Struyve-Hof* (Hindenburg Farm, 1km south of Pilkem), which gave the sector its name of *Abschnitt Struyve*. The concrete bunker on the right is the sole surviving landmark.

The Hell of Passchendaele

On 2 September the division was assigned as *eingreifdivision* to *Gruppe Dixmuide* and moved into accommodation around Jabbeke and Ichtegem. Although safely out of artillery range, the troops could clearly hear the constant thundering of the guns around Ypres. They were dismayed to learn that Langemarck had fallen in their absence. More dismaying yet, 23. RD was assigned as *eingreifdivision* to the embattled *Gruppe Ypern* on 20 September and reached its *bereitstellungsraum* (deployment area for troops on high alert) the next day with one painful exception. III. / RIR 102 had lost thirty-nine men killed or injured in a railway accident at Torhout, and rejoined its regiment near Westrozebeke a day later. Further losses followed due to shelling in the *bereitstellungsraum*, which lay among the German battery positions.

On the morning of 24 September, 23. Reserve-Division took over *Abschnitt Passchendaele* from 2. Garde-Reserve-Division with three regiments abreast. The outpost line was about 100 metres west of the Zonnebeke–Langemarck road, between St. Julien and Zonnebeke (exclusive of both towns). East of the road on the Passchendaele Ridge the *Flandern-I-* and *Flandern-II-Stellung* blocked the way to the ruins of the village itself. Although aircraft and artillery harassment were constant from the outset, the situation seemed 'normal' until hell broke loose on 26 September. From 4am the whole sector as far back as Moorslede was subjected to intense fire for effect, with divisions further left and right also visibly hit. The shelling finally escalated to furious drumfire before the British infantry went in at 5.50am with tank support. Breaking into the lines of IR 392 in the centre, they began to roll up the forward battalions of RIR 102 (left) and GRR 100 (right) from the flank. Uffz. Holland of 7. / RIR 102 described the day's events as follows in his diary, later excerpted in the published regimental history:

At 12 midnight our company sets out in faint moonlight from the bereitschaftsstellung *in single file – silently - in the gloom - among the partially water-filled shellholes. Almost two hours later we are forward in the front line and occupy the murky, damp shellholes. The troops we are relieving advise us to carry out all work (digging, burrowing, fetching food) solely in the dark due to enemy aerial observation. Holes are laboriously shovelled out. At 4am the storm of drumfire erupts. What a terrible hell! Comrades who have been through the 'first Somme' and 'at Langemarck' assure us that never before had the hell-drumming been as mad as it is here. As if all the devils in hell have erupted in frenzy and let loose their bloodthirsty*

The photos on pp.185–188 were taken by a Prussian from IR 128 (Danzig, 36. ID) in the neighbouring sector shortly before 23. RD arrived in September. This concrete command bunker built in the foundations of a ruined farmhouse east of Kerselaere could hold eighty men

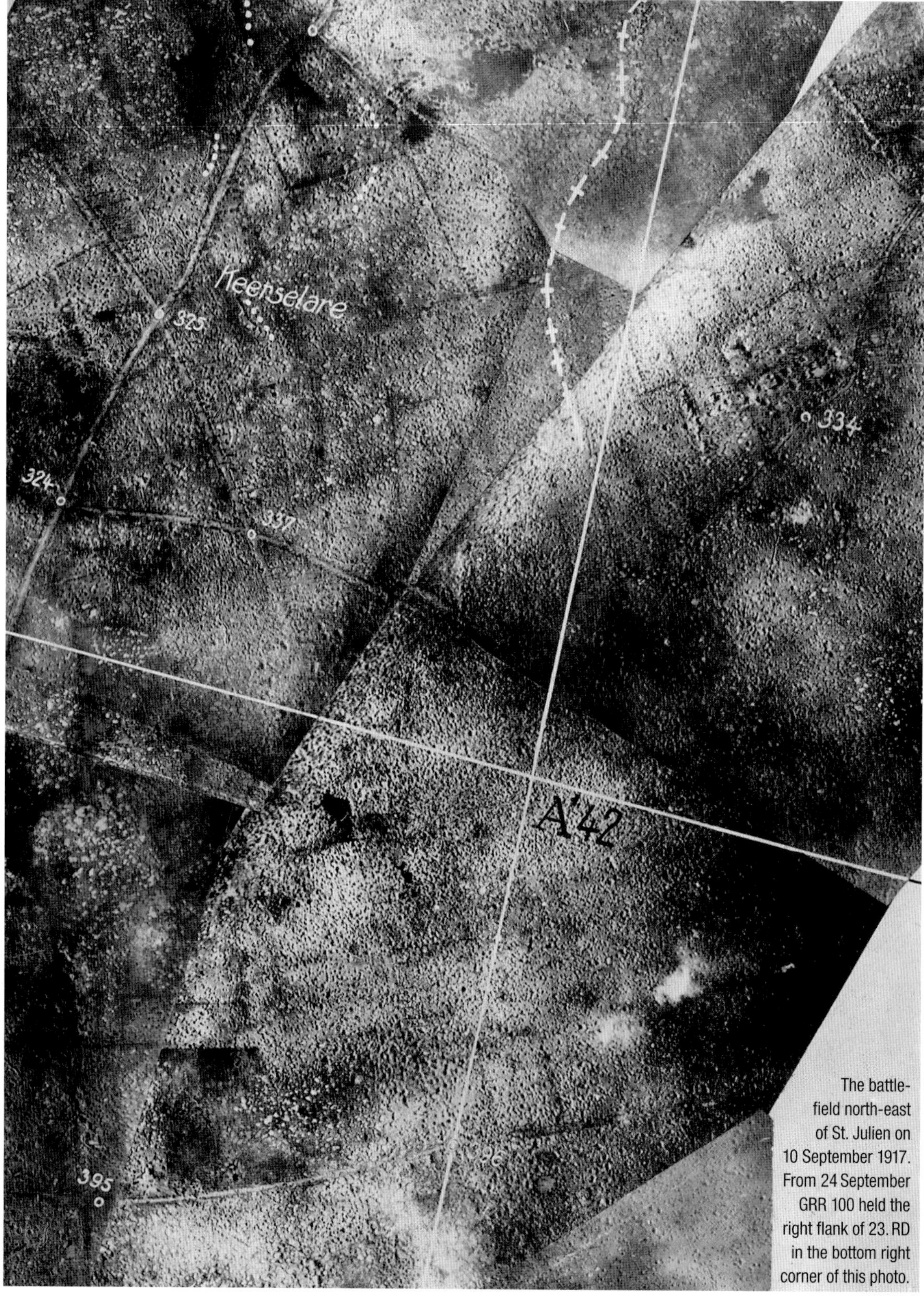

The battle-field north-east of St. Julien on 10 September 1917. From 24 September GRR 100 held the right flank of 23. RD in the bottom right corner of this photo.

vindictiveness, their greed and lust for annihilation with every means at their disposal! Every single kind of projectile, by size, filling or effect; e.g. steel shells, Catherine wheels, boxes of nails, petrels, grenades![4] *Above us the English airmen: directing the murderous fire to the crucial points by firing their machine-guns as a signal. Often one is above me and rattles away, at which the already mad fire at once intensifies still further. Behind a low earth wall we hunch on our knees on the damp ground. We would prefer to bury ourselves in the earth. But we are not allowed to disturb it – because of the airman. Sadly no German airman appears, no matter how dearly we long for one! – Lumps of clay often strike one's steel helmet, frequently with threatening force. The heart trembles, the blood surges. One learns to undergo drumfire and endure it. One thinks of one's loved ones at home, and fervently says one last Lord's Prayer for everyone. Well if it fares ill for us, let us stand firm! Hour after hour trickles by. What will it come to?*

Now and then through the atrocious powder smoke I direct a questioning glance at my neighbour. Right now he's looking backwards. Comrades are rushing toward the rear. A grab for my rifle and then off in giant strides 50m up the slope and I throw myself down in the crater field. Many others have already wrestled their way out this far – among them many dear friends! – The steady pulse of the fighting rings out horribly. The artillery provides the bass notes, the machine-guns and rifles are the tenors. Not many of our brave Seventh are still left holding the upper part of the slope. Often I spring into another crater, to get small sections back together and help them out with cartridges. Shrapnel and steel shells have taken an horrendous toll. Now enemy MGs begin to rage, particularly from the flanks. The last of us frequently glance rearward, to see if reinforcements are coming to our aid. – … but they do not come …

The English annihilation fire is at every range too orderly and target-focused, yet it comes down in a staggered fashion. We pull back to higher ground. Only isolated reserves are slowly able to make it over to the left wing. We run behind a wooden shack, which serves as a refuge for the Red Cross. Many lightly and severely wounded are already laying inside. … They bear their fate with manly dignity. A few still seek to escape, with and without success. Long anxious hours of worry for the future pass for the men crammed reluctantly and oppressively close together in the gloomy shack. The English move closer, a sniper within 50 metres of the hut. The coward guns down yet another of our loyal sanitäter! The fighting rages all day around our shelter, fortunately it continues to be spared from shelling – we

Adjoining HQ and medical bunkers of IR 128 in active use during the attack of British 58th Division on 20 September 1917.

View from the HQ bunker of IR 128 looking toward Passchendaele on 20 September 1917. On the left is the ruined orchard of a farmstead near Kerselaere, on the right the stumps of willow trees along the Strombeek.

have put up the white flag with the red cross. Late in the afternoon both sides open up with drumfire for several hours. Our men are preparing to counterattack. Finally the comforting message comes: our hut is back in contact with our unit. Now finally at evening the way out of the shack is open to us![5]

The line was stabilised by evening with little ground conceded to the enemy, despite grievous losses on both sides. The published history of RIR 102 deemed *'der Tag von Zonnebeke'* the most glorious day in the regiment's history. Published rolls of honour list 125 confirmed dead from GRR 100 on 26 September alone, and 113 from RIR 102. An appallingly high number of them (seventy from GRR 100 and forty-seven from RIR 102) still had no known grave when these appeared in the 1920s and many still do.

After an abortive British attempt to renew their attack on the 27th and a German counterattack on the 28th, the 23. RD was withdrawn and transported to the Eastern Front. Although the last few days had been rainy, the water level was rising in the craters and local drainage systems had long been obliterated, the division thus did not witness the battlefield's final transformation into the near-impassable swamp which bogged down the British offensive. The offensive had cost both sides hundreds of thousands of casualties, and gained the British around 8 kilometres of corpse-choked wasteland.

View looking toward the St. Julien–Langemarck road with a corner of the HQ bunker visible on the right, taken on 17 September 1917.

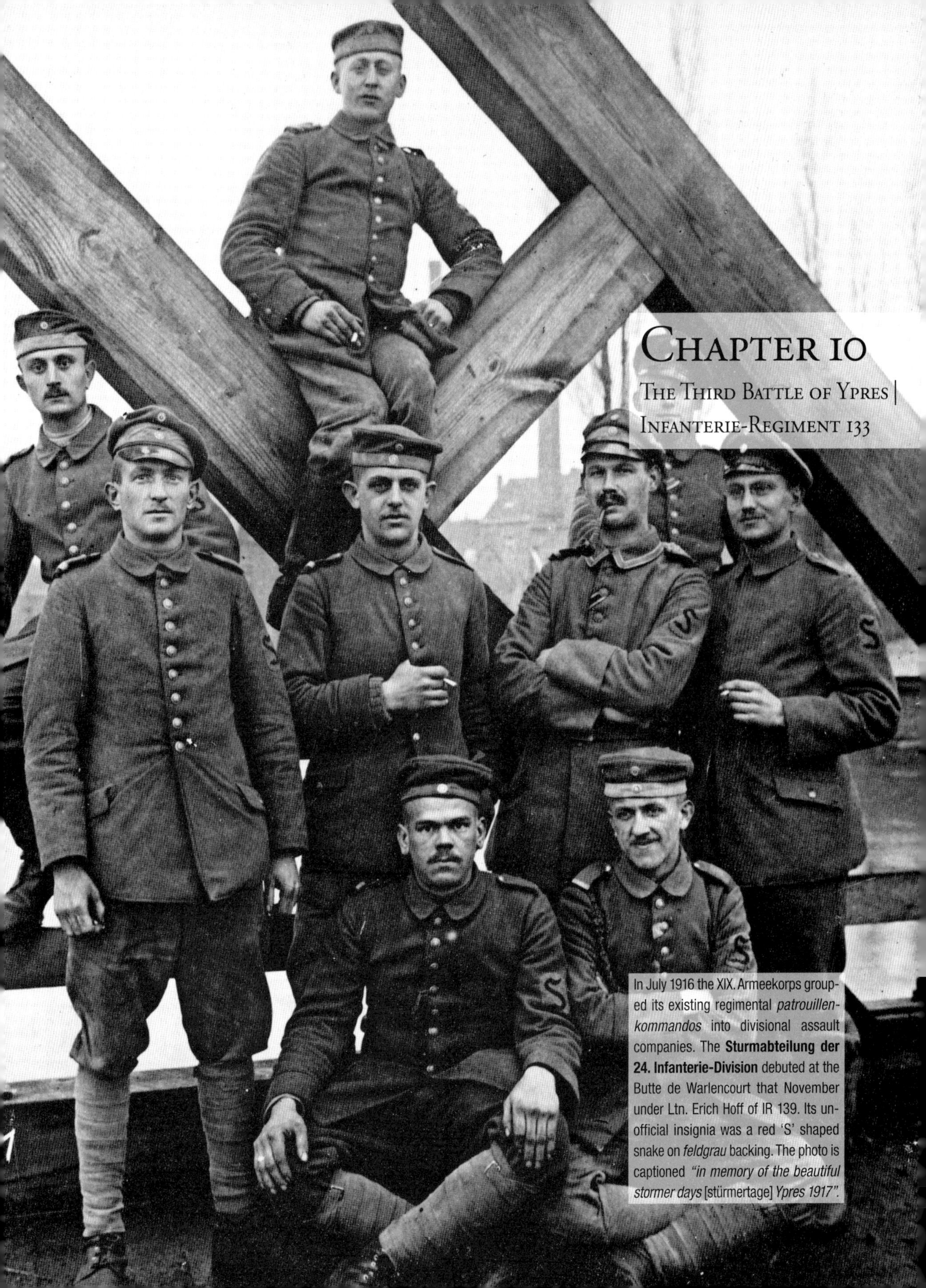

Chapter 10

The Third Battle of Ypres | Infanterie-Regiment 133

In July 1916 the XIX. Armeekorps grouped its existing regimental *patrouillen-kommandos* into divisional assault companies. The **Sturmabteilung der 24. Infanterie-Division** debuted at the Butte de Warlencourt that November under Ltn. Erich Hoff of IR 139. Its unofficial insignia was a red 'S' shaped snake on *feldgrau* backing. The photo is captioned *"in memory of the beautiful stormer days* [stürmertage] *Ypres 1917"*.

The Third Battle of Ypres | Infanterie-Regiment 133

With 24. Infanterie-Division from the '*Kanalknie*' to the ruins of Gheluvelt

In peacetime *Kgl. Sächs. 9. Infanterie-Regiment Nr. 133* (IR 133) was based at Zwickau, centre of Saxony's coal mining and automotive industries. Mobilised in 1914 with 40. Infanterie-Division / XIX. Armeekorps, it fought on the Marne before heading north in October for the storming of Lille and fighting east of Armentières. While the main body of IR 133 took and held a line facing Houplines, elements also fought at L'Epinette and at Frelinghien. Its II. Bataillon spent Christmas 1914 with IR 106 at Ploegsteert Wood, and both there and near Houplines IR 133 was prominent in the fraternisation. The famous account of football with 2nd Argyll & Sutherland Highlanders was related to the BBC in 1968 by retired Oberstleutnant (in 1914 a young *leutnant*) Johannes Niemann, who published a history of IR 133 in 1969. Although transferred to IR 392 (23. RD) in September 1916 and without access to the war diary after 1945, Niemann unearthed some personal accounts from 1917 which are quoted here.

The regiment transferred to 24. Infanterie-Division on 6 March 1915 and extended its sector up to the Lys. As of 31 May it was in army reserve at Haubourdin with IR 134. As such IR 133 briefly relieved the exhausted IR 134 at Givenchy-lès-la-Bassée in mid-June after the Second Battle of Artois and spent most of July in reserve behind Vimy Ridge. On 14 August it rejoined XIX. AK, relieving IR 179 on the left flank at Bois Grenier. In anticipation of an Entente offensive, the staff of 89. Inf. Brig. with IR 133 and JB 13 was transported south of Arras on 1 September. Ten days later the Saxons reinforced 5. bayer. Res. Div. at Beaurains, where the attack of 25 September was decisively repulsed. IR 133 took over 400 prisoners and seven of its officers received the MStHO. Relieved on 18 December, it returned to the line at Bois Grenier on Christmas Day. In 1916 this 'quiet' front was increasingly disturbed by patrols and raids. In one such clash on the night of 13–14 June an unknown 133er became the first German prisoner of the recently arrived New Zealand Division.

XIX. AK was sent to the Somme at the end of July. Before seeing combat IR 133 had the exhausting task of marching back and forth for days on end in the summer heat, to confuse enemy tracking of troop movements. On 9 August it entered the battle on the corps' right flank at Mouquet Farm, where it withstood relentless Australian pressure for over two weeks. Finally relieved over the nights of 26–28 August, it went back into line at La Bassée on 3 September. Here the corps was steadily rebuilt, disturbed only by mortar fire and aggressive patrolling – during which British 30th Division (also convalescent from the Somme) was identified. IR 133 repelled repeated raids on 5, 13 and 15 September. Relieved at the start of October, 24. ID took over from 4. Ersatz-Division at Warlencourt on the Ancre on 15 October. Again on the right flank, IR 133 held the *Belowriegel* near Pys. While the worst of the fighting was further left where 40. ID defended the Butte de Warlencourt, the regiment distinguished itself in beating off British attacks on 18 and 25 October. Over the nights of 26–29 October it was relieved and left the Somme for Flanders, where XIX. AK took over the *Wytschaetebogen* and was designated *Gruppe Wytschaete* in January 1917.

On 14 November 1916, IR 133 took over 24. ID's new left subsector (a line studded with mine craters between the Vierstraat and Kemmel roads) from Württemberg Grenadier-Regiment 123. Here it held the same *Zahnstocherwald* described a year earlier by Ltn. d. R. Pache of IR 182 and became familiar with many places described in Chapter 8. Unknown to IR 133, this subsector was to be the site of six of the great mine detonations on 7 June 1917. Hollandscheschur Farm 1–3 (on IR 133's extreme right, taken over from IR 179 at the end of 1916) and Petit Bois 1 and 2 (in the centre of their front line) were all completed and charged in summer 1916. In September 1916 250th Tunnelling Company R.E. had begun a new gallery aimed at Maedelstede Farm (on IR 133's extreme left) and the *Wytschaeterwald*. Ultimately the latter branch was abandoned, and the charge at Maedelstede Farm ready only just in time for Messines. Fortunately for IR 133, it had by then been relieved.

A note on terminology: German combat doctrine in 1917 emphasised defense in depth. Corps staffs were separated from their organic divisions and became interchangeable command teams for geographical *gruppen*. Each gruppe shuffled its varying cast of divisions between the front and the *eingreif* ('intervention') role, held behind the line to counterattack or reinforce threatened sectors. The forward zone of a regimental subsector was now typically held in depth by one battalion, whose commander served as KTK (*Kampftruppen-Kommandeur*), with tactical authority over all units entering his zone regardless of rank. Further back the commander of the battalion in the immediate support (*bereitschaft*) zone exercised a similar role as BTK (*Bereitschaftstruppen-Kommandeur*), while regimental HQ managed the allocation of reserves.

Offensive preparations and the Battle of Messines: January–July 1917

Winter in the salient saw the usual arduous struggle with the weather. The early months of 1917 were marked by increased forward patrolling and raiding as *Gruppe Wytschaete* sought to quantify and eliminate the mining threat to the Messines Ridge. This included a major daylight raid by IR133 on 8 March, gaining them (according to Niemann and *Sachsen in Grosser Zeit*) thirty prisoners from the 16th (Irish) Division. The raiders had however failed to locate, let alone destroy, the mineshafts threatening their sector.

By April the line on the exposed forward slope of the ridge looked increasingly untenable in the event of the predicted British offensive. Since ceding the ridge posed its own major problems and the full severity of the mining threat was not appreciated, *Gruppe Wytschaete* nevertheless remained in place.

IR133 was relieved on 23 April and billeted in Menen and Bousbecque, the men already suspecting that something was up. On 2 May, due to the insertion of 2. ID between 40. ID and 24. ID, the regiment occupied a new sector between St. Eloi and the Ypres-Comines Canal. Patrols here soon revealed an ominous thickening of the opposing trench garrison, while the British artillery registered on major targets and the billeting areas of Tenbrielen and Kortewilde came under long-range fire. On 21 May, the official start date for the bombardment, IR133 conducted a raid codenamed *'Kirsche'* (cherry). Though nominally successful this found the British second line empty over a breadth of 600m and no prisoners were taken. By 27 May British artillery preparations and troop movements were obvious. 24. ID was relieved by the fresh 35. ID on 31 May and transported by rail to *Gruppe Aubers* in the Seclin area, where it was kept in OHL reserve at immediate deployment readiness *(alarmbereitschaft)* and drilled for defensive warfare. On the night of 6–7 June it was recalled to *Gruppe Wytschaete* during a severe thunderstorm and earmarked to relieve 2. ID. The Saxons heard the apocalyptic mine explosions at 4.10am while marching to billets near Lille and were soon committed to the *Wytschaeteschlacht* (as the Germans termed the Battle of Messines). I./133, I./179 and III./139 joined 1. Garde-Reserve-Division and the surviving Bavarian defenders of Messines in a desperate counterattack that afternoon. Hit by their own artillery, the opposing Australians retired to the *Höhenlinie* around the town perimeter leaving the Germans holding that part of the *Sehnenstellung* (Oosttaverne Line). Here the Saxon battalions held out for three days and nights without food or sleep. Meanwhile as *eingreifdivision* to *Gruppe Wytschaete*, the rest of 24. ID had been committed piecemeal elsewhere.

On 10 June the division withdrew behind the Ypres-Comines Canal. It relieved 7. ID in *Abschnitt Hollebeke* of the new

Purportedly prisoners taken by 7./133 in their raid against 7th Royal Irish Rifles at *Markwald* (Petit Bois) on 8 March 1917. This large group must also include the *"young corporal and nine men of the last draft"*[1] from 6th Connaught Rangers taken by IR 104 early on 9 March (see p.201).

Signaltrupp of IR 139 at Houtem on 14 April 1917 with an M Blink 16. This Morse Code flashing lamp was one of many lower-tech substitutes for the fragile telephone system under battle conditions.

NCOs of 2. Feldkompagnie / Pionier-Bataillon 22 billeted in huts at Korentje near Warneton. This company had been with XIX. AK since mobilisation and was one of two serving with 24. ID in 1917.

This working party from IR 179 seems to have just finished applying cement to this concrete-block bunker in the 'fortified town of Wytschaete' (as the original handwritten caption calls it). Habitually committed on the right of IR 133 in 1917, it initially held the *Bayernwald* subsector.

On 10 April, IR 179 launched its own trench raid codenamed 'Kuckuck' (cuckoo) from the northeastern corner (the so-called *Taleck*) of the *Bayernwald.* The attackers from II. / 179 and the Sturmabteilung der 24. ID claimed to have killed at least eight of the enemy and took two prisoners. The British retaliated on subsequent days with heavy shelling, almost obliterating large sections of the trenches.

German line (Klein-Zillebeke–Houtem–Neu-Warneton–Deulemont) on 13 June with IR 179 on the right at the canal embankment and IR 133 in the centre. Meanwhile the staff of IX. RK relieved XIX. AK as *Gruppe Wytschaete.* A local attack by British 41st Division on the evening of 14 June seized limited objectives in the outpost line at Hollebeke, triggering a counterattack by III./133 after heavy artillery preparation. Advancing to occupy Hollebeke and reinforce the outpost line, the battalion suffered severely from intense defensive fire. In the third wave, 3. MGK lost over sixty men and all its machine-guns. With all telephone lines and relay stations destroyed, III. / 133 hung on alone here in the expectation of a renewed British advance which for now did not occur. The sector was shifted slightly to the right on the night of 16–17 June and the division relieved at the end of the month by 10. bID. Billeted in the Lille suburbs of Loos and Haubourdin, it was designated eingreifdivision to *Gruppe Aubers* (XIX. AK) and its infantry regiments were refilled by its *feldrekrutendepot.* A major all-arms training exercise was conducted on 21 July by the entire division (plus air support).

On the fringe of the Third Battle of Ypres: July–September 1917

British 5th Army launched its long-predicted offensive on 31 July 1917. 24. ID returned to the front line of *Gruppe Wytschaete* on 11 August west of Houtem. IR 133 was on the left at Garde-Dieu, in broken ground rendered swampy by the Wambeek. On 13 August Schütze Karl Franke, a machine-gunner with 3. MGK / IR 133, wrote home:

Since the day before yesterday we are in the fighting line again and in Flanders at that. It looks dreadful here. Our front line is a field of craters. There are no trenches at all. The garrison crouches all day long in the shellholes. You can only stand up at night and it is still not without danger then, as the whole area is constantly under artillery and machine-gun fire. Because we've had so much rain the holes are entirely full of mud. The men don't have a dry rag on them. I only have the gear to deal with this time and as reserve gunner have been allowed to pull back about 1.5km behind the line. I am based here in a ruined farmhouse. At least there I have a roof over my head and a dry place to lay down. Tonight I believe we will be relieved from the front line and move into the 3rd line. The word 'relief' alone has an immediate soothing effect.[2]

On 1 September[3] IR 133 conducted a raid which earned it special commendation (see map). Niemann cites a letter home from a Gefreiter Linke of 6./133:

... Once again I've been in the rear practicing for a patrol in force. What a patrol it was! 88 men strong. Bloody hell!! But I'm sporting a black-white ribbon for it now![4] *Anyway: we were driven forward by truck. About 10 o'clock we got to the front and set out immediately, just as we had practised. Like the old tune 'softly, quite softly'*[5] *we kept going forward in single file, one column on the right and the other about 100 metres to their left. All was quiet, just like every night. About 60 metres from the enemy trenches we lay down. At 11pm on the dot our artillery,* minenwerfers *and MGs opened up (with an absolutely ridiculous din!). Please note though that this fire came down behind the enemy's front line. At the same time our*

Annotated map showing unit sectors at Houtem at the end of August 1917. The Saxon patrol broke in at approximately the point marked 'X'.

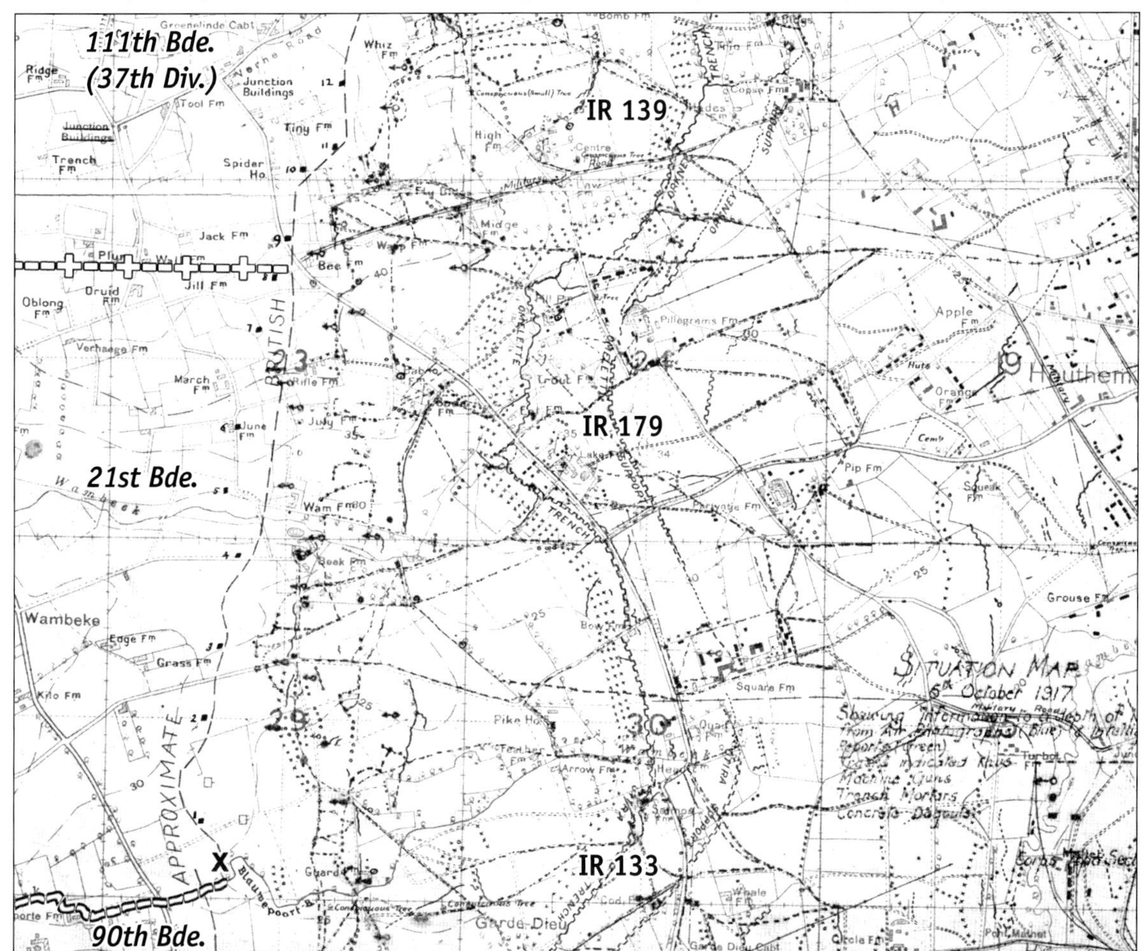

assault troops rushed forward into the enemy trenches, and those opposite us were 'broadly' dead en masse. Many of the enemy were left lying there severely wounded and we had 11 prisoners to book in. These poor buggers had been about to be relieved, and already had their pack and everything hanging on them. I myself lay as liaison post in front of the enemy trenches, so the assault troops could find their way back right away. Once all of them were back though, together with an unteroffizier *I fetched in a severely wounded man who was hanging in the English wire to our front. We had 2 missing(!), 2 severely and 15 lightly wounded. For of course 'Tommy' had noticed that something was up, informed his artillery (as this always works better for them than for us!) and put down heavy defensive fire on us on the way back! Luckily we made it to our KTK all the same. Then we led our prisoners back to the regimental battle HQ, where the regimental commander addressed us. There was tea with rum for everyone (including the prisoners!) and then we drove in motors back home to Wervicq. This afternoon there was a big parade in front of our divisional general, Hammer, who pinned the EK2 on me among others.*[6]

This sector lay some way south of the battlefront, so the British made no attempt to gain ground and only occasionally brought down drumfire. Nevertheless snipers, aggressive patrolling and aerial activity made occupation of the crater line gruelling and lethal. Crouched out of sight in their shellholes the rifle companies were now at least strengthened by the issue of MG08/15 light machine-guns. Leutnant d. R. Albert Oschatz later recalled this period for Niemann's regimental history:

After a thorough rest period southeast of Lille, which relieved us of the heavy impression of the Wytschaeteschlacht *and during which there was plenty of leave to Brussels, Ghent, Bruges and Ostend, on 31 July we heard the opening drumfire to the north which announced the impending Battle of Flanders. We knew that as a division familiar with Flanders we would soon be going into action there.*

On 7 August we were deployed on the Wambeke, west of the town of Houthem which was known to us from the Wytschaeteschlacht, *with IR 179 on our right. There were no longer any lines in the old sense, they had disappeared in the* Wytschaeteschlacht. *The front line consisted of shellholes, there were no wire obstacles left, the rearward positions were grouped as so-called nests of resistance around shot-up farmhouses, in most of which there were concrete dugouts for former command posts and artillery positions. There were still many English corpses left lying in front of our lines from previous attacks. The numerous English snipers made movement by day impossible – all traffic, food transport etc. had to take place at night.*

Attempts were made by means of numerous patrols to get a clear picture of the enemy's distribution of forces, just as the enemy too

Aerial view of the front line and 'dugouts' near Gheluvelt in October 1917, taken from the regimental history of IR 179.

An officer of IR 133 poses with a 10cm K04 gun bogged-down in an open fire position near the Menin Road between Geluwe and Gheluvelt.

harassed us with large-scale patrols preceded by heavy fire, which inflicted many casualties on us in the coverless terrain. Nevertheless we were not yet in the actual area of the major fighting in the battle for Flanders that had been raging since 31 July.[7]

The defense of Gheluvelt – October 1917

24. ID was relieved by 8. ID on 7 October. IR 133 had already been pulled out on 24 September, having lost 211 officers and 907 men in eight weeks at the fringe of the ongoing battle. Although now again designated an *eingreifdivision* it was immediately committed between Zandvoorde and Gheluvelt. This position, a ghastly wasteland of flooded craters punctuated by occasional concrete bunkers, was heavily shelled at all hours of the day and night. IR 133 was in the centre with its right flank near the Menin Road, IR 139 on its left and IR 179 on its right at Gheluvelt (see map p.202).

Another of Gefreiter Linke's letters home paints this period in vividly grim detail, despite his ever-optimistic tone:

In the A-Stellung, 20 October 1917 (Ypres-Menen Road)

Despite so much mud and other hardships I am still well! You can't have any idea what it's like here!! I am a gefechtsordonnanz[8], *and that isn't much fun!! At night we always go out with a flare-gun each, and if we don't know where we are we make a light by shooting a white flare into the sky. We always go about in pairs, as it often happens that one of us sinks up to his armpits in a shellhole! At night every five minutes, or three at busy periods, the KTK shoots a white flare into the air so that the runners etc. can get their bearings, otherwise we would never find our way there at all.*

We lie together with the company commander in a concrete dugout – there are about 10cm of water in there despite vigorous baling, and it is about 300 metres as the crow flies from the KTK. The whole area is ploughed up by shells. The food is pretty good and plentiful (battle supplement!). Just in the A-Stellung *because of transport difficulties there is cold food only, for one day there you get: one iron ration (400g), a litre of coffee, 750g of bread plus something else for the evening meal. Solid spirit stoves are supplied to heat this up. In this position the food is brought up by another company. At night we* ordonnanzen *are constantly taking these carrying parties from the KTK to our company commanders. You should hear the cursing and 'mutinying' if we're not there straight away!! All this aside, there is enough to smoke in all of our positions here!*[9]

Battalion reliefs every two days were necessary due to the mud and severe cold alone, on top of which the garrison was ground down relentlessly by artillery and subjected to massed infantry attacks on 9, 22 and finally 26 October. The last and heaviest was the only one to gain any ground, until a machine-gun in a concrete emplacement at Gheluvelt church mowed down the attackers. IR 133 counted 500 corpses in front of their lines alone. 24. ID had given no ground but was completely exhausted by its ordeal. Ltn. d. R. Oschatz, who suffered a light wound himself on 16 October, described this period as follows:

Battalion staff of IR 133 on duty as BTK at a partly camouflaged bunker complex on the Wervik-Becelaere road southeast of Gheluvelt. The dog with the group on the left is a *meldehund*, trained to carry messages in a metal tube attached to the collar.

After a stronger attack had been beaten off on 1 October we were moved north on 7–8 October, 24. ID receiving the battle zone from Zandvoorde to Gheluvelt. Our regiment lay south of the Ypres-Menen Road, IR139 left and IR179 right, in a completely swamped landscape full of the English fallen. On 9 October an English attack launched after strong drumfire was beaten off with heavy losses for the enemy. Since the heavy MGs would soon be rendered unserviceable by the mud, the crews came inside the few concrete bunkers scattered across our position – which were the constant target of the English heavy artillery, and often overturned and sank into the mire. The regiment lay with one battalion in the 1st line with the so-called K.T.K., a further battalion behind with the B.T.K. and finally a third battalion in the C-Stellung, *in which there had been attempts to create reasonably rain-proof shelters with corrugated iron. Losses were equally severe everywhere in the incessant artillery fire. In the cold, rainy weather the health of the troops deteriorated while constantly exposed in open ground.*

A stronger English attack ensued on 22 October, which collapsed under our MG and artillery fire and further increased the number of corpses in front of our line.

In the night of 25 to 26 October intense traffic behind the English line signalled their offensive intentions. At 6.30 a drumfire erupted beyond anything so far experienced, inflicting extremely heavy losses on us. The attackers were successfully repulsed under our defensive fire, those of the enemy who had broken in were thrown out in an immediate counterattack by our B and C battalions. The brunt of the enemy attack was on the Ypres-Menen Road, where he was able to advance together with tanks and approach the rubble of Gheluvelt, inflicting extremely heavy losses on our sister regiment 179. Our I. Bataillon too in the front line was almost completely wiped out, almost all the officers fell including Ltn. d. R. Fritzsche[10] *who had proved himself in many battles.*

Since the 24. ID had suffered the loss of almost half its combat strength in this heavy fighting, its relief by the 18. Reserve-Division took place on 28 October. The 24. Infanterie-Division, which prided itself on having not lost a single metre of Flemish soil during the weeks of this tour, came southeast of Lille for a few days of rest and refreshment. It received numerous replacements, the officers' corps in particular gained a completely new face due to the arrival of many new comrades from the Saxon landwehr *regiments in the east.*[11]

The division was now transferred to the Vimy sector and remained there until February 1918. After four weeks of training for mobile warfare, IR 133 took part in the *Michael* offensive that March and advanced with 24. ID up to the vicinity of Hebuterne. It was earmarked for the planned *Hagen* offensive around Ypres that July. After this was cancelled however it was steadily ground down opposing allied attacks further south and never returned to Flanders. On 23 November IR 133 returned to Zwickau, having lost a total of 2,835 dead and 861 missing in the course of the war.

Medical orderlies and stretcher bearers of IR 133 manning a dressing station *(verbandplatz)* at *Deimlingseck*, a crossroads 600m southeast of Gheluvelt where Gen. d. Inf. von Deimling of XV. AK was wounded by artillery fire on 31 October 1914.

A rudimentary forward dressing station of IR 133 during the fighting at Gheluvelt in October 1917.

The battle-scarred KTK bunker on the *Divisionshöhe* at Gheluvelt in October 1917. An MG08 sledge mount is set up for high-angle fire on the left; the machine-gun itself is stowed inside to protect it from the mud. The man on the left is operating an M Blink 16 (see p.192).

The *regimentsgefechtsstelle* (regimental battle HQ) of IR 133 in the ruins of the *Jägerhof* (about 1km east of *Deimlingseck* near Oude Hond).

South of the *Jägerhof* was the regiment's *C-Stellung* (the north end of the Zandvoorde Switch, running across the Menin Road to cover Oude Hond and Oude Kruiseik). It is visibly stocked with hand grenades in case of a British breakthrough of the *Flandern-I-Stellung*.

Major Wittich[12] (centre) in command at the *regimentsgefechtsstelle* in October 1917. Note the carrier pigeon baskets stacked to his left.

The remains of a British aircraft shot down at *Nachtigall* (west of *Deimlingseck*).

Decorated members of the Sturmabteilung der 24. ID at Menen in July 1917. Consisting of young, unmarried volunteers temporarily seconded from their regiments, divisional 'stormtroopers' in the 4. Armee area were trained at courses given by Sturm-Bataillon 4 in Oudenaarde.

THE OTHER SIDE OF NO MAN'S LAND

In March 1917 at Wytschaete IR133 faced 16th (Irish) Division, then rebuilding after grave losses on the Somme partly using non-Irish drafts due to the political unfeasibility of conscription in Ireland. The raid on 8 March (and the raids by 40. ID that night) seems to have provoked concern for its current state of readiness up to corps level.

Its war diaries record two intense and precise half-hour bombardments with a fifteen-minute interval. Opposite Petit Bois about 500 yards of forward trenches plus four of the six Lewis Gun posts of the defending 7th Btn. Royal Irish Rifles were "practically obliterated"[13] by artillery and heavy *minenwerfers*, totally disrupting movement and communication. Three parties of at least forty men followed close behind the barrage around 5.30pm. One was stopped by flanking fire, but two broke in among the two weak companies[14] of the Irish battalion and escaped with prisoners before its neighbours could intervene, leaving three dead and four wounded raiders behind. To the surprise of 250th Tunnelling Company the raiders made "no serious attempt"[15] to destroy the Petit Bois mineshaft, although apparently equipped for demolition.

In the raids by 40. ID at 5am that night IR181 had no success on the Wytschaete-Wulverghem road, but *Patrouille Wehmeyer* of IR104 seized ten men and a Lewis Gun from 6th Btn. Connaught Rangers about 500m further south at Peckham (see *fighting the Kaiser's War* pp.138–139). This haul, plus twenty-five men and a Lewis Gun missing from 7th Royal Irish Rifles and two men missing from Y/16 Trench Mortar Battery seems to match the thirty-seven prisoners and two machine-guns claimed by the Germans the next day.[16]

While holding Garde Dieu at the end of August IR133 faced British 21st Brigade of 30th Division. Although experienced on the Somme, this New Army formation had had taken severe casualties for little gain in the first phase of the offensive on 31 July 1917. After relieving 12th Australian Infantry Brigade on 22 August, 21st Brigade held the line from the Blauwepoortbeek in the south to Bee Farm *(Lemmerzahl Ferme/Lemmerzahlhof)* in the north, facing both IR179 and IR133 (see map p.193).

In the southern half of the brigade sector, 2nd Btn. The Wiltshire Regiment found that their new front line was merely shallow interconnected shell holes with very little barbed wire. Movement was impossible by daylight, while at night the German machine-guns were highly active – partly compensating for a German shortage of artillery shells. The Wiltshires had their first encounter with IR133 early on 24 August:

"In the early hours of the morning one man of our patrol, getting slightly in advance of our line, stumbled on 4 Germans who took him prisoner and started leading him away. Fortunately they led him straight into one of our posts. The sentry [being] alarmed, opened fire and the party of 4 were captured except for 1 who escaped. Identification: shoulder straps bearing '133 IR' [sic.] *These men gave much information."*[17]

At about 4:15am on 26 August, a party of about sixty Saxons attempted a silent raid on the left-hand company of the battalion, making *"a determined effort to obtain identifications"*. This failed, and the Wiltshires claim to have killed ten of the attackers, identified as *"179th Regiment (STORM TROOPS)"*. This unusual note suggests that the sleeve badge of the *sturmabteilung* may have been recognised among them.

Although the German sources all state that the raid described by Gefreiter Linke (pp.193–194) took place on 1 September, it can only correspond to an attack described by the British as occurring on the night of 30–31 August. Both of 21st Brigade's frontline battalions were due for relief, and the Wiltshires were awaiting the arrival of 19th Btn. The Manchester Regiment when a *"remarkably accurate"*[18] artillery and machine-gun barrage struck the front and support lines of the right-hand company at about 11:15pm. This forced most of the forward posts to take cover further back, leaving Posts Nos. 1 and 8 exposed to attack by about 100 Saxons. Despite *"a stout resistance with Lewis Guns under heavy shelling and MG fire"*[19] both were overrun and the survivors captured. The British artillery responded immediately to SOS flares, inflicting losses on the withdrawing raiders and allowing one prisoner to escape. Corpses found near the British wire were identified as members of Pionier-Bataillon 22. The Wiltshires reported one killed, fourteen wounded and nine missing, while the Manchesters lost one killed, eight wounded and ten missing.

The British brigade sector was extended a further 550 yards northwards (opposite IR139) on the night of 11–12 September, and 21st Brigade temporarily relieved by 90th Brigade of the same division. After some reorganisation 21st Brigade returned over the nights of 20-22 September; this relief was hampered by severe shelling. On the night of 29–30 September the brigade had a last confusing encounter with IR133 in the northern subsector, again right before a relief. At about 8pm *"a party of the enemy approximately 12 strong walked almost on to No. 13 Post held by the 2nd Bn. Yorkshire Regiment. They were fired on and dispersed, one of the enemy being killed, who was found to belong to the 133rd IR, which suggested that the 24th IR Division had side-slipped northwards."*[20]

Since IR133 had been relieved six days earlier by IR102 of the adjacent Saxon 32. ID and this incident occurred on the British left facing IR139 and 179, this was possibly a mixed group from the *sturmabteilung*.

At Gheluvelt IR133 was affected by flanking and diversionary operations for successive pushes further north. This culminated on 26 October in the Canadian assault on Passchendaele. To the north of 24.ID, 5th Division attacked Polderhoek Wood and Chateau. Directly opposite, 20th Brigade of 7th Division made a frontal assault on Gheluvelt, while 91st Brigade attacked the Saxon line south of the Menin Road. Since 7th Division had twice failed to take Gheluvelt already, its commander Major-General Shoubridge reputedly denounced this operation as suicidal.

It was already raining when 91st Brigade advanced at 06:40 behind a creeping barrage. Severe flooding soon forced the attackers to bunch on the less muddy approaches, becoming even easier targets for machine-guns. Those attackers who got close enough to retaliate found that the mud had also jammed many of their rifles and Lewis Guns. The German defensive shelling too was well-aimed and deadly – on the brigade's left, 2nd Btn. Royal West Surrey Regt. soon lost its frontline observation post to a direct hit. Worse still, the brigade's Stokes mortars could not support this battalion's attack on Lewis House as its men huddled close to the target while the two surviving officers struggled to restore order.

In the centre, 21st Btn. Manchester Regt. came under machine-gun fire before reaching its start line. Lacking any cover and hampered by the mud, the survivors were forced to halt and dig in within half an hour. On their right, 'C' Company of 1st Btn Staffordshire Regt. was repelled from Berry Cottages with hand grenades and virtually wiped out, while 'D' Company was halted by crossfire in front of Hamp Farm. Due to a less exposed approach, 'B' Company successfully stormed 'The Mound', a hillock on the right flank of IR139. Led by a corporal, its survivors dug in and called for reinforcements. However none of their runners reached battalion HQ, and 'The Mound' was heavily shelled by British artillery that afternoon.

Although 5th Division had taken its objectives and now threatened IR 179 from the flank, 20th Brigade was repelled from Gheluvelt. By nightfall, 7th Division was back at its start line. 91st Brigade alone reported 119 confirmed dead, 373 wounded and 482 missing; many of them disappeared into the mud and have no known grave.

The attack of British 91st Brigade on 26 October 1917 against the centre of 24. ID. Although more than mere shell hole lines, the *Flandern-I-Stellung* and the *Gheluvelt-Riegel* (covering the flank of IR 179) were badly flooded and their barbed wire largely submerged in the mud.

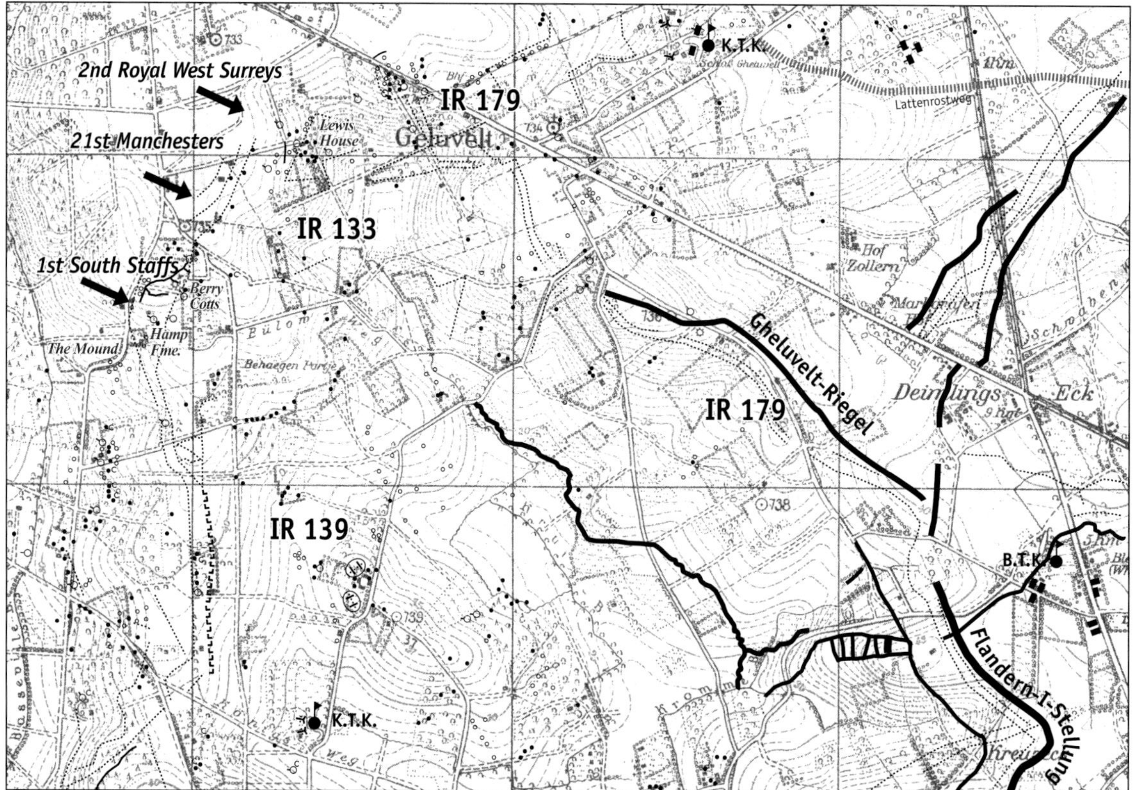

Chapter II

The 58. Infanterie-Division 1917/1918

Aerial photograph taken on 4 November 1917 of the densely cratered area south of Draaibank, where the *Friedrich-Straße* crossed the Steenbeek at the *Sachsenbrücke* (Saxon Bridge). The *Draaibank-Linie* on the right bank was the German front line in September. The sharply angled position behind the stream at top left is the *Merckem-Riegel*, defended by IR 181 of the neighbouring 40. ID in mid-October.

The 58. Infanterie-Division 1917/1918

Houthulster Wald, Poelkapelle und Langemarck

The great British Flanders offensive which opened on 31 July 1917 and raged late into the autumn placed an intolerable burden on the German forces in the west, compounded by the rapid return of the once-mutinous French Army to active combat operations. Every serviceable division available in the west was gradually fed into this relentless meat-grinder of a battle, only to be bled white with alarming rapidity. OHL was obliged to look elsewhere, primarily to the Eastern Front, where the Russian Army's final offensive had collapsed even before the British offensive had begun – and would lead to the demise of the Russian Provisional Government by October. Since however German reinforcements were also needed to prop up the beleaguered Austro-Hungarians against the Italians on the Isonzo, only a modest number of German divisions from the east would arrive in time to take part in the *Flandernschlacht*.

One of these would be the Saxon 58. Infanterie-Division. At its core was the 116. Infanterie-Brigade (formerly 48. Infanterie-Brigade) with IR106 and IR107, which had fought at Ploegsteert Wood and south of Armentieres with XIX. AK in 1914. The new 58. ID was formed at Cambrai in March 1915 with a mixture of Saxon and Württemberg units, with the renumbered Saxon brigade joined by Württemberg Reserve-Infanterie-Regiment 120. The division saw its bloody combat debut against the French offensive between Givenchy-en-Gohelle and Neuville-Saint-Vaast on 9 May 1915. Transferred to 4. Armee in Flanders between 19 and 27 June, it provided working parties to XXVII. RK while rebuilding. At the end of July it travelled to the Eastern Front to take part in the victorious Narew offensive and subsequent breakthrough fighting as far as Wilna (Vilnius). It returned to the West in October 1915, and in 1916 had the unique misfortune to be the only Saxon division committed to both the Verdun and Somme battles. That October between tours on the Somme it spent four weeks holding the line astride the Menin Road. While resting on the now-quiet Verdun front in December, all the division's Württemberg elements were replaced with Saxons. With RIR103 (originally from 23. RD) as its new third infantry regiment, 58. ID was in the Champagne to face the French Nivelle Offensive in April 1917. The victorious but exhausted division went east again in May to hold the Lake Narach sector in Belarus. After seeing brief fighting against the doomed Kerensky Offensive that summer, relief orders reached them on 1 October.

By the time 58. ID arrived in Flanders nearly two weeks later, the objectives of the British offensive had been scaled down due to the weather and ground conditions. The enemy now aimed to reach a suitable line for the winter, and to distract German attention from the French assault on the Chemin des Dames (23–27 October) and the upcoming British tank attack at Cambrai. None of this was apparent to the hapless German defenders of Houthulst Forest, who continually endured the full force of the British and French artillery, seemingly intent on blasting a path through toward Bruges. Here the Saxons of 58. ID (and for a time, the 40. ID alongside them) endured arguably the worst hell they had yet faced, defending one of the most gruesomely devastated stretches of the Ypres battlefield in the face of relentless heavy shelling, copious use of lethal gas, vile weather and determined infantry assaults. After a desperately needed relief in late October, 58. ID returned to the ruined forest in the aftermath of the offensive and struggled to render the sector defensible and habitable for the winter. Although they left the forest for the last time that year at the end of November, the unfortunate Saxons had to leave their rest billets on Christmas Eve to occupy the likewise devastated Poelkapelle-Langemarck sector.

In 1918 the still formidable 58. ID seemed destined to serve in the upcoming German offensives, and spent most of February training for the *kampfdivision* role. Instead it gradually took over the entire 7km front of the former *Gruppe Staden* (including Houthulst Forest) by 3 April, and advanced only when the enemy retired under pressure from the *Georgette* offensive south of Ypres. In mid-May it was sent to defend the gains of *Georgette* on the infamous *Kemmelberg* (Mont Kemmel). Although earmarked and trained in July for the final *Hagen* offensive in Flanders, the demoralised 58. ID was withdrawn in early August when *Hagen* was cancelled. With Germany now entirely on the defensive, the division was committed to shoring up the front west of Cambrai near Bullecourt. For the rest of the year it was gradually driven further and further east, holding successive German defensive lines as its combat strength steadily dwindled in the ongoing absence of replacements. The division ended the war at Ligny west of Namur and marched back to Germany after the armistice, crossing the Rhine on 27 November and entraining in early December for Leipzig where it was finally demobilised.

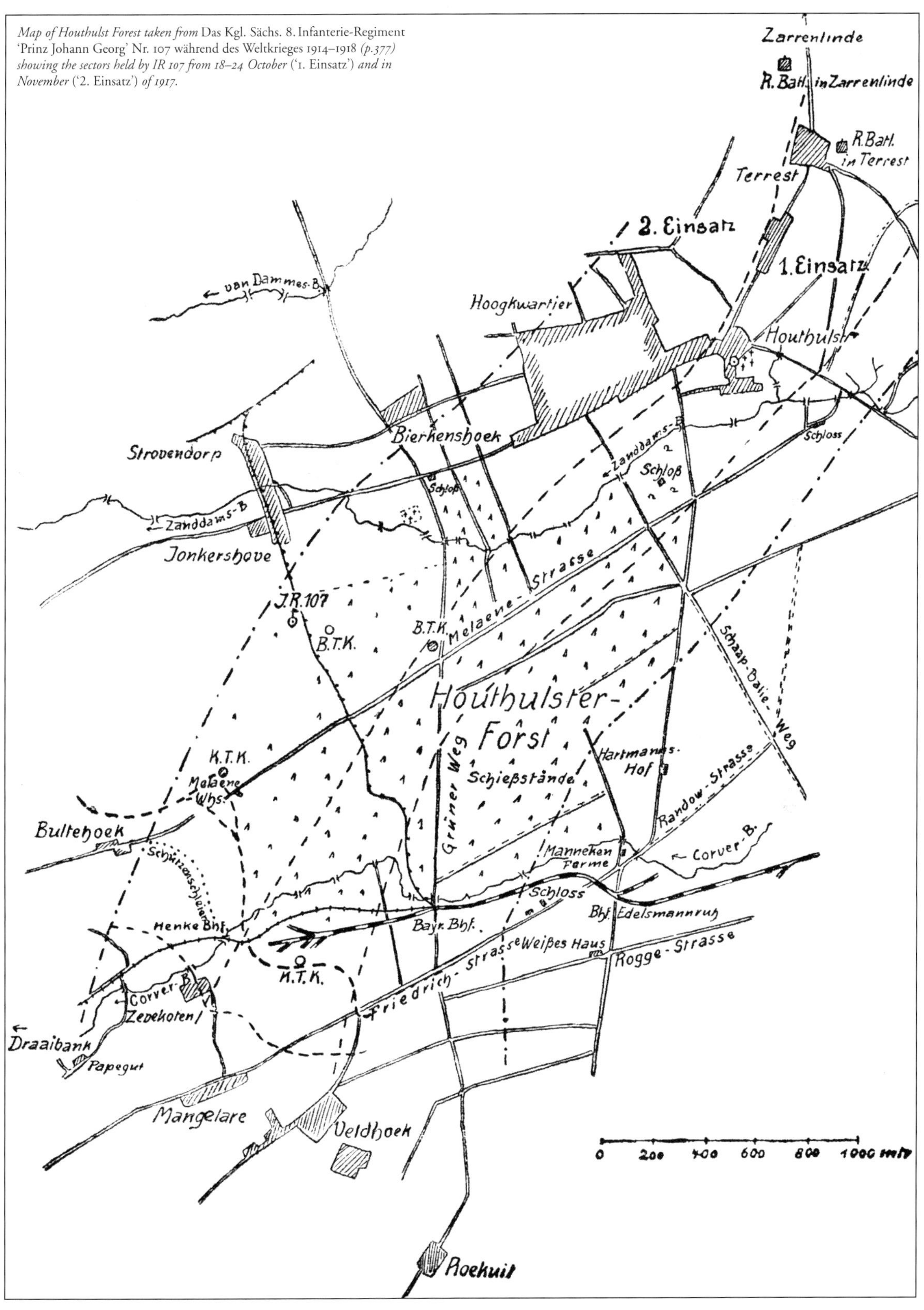

Map of Houthulst Forest taken from Das Kgl. Sächs. 8. Infanterie-Regiment 'Prinz Johann Georg' Nr. 107 während des Weltkrieges 1914–1918 *(p.377) showing the sectors held by IR 107 from 18–24 October* ('1. Einsatz') *and in November* ('2. Einsatz') *of 1917.*

An ominous arrival in Flanders

The trains carrying the elements of the division arrived piecemeal at Torhout and Zedelgem between 10 and 14 October around 120 hours after entraining on the Eastern Front. Due to the critical situation in Flanders, there was no time for the expected rest period – even while struggling to detrain at Torhout station the troops came under sporadic artillery fire.

Briefing on conditions in the west was limited to army orders describing the 'bite and hold' tactics now in general use by the British to counter German defense in depth. The new arrivals were told that a British brigade would attack with three of its four battalions deployed as successive waves and the fourth in reserve. Upon reaching its limited objective each battalion would dig in with heavy machine-guns to repel the expected counterattack of the *eingreif* troops, before the next battalion made a further bound forward to repeat the process.

Army orders recommended faster counterattacks, deployment of the *eingreifdivisionen* closer to the front and stronger counter-battery artillery to protect them. On the ground however there would be no effective answer to 'bite and hold' before the offensive was halted by the weather.

Under current defensive doctrine the front line was a thinly occupied *postenlinie* (outpost line) based around a few machine-gun nests, intended to be held only against local attacks and raids. A few hundred metres beyond was the HWL or *hauptwiderstandslinie* (main line of resistance), occupied by the bulk of the *kampfbataillon* under direct command of the KTK (see p.190). This line was supported by numerous heavy machine-guns and light *minenwerfers* forming interlocking fields of fire without gaps. Even field artillery could be deployed to reinforce the HWL; this would become routine in 1918 as an anti-tank measure. Further back was the *bereitschaftsbataillon* deployed in depth under command of the BTK. The rearward artillery zone contained not only the *reservebataillon* and *regimentsgefechtsstand* but also elements of the *eingreifdivision* with attached *stoßartillerie* (assault artillery) ready for use in counterattacks.

The *Houthulsterwald* (Houthulst Forest) was a wood 3–4km deep which had been firmly in German hands since October 1914. In October 1917 it was actively threatened from the front by the British and French, and later from the right flank by Belgian pressure from the inundated zone

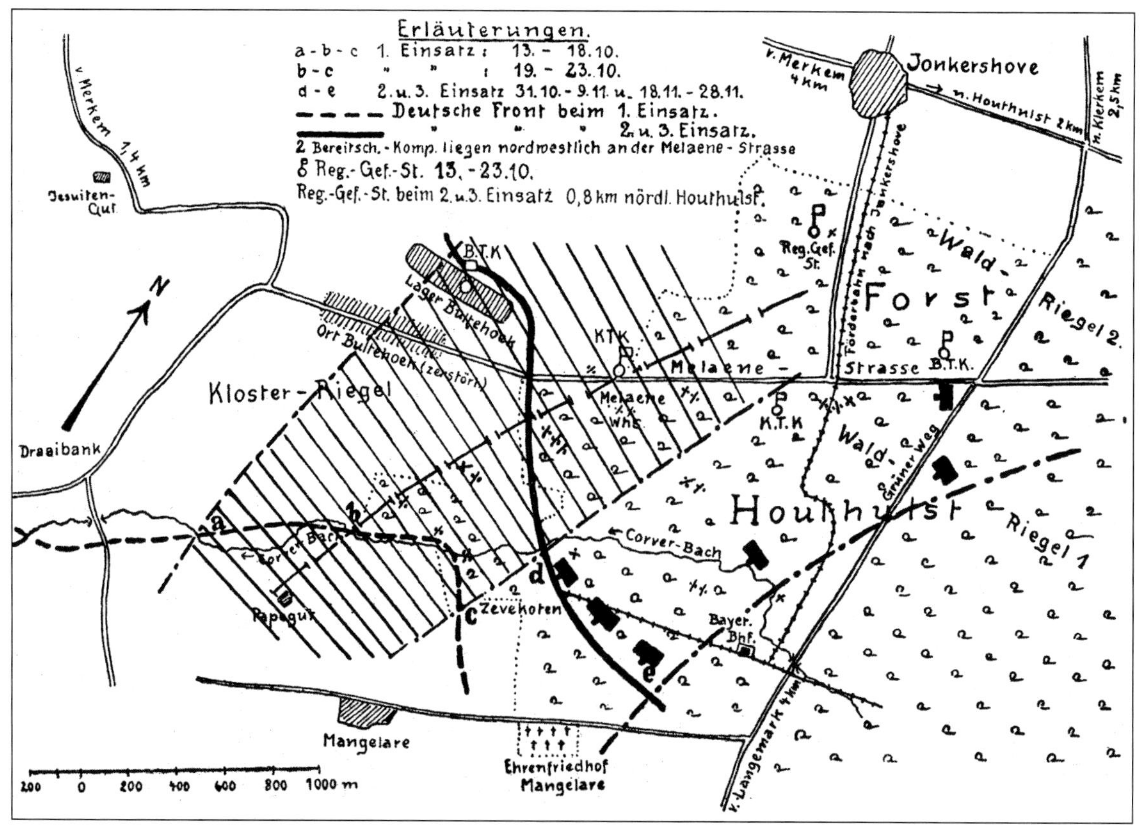

Map of successive sectors held by IR 106 in October–November 1917, also showing the ground lost in their absence on 26–27 October.

The *Melaene-Wirtshaus* (a ruined inn on *Melaene-Straße*) was used by IR 106 before housing the KTK of IR 104 (40. ID) from 19–27 October.

further west. The forest was crossed from southwest to northeast by the *Melaene-Straße* (the present-day Melaenedreef), a major transport artery which suffered almost constant shelling. Near its junction with the north-south *Grüner Weg* (Groenebosdreef) lay a forward dressing station (*hauptverbandsplatz*) and BTK bunker. Just beyond the Corverbeek, *Grüner Weg* crossed a branch line of the Ypres–Staden–Torhout–Bruges railway near a station called the *Bayerischer Bahnhof*[1] on German maps. This line was connected to Jonkershove via a narrow-gauge field tramway. A little further south *Grüner Weg* crossed the *Friedrich-Straße* (Pottestraat) which ran parallel to *Melaene-Straße*.

The only route through the forest which was halfway passable at this point was the *Melaene-Straße*. Around half of the forest facing the enemy had been reduced to a muddy ruin, and the trees thoroughly poisoned by frequent gas attacks. The splintered and fallen trees, bound together with tangles of barbed wire, formed an exceptionally tough obstacle line, backed up by what remained of the rearward switch lines and concrete bunkers constructed in previous years. While the bunkers outlasted the largely obliterated trenches, their foundations in the swampy ground were tenuous and they could and did overturn or shatter under super-heavy artillery fire. Merely to hold the positions on the devastated side of the forest (even without infantry attacks) was a dreadful ordeal, and any attempt at movement exhausting and dangerous.

The battle for Houthulst Forest

While other units of 58. ID were still en route to Flanders, IR 106 was immediately sent forward on 13 October to reinforce the Prussian 119. Infanterie-Division, accompanied by a single guide. During the arduous approach march through the mire in heavy rain many men stumbled into flooded shellholes in the dark, and the regiment took painful losses to artillery fire before even reaching its new positions. The forward zone lay between the Bultehoek to *Melaene-Wirtshaus* road and the Corverbeek, with the enemy 200–300 metres beyond. On the first day here 4. / 106 suffered a direct hit while awaiting orders from the KTK at *Melaene-Wirtshaus*, losing twenty dead and twenty-one wounded. Worse followed on 15 October, a day of heavy shelling with gas and H.E. during which one bunker held by IR 106 was destroyed and a second overturned. Despite repeated attempts and assistance from *pioniere* of 119. ID, it took four days to rescue the two survivors trapped underneath – one of them now showing signs of 'mental disturbance'. On 16 October another bunker was destroyed when an incendiary shell through the vision slit detonated the ammunition inside; a French attempt to advance in the wake of this disaster was repelled with hand grenades and machine-guns, as was a second attempt the following day.

Meanwhile the rest of 58. ID had arrived and was ordered to relieve 119. ID on 16 October. This was cancelled at the last minute in favour of inserting 58. ID between 119. ID and the Württemberg 27. ID, under the command of the Garde-Reserve-Korps (*Gruppe Staden*). Despite darkness, thick fog and heavy shelling this difficult operation was successfully completed on the night of 18–19 October almost without casualties. IR 106 now held a reduced sector on the right, with IR 107 in the centre and RIR 103 on the left. Simultaneously 119. ID was relieved by 40. ID (and 27. ID by 26. RD), placing the forest almost entirely in Saxon hands. Further back, the divisional Feldartillerie-Regiment 115 gradually deployed between 16 and 22 October in wretched open positions. Where the ground was too swampy, guns had to be mounted on plank foundations and ammunition kept in raised boxes covered with roofing felt. Survival here depended on camouflage and regular movement. With telephone lines frequently broken, the gunners had to organise their own forward patrols to locate the friendly and enemy lines.

20 and 21 October saw increasingly intense shelling with aerial observation, heavy use of gas and a weak French probe against 40. ID as the enemy visibly massed for a major attack. The subsequent 'Action of 22 October 1917' was the worst day of the battle for 58. ID, as one French and three British divisions set out to clear Poelkapelle and gain a foothold in Houthulst Forest. From 3am a huge swathe of the German line including the whole divisional sector was subjected to devastating drumfire, and visibility greatly reduced by smoke and rain. Infantry attacks followed shortly before 7am. West of Veldhoek the French 1re Division d'Infanterie seized largely undefended ground on the edge of the IR 104 and IR 106 outpost zones, then moved to assist the advance of British 35th Division into the forest. Although far beyond their objective line, some of the enemy broke through the lines of RIR 103 as far as the *Bayerischer Bahnhof*, forcing the flanks of IR 107 on their right and Württemberg RIR 121 on their left to fall back in support. By 8am the enemy had stopped to dig in. The threatened area was quickly reinforced by II. / 106 and II. / 107, while Württemberg Grenadier-Regiment 123 stood ready in support. Amid a ferocious artillery duel, a divisional counterattack was launched at 6.30am on 23 October under overall command of Major von Krauss (RIR 103). The enemy was found beyond the old German outpost line in shellholes about 50m south of *Friedrich-Straße*, and after bloody fighting throughout the day they were still there at nightfall. Relief of 58. ID by 35. ID (its designated *eingreifdivision*) began that evening, with 58. ID assuming the *eingreif* role. As such its infantry were frequently moved around behind the front and had no opportunity to rest and recuperate.

Krankenträger (stretcher-bearer) Paul Kahlert of 1. / RIR 103 sent this photo to his mother and siblings with the following comments: *"here I am sending you a view of the embankment near the* Bayerischer Bahnhof*. On 22 October I was stuck bandaging [the wounded] behind this derailed carriage. There I spent the most dreadful hours of my life. Please put the card aside for me."*

German aerial photo taken at 4000m just north of Draaibank on 4 November 1917. The western edge of the forest is visible on the right.

As usual the divisional artillery were actively engaged for longer. On 28 October 2. Battr. / FAR 115 had a narrow escape at its much-shelled position near the Pierkenshoek crossroads north of the forest. The battery had just taken delivery of 800 rounds of gas ammunition when the British drumfire erupted again. With no time to store the gas shells safely, half of them were dumped in old shot-up stables where hundreds of high explosive shells were already stored. Inevitably one of the stable buildings took a direct hit and erupted in flames. The resulting thick cloud of smoke violently punctuated by fizzling cartridges and exploding shells attracted still heavier enemy shelling. Knowing that if the fire reached the gas shells it could put every battery downwind out of action, the gunners of 2. / 115 rushed from their dugouts to fight the fire in defiance of their battery commander's orders. Frantically hauling the shell baskets away from the stables and throwing buckets of water from shellholes into the flames, they somehow succeeded in their seemingly suicidal task. Many promotions and decorations followed. *Zugführer* (two-gun section leader) Leutnant d.R. Seyfert was recommended for the Saxon *Albrechtsorden*, only to be killed by artillery fire the next day.

Houthulst Forest in the aftermath

On 31 October the 58. ID returned to Houthulst Forest, relieving 35. ID. During the preceding week the French had substantially pushed back 40. ID in their last offensive effort of the battle, so that the front line now bent sharply northwards at Zevekoten and the *Melaene-Wirtshaus* barely remained in German hands (see map p.206). IR 107 was on the right, IR 106 in the centre and RIR 103 on the left, each holding a front of about 750 metres with a *hauptwiderstandslinie* and an outpost zone 200–300 metres in depth. The rudimentary 'positions' were now in an even worse state than before. There was no barbed wire at all to protect the muddy shellholes occupied by IR 107, but the flooding was so severe that a renewal of the offensive in this sector was (correctly) considered highly unlikely. Both IR 106 and 107 sent patrols forward at night to the ruined bunkers in the swamp, where they fired off signal flares to simulate the existence of a garrison. Offensive action was now limited to shelling and raids by very small groups aimed at taking prisoners.

On 6 November the brigade commander Oberst von Zeschau appealed urgently for relief, stating that the infantry could only hold out for a maximum of two days at reduced capacity. His infantry regiments were now below half strength and the health of the troops very poor, with numerous cases of gastric illness due to the insanitary conditions. The division was relieved on 9 November and finally received a proper rest and refit for the first time since arriving in Flanders. Due to a shortage of trucks, IR107 was forced to march all the way to Bruges for its much-needed delousing.

Somewhat refreshed, the division returned to Houthulst Forest on 18 November and found the situation slightly improved. The ghastly shellhole line was now fully wired and hot food regularly available. Patrols went out regularly, not only to monitor the enemy's work on their own line but also to salvage the wealth of abandoned materiel in No Man's Land. Even in this 'quiet' period IR106 suffered losses on the first day to a grievous accident. In their absence the *pioniere* of 35. ID had rigged concrete bunkers in the sector for demolition in case they had to be abandoned to the enemy, and IR176 had failed to warn IR106 when handing over the line. Consequently the crates containing the demolition charges were used as seating, or propped against the wall alongside cases of signal flares. In one bunker occupied by 3./106 a falling candle lit a flare and in turn set off the charges. The ten men inside died instantly and were virtually incinerated, while another man in the doorway was hurled out by the pressure wave and survived to report the tragedy.

The regimental history of IR106 includes this vivid description of Houthulst Forest in November 1917:

Countless metre-deep shellholes, torn into the ground by the heaviest calibre [shells], *filled to the rim with dirty-brown or sulphur-yellow liquid mud. Splintered, half-submerged, uprooted tree-stumps. Sparse wreckage of duckboards and planks. Grotesquely bent and turned-up rails. Churned up gravel embankments. A few ungainly concrete boxes hit by the heaviest calibres, displaced or half-overturned. Houthulst Forest at dusk. The enemy fire on the company sector has died down. Now the falling shells sweep over their heads deeper into the wood. They are directed at the brave men who are hurrying to the front with ammunition, food and the mail from home. – Mud-covered figures with grey, sunken faces show themselves at the entrances of the concrete bunkers.*

The typically devastated and flooded area around one of the bunkers at Houthulst Forest in November 1917.

A designated *mannschafts-unterstand* (other ranks' dugout) of the *Flandern-I-Stellung* on the forest's eastern edge, in use by IR 106.

The KTK bunker of IR 106 near the Jonkershove road (see map p.206), camouflaged from aerial observation with branches and wreckage.

Oberstleutnant Georg Bock von Wülfingen (middle), commander of IR 106 since April 1917, with his staff at the *regiments-gefechtsstand.*

A member of IR 107 crouches in a shellhole at a *pionier-park* (engineering supply dump) in the dead forest.

The only Saxons left in the forest on 21 December 1917 were radio operators of Divisions-Funker-Abteilung 14, seen here at a KTK.

Now one can stretch one's limbs again for a little while. Gas alarm posts and signal flare posts will be reinforced. A section makes ready to relieve the isolated concrete boxes in the completely swamped outpost zone. Then the ration carriers approach from the rear between the shot-up trees. Rushing, jumping – their pace hampered by the tenacious mud – laden with sandbags, canteens and pails of food. Around the water-filled craters they go to the individual concrete boxes and sentry holes. Only a short halt. Empty canteens and mail for home are pressed into their hands. A brief exchange of greetings and on they go again. They have at least brought glad tidings. The regiment is to be relieved and go for a rest period at Torhout.[2]

This relief came for the infantry on the night of 28–29 November. During the subsequent rest and training period the troops were accommodated in the area of Zedelgem, Aartrijke, Torhout and Ruddervoorde, with opportunities to visit Gent and Bruges. Training focused on the expected renewal of mobile warfare in spring 1918, and included such novelties as shooting with light machine-guns while advancing. This pleasant interlude came to an unwelcome end on Christmas Eve, when advance parties went to reconnoitre the division's new sector. The relief (of Württemberg 204. ID) was completed over the next two days.

Three *feldgrauen* enjoy the view from the church tower in Aartrijke.

At Poelkapelle and Langemarck

The new sector lay in a lifeless, heavily cratered wasteland east of Poelkapelle, with the ghastly remains of Houthulst Forest clearly visible further to the right. The *hauptwiderstandslinie* ran along the southward road from Schaap Balie with a weak outpost line occupied only at night about 150 metres further forward. IR 106 was in the centre holding *Abschnitt A Mitte* (see map below), north of the road which led from the enemy-held rubble of Poelkapelle to Westroosebeke and beyond to Hooglede. Both IR 106 and RIR 103 on its right enjoyed the additional security of partial flooding in front of their lines, partially compensating for a lack of barbed wire. This was less pronounced for IR 107 on the left flank, which instead benefitted from the greater concentration of concrete bunkers in the ruins of Spriet. Each regiment held about 1km of frontage, with positions inevitably consisting merely of shellholes and shelter from the elements limited to sheets of corrugated iron. Bunkers in the forward area mostly housed HQ elements and machine-gunners. The sector had seen intense fighting and was still judged at risk due to the value of the high ground at Westrozebeke. The *hauptwiderstandslinie* however was lower than the enemy line (about 500 metres away), so that movement by daylight was nearly impossible. At first a persistent light frost kept the ground firm, and the floodwater in No Man's Land was frozen solid. The thaw began on 12 January, followed by rain three days later, flooding the shellholes and turning the ground back into a swamp interspersed with large areas of standing water. Soaked to the skin, sentries were forced to stand upright to avoid drowning and became dangerously exposed. Under such conditions an enemy attack was judged impossible, and the temporary evacuation of parts of the forward zone was authorised.

Each regiment was temporarily divided into a *kampfstaffel* (fighting detachment) and *ruhestaffel* (resting detachment) of six rifle companies each, which changed places every four days. Due to these frequent reliefs and the exhausting 12km march between the front and the rest area around Hooglede, it proved impractical to hold training exercises for the 'resting' troops; instead sport was used to loosen

The various sectors occupied by IR 106 between Christmas 1917 and mid-May 1918.

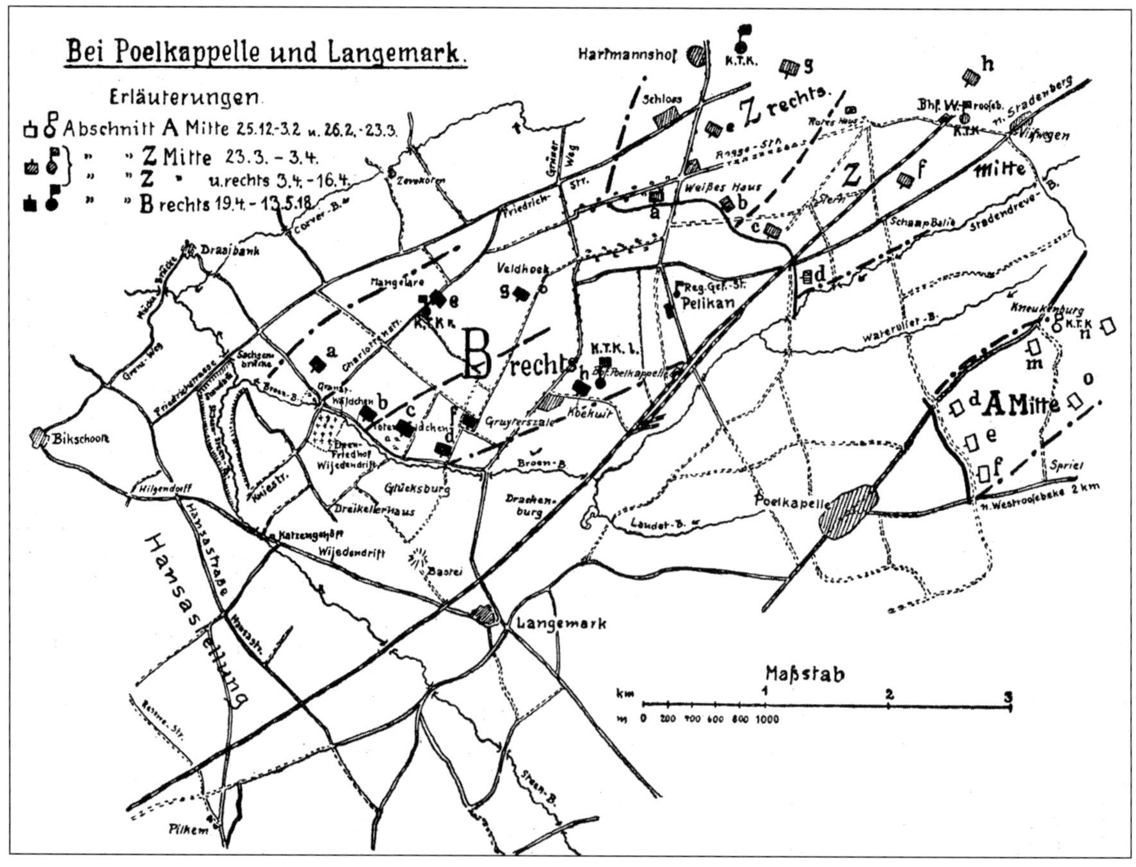

A full company of IR 106 with its two MG08/15 light machine-guns. 58. ID received twelve per infantry regiment on arrival in Flanders.

up muscles stiffened by days spent crouching in wet shell-holes. Nevertheless, the health of the troops was poor, with many cases of skin, foot and gastric complaints; this would gradually improve with the approach of spring. Offensive action was predictably limited to patrols and small raids, as both sides struggled to restore such basic facilities as dugouts, communication trenches and barbed wire. As at Houthulst Forest, much valuable materiel was regularly salvaged from the battlefield, and patrols often returned with rifles collected from the dead. One of the division's first construction projects was a simple wire fence, erected along the divisional front at night in the first week of January, and intended to prevent men wandering (accidentally or otherwise) into No Man's Land or even into the enemy lines in the near-featureless landscape.

Losses in this period were limited but nonetheless tragic, caused by routine shelling or accidents. For example Ltn. d.R. Wittrock, the regimental *minenwerfer* officer of IR106, was fatally injured on 14 January when he slipped and fell awkwardly onto his camera while leaping over a trench. The enemy artillery remained moderately active and was never entirely silent for long. On the Saxon side FAR115 limited itself to nuisance fire, bombardment of visible enemy traffic and occasional support for offensive patrols aimed at taking prisoners. Between 8 and 11 January the British artillery grew far more aggressive, with occasional hurricane barrages and long-range shelling of Westrozebeke. German retaliation restored the situation to normal, but not before a surprise attack by a heavy battery against 5. Battr./FAR115 on 11 January with no discernible pre-registration. Two guns were knocked out and others lightly damaged, though no crew were harmed as the battery was not in action at the time. It was suspected that 5./115 had attracted attention by firing more than usual since December, while in use for the practical gunnery training of H.M. Prince Ernst Heinrich of Saxony (see pp. 216–217)

Three examples will serve to illustrate the lively patrol activity in this period. On 21 January a group from the *sturmtrupp* of I. Batl./IR106 under Uffz. Thiessen was lost behind enemy lines and written off as captured or killed. After ten hours they reappeared the following morning in the neighbouring divisional sector at Houthulst Forest, having evaded capture by stealth and intermittently feigning death. Their report was reckoned highly valuable and earned them commendation and decorations. On 2 February RIR103 launched a larger scale trench raid codenamed 'Franz Theodor' with artillery support. The raiders breached the British wire and returned with a British machine-gun plus a corporal and a private soldier of the 35th Division, confirming an identification previously obtained by Vfw. Weiss of RIR103 on 24 January. The ironically named *'Glückskind'* (child of fortune) launched by IR107 against a British blockhouse on 1 February was far less successful, owing to German artillery drop-shorts scattering the raiders.

BIOGRAPHICAL NOTES

HRH Prince Ernst Heinrich of Saxony (9 December 1896–14 June 1971), the youngest of three sons of King Friedrich August III, held the rank of oberleutnant with Leibgrenadier-Regiment 100 at the outbreak of war. In September 1914 he joined the staff of XIX. AK, and later claimed to have visited the British trenches opposite IR 107 during the prolonged post-Christmas truce period there. He transferred to the staff of 24. RD just in time for the Battle of the Somme, and spent six weeks as company commander of 9./RIR 104 in Galicia in May–June 1917. After convalescing from an illness, he persuaded his father to let him command troops on an active front – a position denied to his older brothers. Assigned to FAR 115 in Flanders in October 1917, he joined them in the field in December after retraining as an artillery officer. In May 1918 he took up a squadron command with the Garde-Reiter-Regiment in northern Russia and the Baltic, finally returning with them to Saxony in December 1918. After the war the prince was involved in conservative-monarchist politics. Repeatedly arrested in the Nazi period, he was saved by his royal status. The memoirs quoted here were written in exile in Ireland near the end of his life.

"My father had me transferred to the 58. Division, whose commander, Graf Vitzthum[6], enjoyed his special confidence. This formation lay in Belgian Flanders facing Ypres, and I was immediately ordered to the artillery school at Thimougies near Kortrijk in Belgium, where I received theoretical and practical training in this interesting arm of service. Then I was assigned command of 9. Batterie / Artillerieregiment 115, which was equipped with 10.5cm howitzers. I took it over at Poelkapelle in front of Ypres. There we had a deep dugout, in which the battery crew was relatively safe from heavy calibre shelling. We lived in it like rabbits in a burrow. When there was nothing to do, we sat in the narrow little rooms with bad air, lighted by acetylene lamps. There was a main exit and a small emergency side exit. As we were 'below' one day due to intense shelling by English heavy calibre guns, we suddenly heard a heavy impact which made the whole dugout tremble and shake. A pressure wave extinguished all the lamps. It was pitch-black, even in the entrance gallery. Then we heard a trickling sound, which grew louder and louder. We rushed over and established under the light of our pocket torches that our entrance gallery had taken a heavy direct hit and we were buried alive. So as not to be cut off from the side exit by the slipping earth, we rushed out at once via the escape hole, as it would be called in a rabbit's burrow. The battery was all in order, there were just a lot of small impact craters to be seen; the telephone line was also cut. When it was quiet again, we went straight to work shovelling the entrance clear.

Naturally the enemy had found the battery's exact location by observation, sound and flash location. We received regular thrashings, which were supposed to silence us as far as possible.

I received the order to dispose of an English battalion staff by means of gas. This task was highly disagreeable to me, but orders are orders. … So I observed the British command dugout and ranged the gun in exactly with high explosive shells. When the concrete blockhouse was occupied, I shot first with irritant gas and then with the lethal Green Cross, whereby the garrison was finished off – to my consolation probably very quickly.

As strange as it sounds, it was a relief that the enemy was likewise constantly seeking our lives, otherwise one would have had the feeling of committing murder. One felt no hatred or aversion for the so-called enemy. Here men stood facing each other, with a dispassionate duty on both sides to destroy one another. What insanity!

From Poelkapelle the battery came to Houthulst Forest, not far from Langemarck. This was the area where in 1914 in an un-

HRH Prince Ernst Heinrich (left, uniformed as an *oberleutnant* of LGR 100) in the dugout of his *'Prinzenbatterie'* in January 1918.

The prince with one of his battery's four 10.5cm light howitzers, deployed in a rough open position in the dead forest in spring 1918.

paralleled action the German volunteer regiments … bled to death in front of the battle-hardened English troops. In 1915 the same sector was the scene of the first gas attack, which caught the French troops there wholly unprepared and unprotected. At that time the Flandernschlacht *raged there: the tremendous artillery fire ploughed up the ground completely and turned the area into one continuous crater field. Gas shells did the rest. In Houthulst Forest not a single tree remained which was not splintered and dead. No bush sprouted, there were neither grass nor flowers, the birds shunned the area completely. The fury of war had not only struck humanity, but also wiped out every other form of life. Death permeated the entire landscape. …*

Close to the new fire position in Houthulst Forest I came upon a small infantry bunker with a floor space of only 25 square metres. When I entered it in the evening, I saw a strange phosphorescent glow on the ground at the entrance. We investigated the next morning and discovered that it was one of the fallen, who had lain there perhaps since 1914 and was only lightly covered with earth. However when we picked up the corpse to bury it, the body crumbled to dust. …

Houthulst Forest was a 'windy corner'.[7] *We received fire of all kinds, very often from medium artillery with gas shells. The open gasmask* [canister] *was our constant companion. Once we were subjected to gas shelling from the afternoon until well into the night and had to wear gasmasks throughout. That was almost unbearable, because breathing was greatly restricted; it was warm and musty inside the mask and stank of leather and rubber. The choice however was to endure these discomforts or die on the spot.*

English flyers frequently attacked the battery from a height of 50 metres. They dropped numerous small bottle-sized bombs. I shot at them myself with a machine-gun fitted with ring sights, but none was ever shot down – although at such a low height I certainly scored some hits. Most unpleasant of all was the shelling of the so-called klauengeschütze.[8] *These were long-barrelled 28cm guns mounted on railway carriages. On several occasions we were graced by these big boxes, often striking only 30 to 50 metres away from our bunker, which trembled and swayed on its foundations each time. After the first bombardment we added a two metre layer of stones to the roof of the bunker, but had to accept that in the event of a direct hit of such a calibre the whole bunker would burst open. However it did offer protection against splinters and shrapnel, with which we were frequently bombarded.*

With a floor space of only five square metres and a two to two and a half metre ceiling I managed to shelter 25 men. We stood so close together that hardly anyone could move. Each night four men at a time took turns to sit down, we called it the proscenium box. I was the only one who had no-one over me, since I had the telephone and maps beside me and often had to write it down when an order was received. Instead however I lay so to speak at the breast of one of my gun commanders, whose arm in turn lay across me. We slept like this for almost three weeks. This brave unteroffizier *was a miner in the Lugau-Oelsnitzer coalfield. We had long conversations; soon I knew his whole life. That was simply the comradeship of the front. Everyone had the same worries, was constantly in the same danger and each was reliant on the other. Everyone lived from one day to the next, no-one gave a thought to the future or the past. The present alone was supreme.*[9]

Hooglede, a major billeting area used by the 58. ID which was still less damaged than its bigger neighbour Roulers in early 1918. On the back Paul Kahlert of RIR 103 wrote home on 29 January 1918 as follows: *"Here I am sending you a view of Hooglede, where I am staying at present. At midday on the 28th the English bombarded a dummy tank here from the air. Our regiment had eight dead in the process."*

This period also saw significant aerial activity, opening on 6 January with the year's first appearance of a British aircraft directing hostile artillery fire. A German aircraft which attempted to intervene was forced down by fifteen enemy machines. Enemy aircraft were shot down over the 58. ID sector on 18, 24 and 25 January; on this last occasion an enemy observation balloon broke its moorings and flew over the Saxon lines, while two hostile aircraft were downed. As mentioned by *Krankenträger* Paul Kahlert of RIR 103 (see photo above), Hooglede was attacked by British bombers on 28 January, inflicting heavy losses on the 'resting' troops there. The regimental history of RIR 103 does not give casualty figures, but that of IR 106 records five dead and seven wounded. The following day an enemy aircraft was brought down east of Stadendreef Chateau and secured by a patrol from IR 106. Most lastingly significant however was the crashed British aircraft seen just in front of the enemy lines opposite IR 107 when the division arrived in December; this became a persistent landmark and target for patrols, as it was guarded by a small British sentry detail.

On 2 February the division was relieved by Württemberg 204. ID and sent for a planned four weeks of training for mobile warfare in the area south of Bruges. This included divisional wargaming of the breakthrough battle with all staffs down to battalion level, and two massive corps exercises on 16 and 23 February in which the entire 58. ID conducted a simulated breakthrough alongside two other divisions. At lower level individual infantrymen were drilled in musketry and use of the compass, while small units were trained in fire and movement techniques such as rushing through the enemy's defensive barrage zone and both attack and defence of isolated pockets. Both light and heavy machine-gun crews practiced close support of the infantry attack, as well as anti-tank defence with armour-piercing ammunition. Every effort was made to ensure that the tactical principles of Ludendorff's planned spring offensive were internalised at every level of organisation from section up to corps.

This training was cut short on 26 February when 58. ID was sent to relieve 204. ID again in the Poelkapelle sector. They found ground conditions much improved (due to drier weather) and the enemy increasingly jumpy in expectation of a potential German offensive. The German *hinterland* came in for scattered shelling every night, and the area immediately behind the front line suffered intense barrages at daybreak to catch any troops massing for an assault. Patrol activity was lively, overwhelmingly from the German side. For instance on 18 March the *sturmtrupps* of I. and III. Batl./RIR 103 conducted a raid code-named *'Felix'* which brought in three Scottish prisoners from the 1st Division.[3] A major operation by IR 106 code-named *'Speiseträger'* (food carrier) against a British post on the Poelkapelle–Kneukenburg road was far less successful. This involved six sections from the *sturmtrupps* of I. and III. Batl./IR 106, reinforced by two light machine-gun sections and a demolition team from Pionier-Kompanie 115. Precisely at the appointed time for the raid on the evening of 3 March the enemy opened a ferocious defensive barrage and *'Speiseträger'* was called off. At first it was assumed that careless telephone conversations had betrayed the operation, but it was later discovered that much of the population of Roulers knew all about it. The regimental history laments *"seemingly incurable German talkativeness and indiscretion"*.[4] A renewed attempt was made on 7 March, but failed when the raiders encountered a newly erected and formidable wire obstacle. Due to the non-appearance of the assigned *pioniere*, the party lacked the wire cutters and charges needed to breach it. They returned empty-handed, little comforted by the fact that their supporting light *minenwerfer* and heavy machine-gun barrage had been laid down precisely as planned. A third attempt at *'Speiseträger'* followed on 20 March, with some initial success. The raiders reached their objective, seized four Tommies and beat off a group of eight to ten more who rushed to intercept them. However while the light *minenwerfers* and heavy machine-guns again performed flawlessly, the box barrage laid down by the artillery came down short in No Man's Land, hitting both the returning raiders and the two rifle and two light machine-gun sections which were covering their flank and rear. Eight men were killed or missing and a further five wounded, all due to friendly fire. All four prisoners were killed or wounded and had to be left behind. The bodies of those slain in this misadventure would not be recovered until the advance on 21 April.

The opening of the *Kaiserschlacht* on 21 March forced OHL to economise on troops on the currently inactive fronts. On the right of 58. ID, the Prussian 11. Reserve-Division was ordered to be withdrawn without replacement, and the Saxon division to extend northwards accordingly on the night of 23–24 March. This was followed by the withdrawal of 38. ID on its left, obliging 58. ID to extend southwards on the night of 2–3 April to occupy the entire (approximately 7km) frontage of the former *Gruppe Staden* alone. IR 106 was now on the right at Houthulst Forest, RIR 103 in the centre and IR 107 on the left a few hundred metres south of the positions it held in January (this time

On the back of this photo of his billet, Leutnant d.R. Hans Rüger of Reserve-Infanterie-Regiment 103 whimsically describes it to his parents at home as a *'lustschloss'* (pleasure palace) and expresses concern that it is likely to become a *'luftschloss'* (castle in the air).

on higher and drier ground). When the *Georgette* offensive around Armentières was launched on 9 April, the severely overstretched division was also expected to be ready to advance as soon as the enemy began to withdraw from the Ypres Salient. Under these uncertain conditions patrol activity was intense, but German raiders frequently found forward sentry posts unoccupied. A failed British raid on 11 April left a prisoner from 18th Battalion / King's (Liverpool) Regiment in the hands of RIR 103, identifying the 30th Division (recently mauled at St. Quentin). At Houthulst Forest, IR 106 confirmed that Belgian troops lay opposite. Meanwhile the Saxon lines were repeatedly gassed, and their rear areas subjected to heavy shelling. On 13 April the enemy artillery was so quiet that 116. Infanterie-Brigade ordered the infantry to establish whether the withdrawal had begun. A four-man patrol from 9. / 106 got within 200 metres of the enemy line before they were all wounded by small-arms fire. Seven unarmed men who bravely went out to rescue their comrades were permitted to bandage them and carry them back to the German lines without interference from the Belgians. An officer's patrol from 6. and 7. / 107 was far more successful, pouncing on a three-man advanced post and bringing back a British prisoner from the previously unidentified 41st Division.

The anticipated enemy withdrawal was carried out with remarkable stealth on 16 April, and discovered by a patrol led by Ltn. Wagner of 10. / 107 on the division's extreme left flank about 3pm. Uncertain and taken by surprise, the divisional staff finally gave all regiments the codeword *'Blücher'* to begin the pursuit around 6pm. Despite pitch darkness, treacherous ground without landmarks and resistance from rearguard machine-gun nests the Saxons made steady progress. By about 8pm IR 107 had reached the obliterated site of Poelkapelle, and later advanced as far as the Steenbeek, beyond which the enemy had dug in again – shattering initial hopes that they had retired beyond the Yser Canal. In the centre RIR 103 had occupied the unrecognisable remains of Langemarck, which were intermittently subjected to severe enemy shelling. On the right IR 106 had reached a point slightly north of the confluence of the Steenbeek and Broenbeek, before going to ground upon encountering the new and strongly defended Belgian front line.

To their great disgust the Saxons found the abandoned enemy positions full of unburied corpses, which had even been heaped up to form barricades covering the (naturally German-facing) entrances of the German bunkers reused by the British. Near Poelkapelle IR 107 discovered wrecked tanks lost in the autumn fighting, in which the crewmen still lay rotting. According to its regimental history, IR 106

Men of IR 107 near Westrozebeke, in the gun lines of FAR 115 (hence the pile of shell cases). Although this concrete blockhouse was originally concealed inside an existing brick building, it has since been largely stripped of its disguise by enemy shelling.

Pelikan or Egypt House, a three-room concrete pillbox housing the *regiments-gefechtsstand* of IR 106 in April–May 1918 (see map p.214).

alone buried 107 British and nine German dead, plus several others who could not be identified even by nationality. RIR 103 buried 320 corpses, 230 of them British. Many of these would be interred in German cemeteries. The regimental history of IR 106 vividly describes the grisly scene found at the bunker shown in the photo above, by all accounts already in a horrific state when it fell to the Guards Division on 9 October:

As the staff began bailing out the shellholes at the English aid post 'Egypt House', now Regiments-Gefechtsstand *Pelikan, a task at which the regimental commander and officers of the staff also diligently assisted, we found besides severed limbs a number of dead Tommies in the drained craters, which the medical personnel had disposed of in this simple manner. The stinking used dressings lay in a vast heap, and in a nearby funk-hole destroyed by a direct hit the half-decayed corpses of five Englishmen grinned at us.*[5]

Conversely, the regimental history gives the British credit for their well-maintained duckboard paths and creative use of camouflage. The Saxons marvelled at a metal observation post so convincingly disguised as to pass for a dead tree even at close range. Masses of abandoned machine-gun ammunition were eagerly plundered for the copper, with some diligent soldiers collecting enough to earn as much as 100 Marks each from the *sammelwesen* (salvage service). Rubber boots and mackintoshes were also prized, either for use or recycling of a material now very scarce in Germany. To general disappointment, there were very few tins of corned beef – a mundane staple to the British, but a great favourite of the Germans.

Abortive attempts to cross the Steenbeek began on 17 April and were called off two days later. Allocated as *eingreif-division*, the low-grade 83. ID proved an outright liability. Having been exclusively on the Eastern Front from October 1914 to March 1918 and only in Flanders for a week, it was wholly unprepared for local conditions and served only to create traffic jams in the rear. Desertion and even open insubordination were reported before it was withdrawn. After a further British withdrawal, IR 107 finally took the west bank on 27 April.

The relief of 58. ID began on 12 May. Although not critically depleted it was exhausted, and received replacements and a week's rest before it was committed to the infamous *Kemmelberg* (see *Fighting the Kaiser's War* for details and a personal account). Leaving Flanders in August, it was ground down in bloody defensive fighting near Cambrai and the subsequent retreat, before the survivors were finally able to return to Saxony.

H.M. the King of Saxony takes the salute of IR 106 during the divisional parade on 16 May 1918 at *Flugplatz* Abeele. This airfield near Izegem was the only large open space in the area where crop damage was not a concern. Due to delays, the monarch and his troops were still present for the inevitable enemy bombing raid on the aerodrome that afternoon and had to take cover together. Luckily there were no casualties.

Having mercifully survived his ordeal at Houthulst Forest, the subsequent spring advance and the *Kemmelberg*, Paul Kahlert wrote home to his parents in June 1918 from rest billets at Wevelgem. Sadly we do not know which of these medical orderlies from RIR 103 is him.

Chapter 12
Those who remained in Flanders

NCOs from Reserve-Infanterie-Regiment 243 tending the freshly decorated grave of their comrade Unteroffizier Emil Friedrich Krauss in Moorslede. Born in Mittweida, he was killed on 6 February 1915 – a day of routine trench warfare, while RIR 243 was holding the line immediately north of *Calvairewald*. Krauss is now buried in the mass *kameradengrab* at Langemark.

Those who remained in Flanders

Saxon Graves and Cemeteries

In the relentless mobile warfare of summer 1914 it was rarely possible to treat the fallen with the expected degree of military honour. Advancing units often had to leave the dead of both sides on the battlefield to be buried in haste by others following behind, so that their path was marked by a scattering of individual and mass graves with roughly improvised crosses. Despite the universal issue of *erkennungsmarken* (dog tags) many of the dead could not immediately be identified and were interred as 'unknown'. The expectation was that permanent cemeteries would be established at the end of a short and victorious war.

In the early stages of static trench warfare the dead were still generally buried in battlefield graves close to where they had fallen, potentially turning the entire trench system into a graveyard. However official acceptance of the need to plan for long-term occupation soon led to the creation of proper cemeteries behind the front. Initially these were established spontaneously at unit level with no design guidelines, higher organisation or thought for expansion. Such unplanned cemeteries soon came in for criticism, among others from landscape architects, for their undignified and unaesthetic appearance. It was widely felt that a military cemetery should convey an orderly unified impression and deeper significance, rather than being a mere collection of graves.

Like so many other initially improvised aspects of the war, the construction, layout and management of cemeteries became increasingly regulated over time. Although they always retained individual peculiarities due to size and location, common design elements soon developed. A wild variety of materials, shapes and designs for grave markers was gradually superseded by a simple uniformity of design within each cemetery, representing the common attachment of the soldiers (regardless of rank) to their unit even in death. This impression was reinforced by the orderly planting of decorative trees, bushes and flowers, and by the use of neat boundary walls or fences. Nevertheless each grave still had space for the planting of additional flowers as an individual expression of remembrance. The design of the main gateway was also unique to each cemetery, made of wood or brick and typically bearing the names of the unit and location together with a biblical or soldierly quotation. This gateway usually opened on a central avenue, with a high cross or a memorial at the far end.

When circumstances permitted, funerals were held with full military honours, attended by divisional chaplains, senior officers, regimental bands and a large honour party from the unit in question. While individual ceremonies were possible in routine trench warfare, battles were followed by mass funerals (provided the battlefield was in German hands). Printed images of these dignified occasions and of the well-ordered cemeteries were widely used to offer comfort and reassurance both to families at home and to comrades in the field, in the face of impersonal slaughter on a scale which threatened to rob individual tragedies and sacrifices of all meaning and identity. The hackneyed but emotionally necessary mythology of heroic death in battle[1] and the painstaking memorialisation of each individual as an integral part of his regiment's history sought to restore human dignity and identity to the relentless bodycount, and to motivate the living to fight and face death without fear as part of something larger than themselves.

In addition to cemeteries for units and arms of service, *sammelfriedhöfe* (gathering cemeteries) were established to give dignity to the dead with no other home – members of units with no cemetery in the area, the unidentified and the enemy. However it was the *regimentsfriedhöfe* (regimental cemeteries) which had the greatest emotional significance. The sense of comradeship and mutual belonging with the dead which was fostered there motivated painstaking efforts – and even personal sacrifice – to retrieve and identify bodies for burial with their regimental comrades. It also created sacred ground which had to be defended in order to keep faith with the unit's fallen. The enemy's perceived contempt for the unburied dead (see pp.105–106 and 221) prompted intense revulsion and anger, but the mass destruction of these sacred places in Flanders by shelling in 1917 produced a profound grief and despair.

After the war the dead from these devastated sites were systematically transferred to the surviving German cemeteries, with individual graves wherever possible. The gradual process of consolidation (in part due to the financial demands of ground rent imposed by host countries) culminated in 1955–1957 in transfer to huge mass graves in a small number of concentration cemeteries, where the burial of newly discovered German dead intermittently continues to this day. While these cemeteries are more numerous in France, in Belgian Flanders there are now only four – Vladslo, Hooglede, Langemarck and Menen. No trace of unit affiliation or original place of burial remains on their spartan grave markers.

The two Saxon corps in Flanders from 1914 to 1916 inevitably left thousands of dead in their operational areas. Since its front was static from the end of 1914 until its departure at the end of July 1916, XIX. AK established cemeteries early on at locations such as Quesnoy-sur-Deûle, Verlinghem, Lambersart and Lomme. The first cemeteries of XXVII. RK were expanded and new ones created after the advance of May 1915, when many unburied dead of both sides from 1914 were finally recovered; its main cemeteries were found (among others) at Broodseinde, Moorslede and In de Ster Cabaret. Outside these two corps, IR 105 (the sole Saxon regiment of Prussian 30. ID / XV. AK) buried many dead at *Drei Häuser* east of Hill 60 in 1915. The regimental cemetery of RIR 245 was known as Hollebos or Holle Bosch for its location in the (no longer extant) wood on the current Markizaatstraat north of Becelaere. Like most of its kind it was run by and for its regiment, but inevitably included a few other burials. Established early in 1915 when Holle Bosch still held the battery positions of 5./RFAR 54, it was enlarged that May. Even after RIR 245 left Flanders in 1916 its *friedhofskommando* remained on site led by Wehrmann Richard Frensch, until the British offensive in 1917 laid waste to Holle Bosch. In the following article from the veterans' newsletter *Was wir erlebten*, Frensch describes his typical working day.

A day with 245's *friedhofskommando*

Silent images of the war by Richard Frensch, Leipzig

Far from the bustle of publicity the friedhofskommando *of our regiment laboured close behind the front. Only occasionally did news of it reach those most closely concerned with its work in the homeland. For the task that it performed was a harrowing one – the last comradely service. And why shouldn't a few short lines also be devoted today to this unit, whose activity was so infinitely significant for thousands at home?*
It is 7 am. The totenholer *['corpse fetchers'] are not reporting for cemetery work today. Already at 4 am they were called to their sad duty in the trenches, to recover a comrade from the danger zone of fixed-line fire and shells in a self-made wooden handcart. Late yesterday evening the trench telephone had reported yet another dead man, who had been transported back to the* Gelbes Haus *[Yellow House]. Naturally after many months of positional warfare everyone knows this house, which is under enemy observation and only advisable to approach at night – during the day shrapnel has been known to be directed even at individual men. A yellow-stained wall fragment gives it its name, as ever soldier's parlance helps coin curious designations for official adoption. An estate that happens to be mov-*

Exterior view of the regimental cemetery of RIR 245 in Holle Bosch in March 1915, still within its original boundaries.

The same cemetery in spring 1915, now with a more elaborate fence around its original perimeter and new rows of graves already established outside it. Hidden among the trees on the right is the *'Feuerturm'*, a regimental dressing station during the First Battle of Ypres.

ed into at Easter thus becomes the Ostergut *[Easter Manor]. A house long-since smashed up by English sulphur shells*[2], *the* Stinkhaus. *A farmyard in which an old lime tree stands, the* Lindenhof *[Lime Farm]. A waterhole alive with toads, the* Unkenteich *[Toad Pond].*

The gardeners and helpers proceed to the nearby cemetery. There are no jobs for slackers in the kommando. *– The* ausgräberkommando *[exhumation party] receives precise instructions and heads off to its arduous work, requiring nerves of steel, at the sites of the regiment's previous battles – the 'contemplation of Becelaere', where there are still old trenches to be probed. It's the pride of the* kommando *to know each of our brave fallen is at the common resting place, where cross upon cross line up in alarming numbers. No wonder then that each man does his job all of his own accord with a certain detective interest. Already there is a comrade from the neighbouring division at the door of the orderly room with an enquiry whether his brother-in-law has been recovered yet. The lists do not show the man's name; so it's time for detective work. In the back and forth suddenly apropos of nothing mention is made of his conspicuously tall, strong build and full black beard. Stop, there we have it. The very same, so frequently pondered description leads to one man in the list of still unidentified dead from our first days at Becelaere. The corresponding grave number is quickly hit upon. The place of discovery matches, likewise the personal description. –"Do you also know of anything he may have had about him?"– A moment's thought. "I had given him a silver cigarette case before the mobilisation – it's about..." "Yes! That's also among the findings! So if the other objects match up, your brother-in-law is lying in grave 802, fell at B. to a neck shot on 29 October 1914 and was transferred to the* regimentsfriedhof *on 5 May 1915. The desired photograph can be taken in a couple of days after production of the cross ---" The telephone rattles. Railway station X reports the arrival of a wagonload of ornamental shrubs and roses, obtained by the thoughtful head of the* kommando *at a large local nursery as a gift of love for the heroes' graves. The telephone immediately transfers to the nearby* fuhrparkkolonne, *which helps us pick things up by horse and cart in such cases. ... An identification of the dead doesn't always go so smoothly; there is often the need for fresh exhumations, comparisons, dozens of queries, investigations and examinations, and heaps of files are built up on some of the dead before their identity is finally unquestionably established. The painter collects texts and further particulars for fresh crosses and the photographer brings completed grave pictures. With a few warm words these will be sent off as*

The white shield of the original entrance gate in front of the treeline reveals the extent of expansion in this photo from September 1915. The new graves now show a rigorously uniform design and arrangement, and the perimeter fence is neatly reinforced with barbed wire.

precious keepsakes to the relatives waiting in the homeland. Meanwhile the totenholer *have returned with their tragic burden; instead of one body they sadly bring two. An unscheduled English surprise barrage has left them in dire distress themselves. One of the dead is from my company. Poor wife, who is not yet aware that she is now a widow with four orphans. – A report is logged, the required notifications are made to the regiment, money, watch and wedding ring are forwarded against receipt to the* regimentszahlmeister[3] *to be sent on, and blood-soaked correspondence and family picture put in the grave with the body. At the same time the* divisionsgeistliche[4] *is asked by telephone to attend the funeral, and the time is communicated to the participating companies for the formation of the honour party. The mail carrier hands out the post for the* kommando. *I know that once again in this little heap all the sorrow of humanity is huddled together. Here a young widow does not want to believe that her one and only rests in the damp earth of Flanders. She desperately clings to a small discrepancy between comrades' accounts and the official report, hoping that her husband has after all been taken prisoner and only prevented from writing for some reason. We have already had the body exhumed twice on new grounds each time, und today the regimental dentist is summoned for the third exhumation. On the basis of an infallible dental chart sent over yesterday, the last fading ray of hope will now be tested, if not snuffed out. Here a young wife asks for particular grave decoration on her husband's birthday. The wish is noted down in the great list of miscellaneous requests. A wreath arriving at the same time will be placed on the grave at once.*

A bride appeals to our sympathies for the most exact details of her fiance's death. However the most painstaking enquiries to companies and comrades do not yield any clues. Unfortunately, we can only inform her that in those hot days everything was in total disorder, and that she must content herself with knowing that he is in the mass grave at the church in Becelaere. A hard-hit father, himself a landsturmmann, *who approaches us with a similar request, is more fortunate. A man from the* kommando, *who fought in his son's section, still remembers the exact circumstances. The brave* landsturm *comrade learns that his only son got lost while carrying food in the dark, ended up in front of the enemy trenches and was later found in a shellhole with four gunshot wounds.*

An official letter brings the settlement of an embarrassing case. A father complained about the substantial amount of money, which his son was allegedly supposed to have had about him on the day of his death, but which the father found missing in

In 1916 or 1917 the Holle Bosch cemetery received this regimental memorial donated by Hptm. Reichel of 8./245.

The new entrance gate for the enlarged cemetery. Graves here were typically edged with the roof tiles seen stacked to the right of the gate.

the estate he received. A comrade had told him this in a letter. The investigation demanded by the kommando *has now revealed that the son's companion, as in most such cases, had only heard that someone had repeated this, that a fourth man had... etc. – Our curse is a heartfelt one which wishes the thoughtless self-important fool in the land of pepper*[5].
A mother asks if she can visit her son's grave. The response must be to decline her request. The cemetery is located in the area of operations and under enemy fire. Outside hoofbeats patter in the mire. Out of the splendid cavalcade an adjutant calls for the kommandoführer. *His Excellency*[6] *wishes to see the cemetery, which is widely known for its beauty. Under expert guidance steed and knight*[7] *disappear into the nearby cemetery. In the afternoon the* ausgräberkommando *returns with*

Since his death on 25 October 1914 long preceded the existence of RIR 245's regimental cemetery, the body of Sold. Max Engert from Langenleuba-Oberhain was presumably either exhumed from a grave elsewhere or recovered after the advance in May 1915; he is now buried at the *soldatenfriedhof* Menen. His cross is this cemetery's later standardised type as seen on p.227. This is one of around 2,800 grave photos taken by official cemetery photographer Kurt Engel, who served from May 1915 successively with the *friedhofskommando* of RIR 245, the divisional *friedhofskommando* and Gräberverwaltungsbezirk 3 of the centralised *Gräberwesen*. These pictures were supplied free of charge to relatives of the deceased.

Kriegsfreiwilliger Richard Preussler from Hohenstein-Ernstthal was killed with 6./245 on 3 June 1915 and now rests at Menen.

five members of the regiment, unfortunately only some of them identified. They have already laid out three dead of other regiments ready for collection. The friedhofskommandos *responsible for them will be notified. In a grave whose cross inscription speaks only of 'a soldier' they have found a long sought-after oberstleutnant of the then-neighbouring regiment, a grave allegedly with 'two German heroes' was filled with ten Englishmen etc.*
Meanwhile the feldgeistliche *and the dentist report to the cemetery, and the two honour parties deploy for the simple funeral service. It is a short but impressive affair, with gunfire from the nearby front in the background. – Then a short time later the orderly room also knows that the dentition of the said deceased (luckily the shell was merciful!) has been found to be an exact match with the records, so the poor widow must bow to the bitter fact. The notification will not be easy for us; indeed we know the street and house in Leipzig, where within a few days every hope must now come to an abrupt end.*
Again the telephone buzzes. A message from R. announces the official of the 'Pietät' *institution, who is expected tomorrow with exceptional permission for the transportation of a corpse back to the homeland, and wishes to confirm what he has to bring with him besides the zinc coffin. – "Soldering gear", the reply reads, soldering tin and hydrochloric acid.*

Dusk has descended. The captive balloon comes down, our airmen return. The artillery fire erupts into frenzied violence. A shell bursts near the cemetery. The trenches report a death.

State of the *friedhof* Hollebos in 1918

Report by Richard Frensch

The extent of the destruction grows as we approach the village of Terhand. We're on the edge of the cratered zone. – And suddenly we see by the well-known concrete towers and the badly damaged concrete monument of a destroyed cemetery that we are already right in the middle of the former village. Nothing bears witness to the village itself, no tile, no fragment of a wall, no trace of a house. The road itself meanwhile has come to an end in the chaos of the crater field. An eerie confusion of swamp, barbed wire, trenches, shot-up funk-holes etc, surrounds us. In vain the horrified eye seeks the orientation point of our route, the familiar ruined church of Becelaere. No trace of it can be seen. In rigid lines, the bare hills from Gheluvelt to Broodseinde frame the gruesome wasteland. Half-left the infamous 'Kemmel' stretches into the picture like a threatening admonition. Two track sections from the field railway staring up out of the valley toward heaven as if in accusation finally show us our way onward. We arduously clamber around the shellholes and fortunately find a new duckboard path, which finally leads us past unburied Englishmen through expanses of horror to Molenhoek. Here too is chaos. Right into the wasted village, up to the narrow connecting path from the main road leftward to the church of Becelaere are the track marks of tanks. The ruined church itself has shrunk to a three metre high pile of rubble, so no wonder the area lacks its familiar landmark. We clamber further rightwards through the weed-choked crater zone to the 'Hollebusch' *copse. But what remains of the so familiar copse, on the edge of which our cemetery huddled? Are the few tattered little trunks among which we stand, perhaps supposed to be the* Hollebusch*? There is no possibility of doubt, it was the* Hollebusch*! It has emerged from the horror of the attacks in a heartbreaking state of disorder, as has the small avenue which leads along its flank past the* Reservehof *to fiercely contested Reutel. And now we stand in the cemetery itself, that is to say we merely surmise that we are standing in it, since apart from six apparently freshly renewed crosses there is almost no trace in the repeatedly upturned mass of shellholes of the circa 1,500 graves. It had reached that many over time. I do not wish to go into detail. Every informed individual already knows from what he has heard: our cemetery, once called the most splendid place for the honoured dead on the Western Front, has like so many others been irretrievably annihilated.*

The cemetery in Terhand mentioned by Richard Frensch, seen in 1918 after its ruination in the Third Battle of Ypres.

Other Saxon graves and cemeteries

Battlefield graves of Jäger-Bataillon 13 after the third attack on L'Epinette on 23 October 1914. The practice of adorning graves with the *pickelhauben* (or in this case, *tschakos*) of the dead was later prohibited as wasteful, but reappeared in the Second World War.

Some of those killed when IR 181 stormed the Porte de Douai at Lille on 12 October 1914 were buried and memorialised on the spot.

Battlefield graves near Broodseinde of members of RIR 241 and RJB 25 killed on 26 October 1914 in one of the numerous bloody assaults on the crossroads, including Hptm. Gerd Sabinski of 11./241 and Ltn. Kurt Eichler of 3./25.

Following the advance in May 1915, medical personnel of RJB 25 search the thoroughly devastated crossroads for unburied corpses.

The *Jägerfriedhof* established at the crossroads by RJB 25, which had left many dead here after the abortive attack of 25 January 1915.

Directly opposite the *Jägerfriedhof* at the southwestern corner of the crossroads was the principal *sammelfriedhof* of XXVII. RK. Besides miscellaneous German dead from the corps sector (all now at Menen), British and French soldiers were also interred here.

The initial battalion cemetery of RJB 26 on the present-day Slangenmeersstraat, about 500 metres northeast of RIR 245's cemetery.

By summer 1915 this cemetery too had been greatly enlarged, gaining a substantial entrance gate. The once-dominant cross in the background shows the scale of the expansion. Here too a *friedhofskommando* remained active on site until the cemetery's destruction in 1917.

Oberjäger Otto Hertel from Dittersdorf in the Erzgebirge mountains reached Becelaere on 24 December 1914, as one of 320 men who formed the first major replacement draft for the gravely depleted Reserve-Jäger-Bataillon 26. That evening he wrote home as follows: *Christmas Eve, 8.30 pm. Dear brother! Arrived at our destination at 1 pm today, we will probably celebrate Christmas in dismal style as we have to get ourselves set up first.*

This was probably one of his last messages to his family, as his fate was sealed by a shell three weeks later. The battalion's published history states: *14 January was to be a particularly black day. Around 2 pm about ten shells hit the* Jägerheim. *The very second shot hit a cowshed occupied by a platoon of the 4. Kompanie. Two* oberjägers *and six* jägers *suffered a hero's death, and a further twelve men were wounded. As a result the construction of shellproof dugouts began with all haste.*[8]

Hertel and his fellow victims were presumably interred nearby, and later moved to a communal grave at the *Jägerfriedhof* of RJB 26 in Becelaere-Lichtenstein (shown on the previous page) when this was established. Although severely damaged in 1917, the battalion cemetery was restored – only to be closed in 1930. The dead were moved to Holle Bosch, but sadly not all of the bodies could be found and identified. When the Holle Bosch cemetery was closed in the 1950s the identifiable bodies were reburied at Menen. What remained was interred in the mass *Kameradengrab* at the *soldatenfriedhof* Langemarck; since he now has no known grave, this presumably included the mortal remains of Otto Hertel.

The *sammelfriedhof* at In de Ster held many of the dead of October 1914 to May 1915 recovered in this area, including French and British soldiers. The memorial text is from John 15:13 – "Greater love hath no man than this, that a man lay down his life for his friends."

The grave of Hptm. d. L. a. D. Dr. Oskar Dähnhardt (centre) in the regimental cemetery of RIR 242, adorned with a wreath from Landsturm-Infanterie-Bataillon Wurzen XIX.9. The 44-year-old retired *hauptmann*, philologist and teacher voluntarily left his post with this rear-area security unit in February 1915 to serve at the front. He was killed in action as commander of 12./242 on 23. April 1915 (see pp.102–103).

As a major billeting area and the site of Reserve-Feldlazarett 91, Moorslede inevitably contained numerous cemeteries, especially those of the Saxon units of XXVII. Reservekorps. The regimental cemetery of RIR 242 at the Passchendaele-Moorslede railway station was dominated by this imposing brick pyramid.

Like many others which came within range of the enemy guns during the offensive, RIR 242's cemetery was devastated during the Third Battle of Ypres. In this sad photo taken at the end of 1917, it can nevertheless still be identified by the remarkably preserved pyramid.

The *Friedhof der schweren Artillerie* (below) was established at Waterdamhoek in 1915/1916 as a dedicated resting place for the – by infantry standards – not very numerous dead of the *fussartillerie* (heavy artillery). It proved highly challenging to gather the fallen of many small units from widely dispersed field graves. The three typical graves above belong to members of Mörser-Batterie 201, an independent 21cm battery formed by Saxon Fussartillerie-Regiment 12 in Metz which fought with XXVII. RK in 1915 and in the neighbouring Hooge-St. Eloi sector in 1916.

Iseghem

The establishment of major medical facilities in a rear-area town was inevitably followed by the establishment of cemeteries for the patients who died there. As the long-term base of operations for Kriegslazarettabteilung 127 of XXVII. RK, Izegem was no exception.

Graves of deceased patients of Reserve-Feldlazarett 92 in Moorsele churchyard. Besides the expected Saxons and Württembergers of XXVII. RK, there are also members of the Prussian 38. Landwehr-Brigade which fought alongside them in the first two battles of Ypres.

Numerous cemeteries were established for the dead of XIX. Armeekorps in its rear area north and east of Lille in late 1914 and early 1915. This is the regimental cemetery of Infanterie-Regiment 133 in the field opposite Verlinghem church.

H.M. the King of Saxony and his entourage visiting the regimental cemetery of IR 133 on 20 March 1916. The following day the royal party was given a tour of both of the breweries and the mine craters at Frelinghien (see p.25).

The *soldatenfriedhof* established by the Germans in French Comines in 1915 remained undisturbed until 1956. The dead were then moved to the *soldatenfriedhof* St. Laurent Blagny and this site was reused for the present civilian Cimetière nord à Comines. The massive German memorial seen here at top left was magnanimously preserved by the French and can still be seen there.

A mass funeral at the *soldatenfriedhof* Comines. Many Saxons killed at Wytschaete, St. Eloi and Messines in 1915–1917 were buried here.

The *ehrenfriedhof* in Quesnoy-sur-Deûle was established in 1914 by extending the civilian cemetery eastward. It still exists, holding dead mainly of 40. Infanterie-Division from 1914–1916 (including some moved from the civilian cemetery) and a preserved divisional memorial.

These comrades of the late Uffz. Albert Engler of 10. Komp./Infanterie-Regiment 104 (KIA 6 June 1915) have added a memorial board carrying a personal 'last salute' *(letzter Gruss)* to his grave in the cemetery at Quesnoy-sur-Deûle.

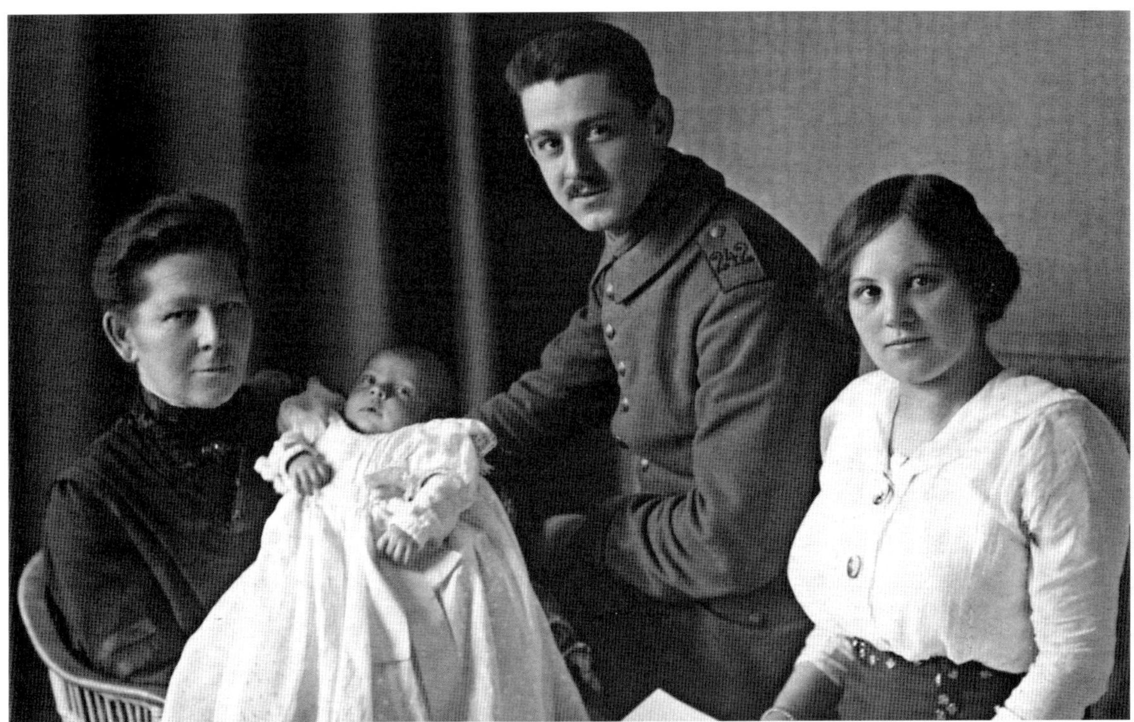

Ersatz-Reservist Friedrich Balz from Berlin with his wife, mother and five-week-old baby son during home leave. Balz was mortally wounded with 10./RIR 242 and died on 16 June 1915 at Feldlazarett XII.3 in St.-Eloois-Winkel. He is now buried at the *soldatenfriedhof* Menen.

Regimental commander Major Kirsten[9] of IR 177 was killed by a sniper at Warneton on 10 December 1917, and received a funeral with full military honours. After the service in the church at Bousbecque his body was transported home at his family's expense for burial in Saxony.

Since the interment of the overwhelming majority of the dead in foreign soil left their families without a readily accessible grave as a focus of mourning, *gedenkblätter* (memorial certificates) were produced for framing and display in the home. In addition to a universal *gedenkblatt* commissioned by the Kaiser and bearing his signature and selected bible verse, the version on the left with the signature of H.M. Friedrich August III and the motto *"Getreu bis in den Tod"* (faithful unto death) was printed for the Royal Saxon Army.

Much rarer are *gedenkblätter* produced for specific units, such as the example on the right designed by Arthur Schott, the prolific regimental artist of RIR 244 (also known for his postcards). Besides depicting the ruins of Becelaere (left) and Ypres, Schott has also included space to attach photos of the cemetery and grave (in this case in Ledegem).

3. Komp.
GEDENKBLATT
* 14. Sept. 1894. Sold Otto Tellert † 6. Mai 1915.
R.J.R. 244
1914
SCHOTT
Sei getreu bis an den Tod,
ſo will ich dir die Krone des Lebens geben.
Offenb. 2, 10.

A HUNDRED YEARS LATER

In Ledegem since 2014 stands a monument constructed from salvaged gravestone fragments found at the site of the old *lazarettfriedhof.* These include the grave cross of Oberleutnant Benno von Minckwitz, company commander of 4./RJB 25. Born into an old Saxon noble house at Nowosiolke in Galicia (Austrian Ukraine) on 26 May 1883, he was mortally wounded at the head of his company in the assault on Verlorenhoek on 9 May 1915. Although carried under fire from the battlefield by his loyal batman, he died two days later at Reserve-Feldlazarett 94 in Ledegem; his place of death is falsely cited as Görlitz in the *Helden-Gedenkmappe des deutschen Adels.* When the *lazarettfriedhof* closed in the 1950s the identifiable bodies were reinterred at Menen, where Benno von Minckwitz now rests.

The monument, with the von Minckwitz cross at the near end.

Mass grave marker at the *soldatenfriedhof* Menen.

A ward of Württemberg Reserve-Feldlazarett 94 in Ledegem church, where both Oltn. von Minckwitz and Hptm. John (see p.82) died of wounds.

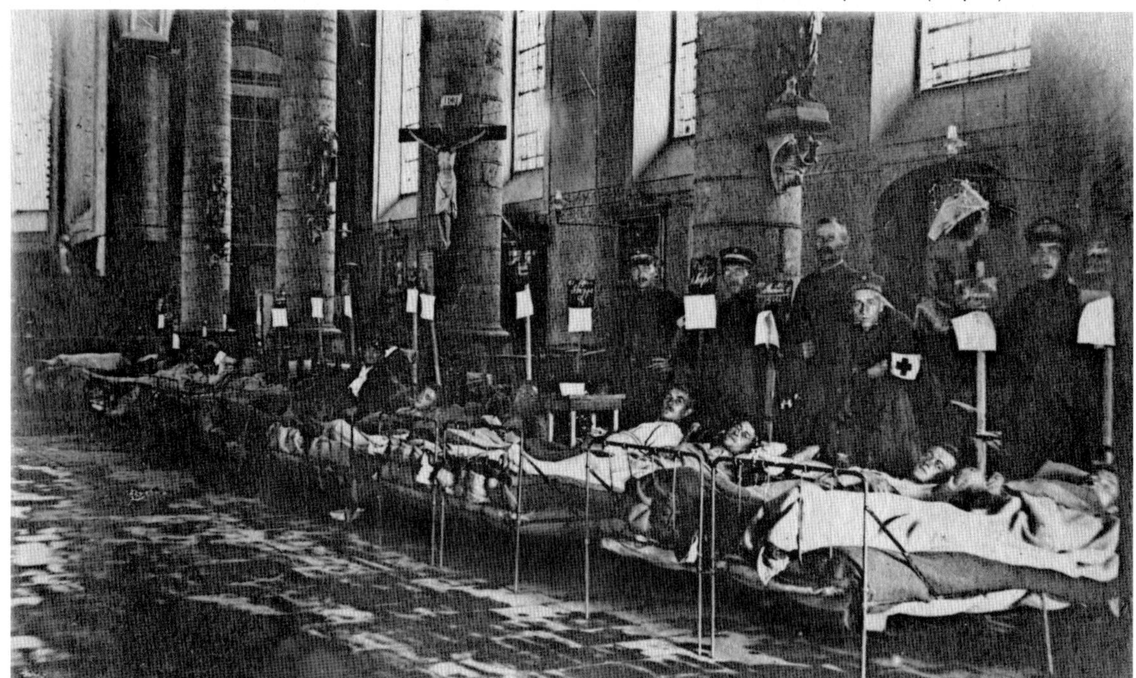

Appendices

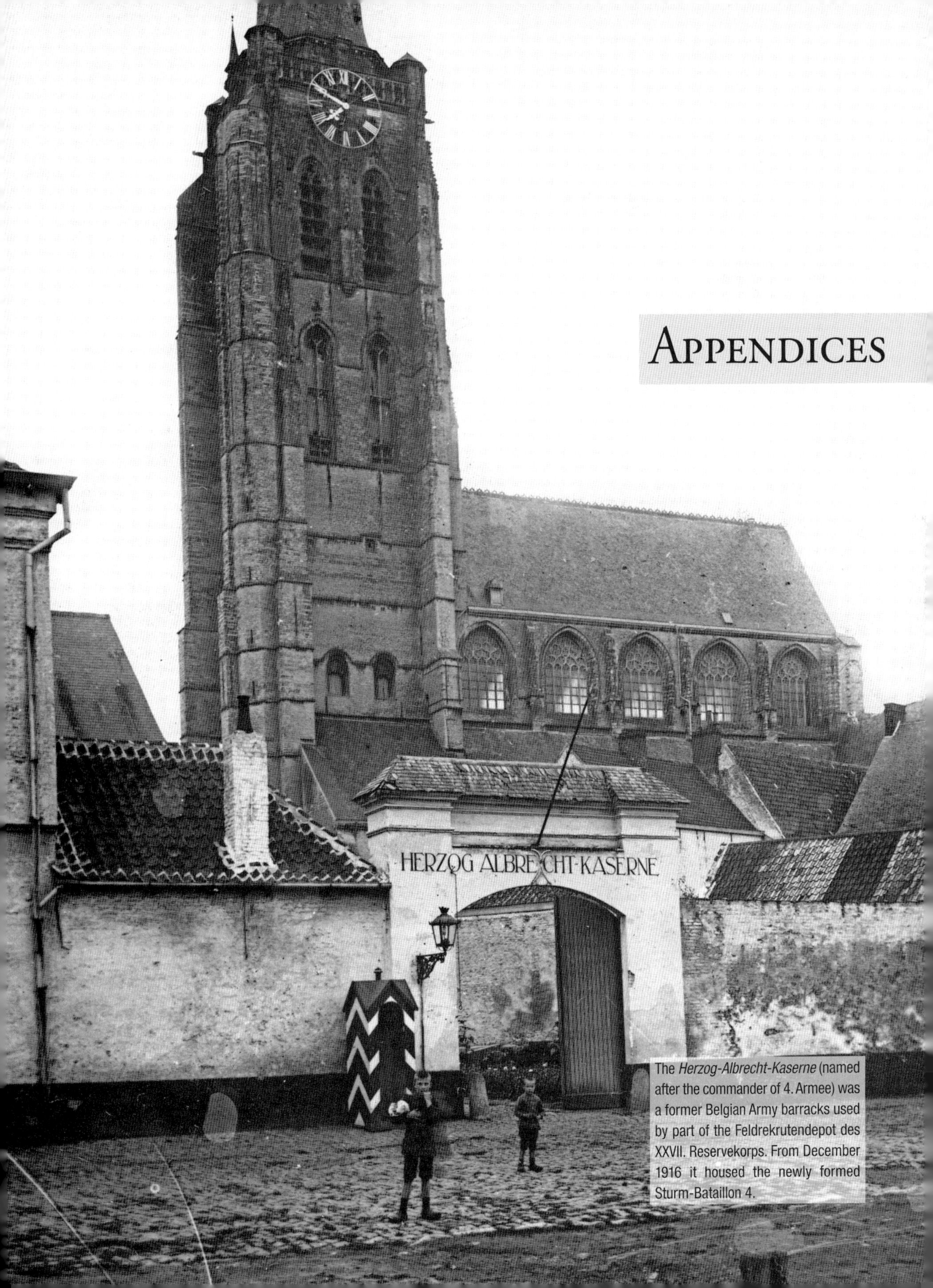

The *Herzog-Albrecht-Kaserne* (named after the commander of 4. Armee) was a former Belgian Army barracks used by part of the Feldrekrutendepot des XXVII. Reservekorps. From December 1916 it housed the newly formed Sturm-Bataillon 4.

Notes

CHAPTER 1 – The beginnings of trench warfare | Jäger-Bataillon 13

1 Bucher, *Dienstunterricht des Königlich Sächsischen Infanteristen* (p. 194).
2 Bucher, op. cit. (p. 199).
3 Soft-nosed or hollow-pointed 'dum-dum' projectiles had been banned by international convention since 1907, but in 1914 both sides were convinced (apparently falsely) that their opponents were using them and put much effort into proving it. Much of this belief seemingly stemmed from unfamiliarity from the wounds modern small arms could inflict, especially ricochets.
4 'cooking pot candidate', a popular witticism based on *offizier-aspirant* (officer candidate).
5 Individual or collective gifts from home, gathered by organised charitable initiative.
6 "*Schwefelgranaten*" (sulphur shells) were British HE rounds filled with Lyddite, which stained the target area (and the skins of munitions workers) yellow.
7 Freiherr von Uslar-Gleichen, K., *Das Kgl. Sächs. 2. Jäger-Bataillon Nr. 13 im Weltkriege* (pp. 37–42).

CHAPTER 2 – The Breweries at Frelinghien

1 Wolff, L., *Das Kgl. Sächs. 5. Inf.-Regiment „Kronprinz" Nr. 104* (vol. I p. 100).
2 War diary of 2nd Btn. Seaforth Highlanders [WO 95/1483/1].
3 Schatz, *Das 10. Kgl. Sächs. Infanterie Regiment Nr. 134* (vol. II p. 52).
4 Niemann, *Das 9. Königlich Sächsische Infanterie-Regiment Nr. 133 im Weltkrieg 1914–18* (p. 27)
5 Freiherr von Uslar-Gleichen, op. cit. (p. 85).
6 Freiherr von Uslar-Gleichen, op. cit. (pp. 89–90).
7 Wolff, op. cit. (vol. I pp. 128–129).
8 Wolff, op. cit. (vol. I p. 129); Ltn. d.R. Erich Engler, another peacetime architect serving with PB 22, had received the MStHO on 2 December 1914 for leading three men in a daring bombing raid on a British position opposite IR 104 on 6 November.
9 Wolff, op. cit. (vol.I p. 129–130).
10 *Regiments-Zeitung für die Angehörigen des ehemaligen Landwehr-Infanterie-Regiments Nr. 77*, (vol. I p. 26).
11 Wolff, op. cit. (vol. I p. 130).

CHAPTER 3 – At Ploegsteert Wood

1 The titular commander Oberst Rudolf Hammer was still convalescing from a head wound suffered while leading an assault in August. He returned to IR 104 in mid-December 1914 with the rank of *generalmajor*, but was promoted to command 89. Inf. Brig. on Christmas Eve. He later briefly commanded 32. ID and then 24. ID from May 1916 until demobilisation, ending the war as a *generalleutnant*.
2 Wolff, op. cit. (vol.I p. 99); 104er Gut (Plantation Farm), southwest of Pont Rouge on the road to Le Touquet, was adopted as regimental battle HQ on 20 October 1914. When IR 104 ceased to use the farm it became the *Regimentsgut* (see the aerial photo on p. 63).
3 Böttger, *Das Kgl. Sächs. 7. Infanterie-Regiment König Georg Nr. 106* (p. 41).
4 *Fighting the Kaiser's War* (p. 206); as early as 5 November Kaden noted severe tension between the pessimistic Gen. der Kav. Krug von Nidda of 24. ID and the aggressive corps commander. Gen. der Kav. von Laffert continued to command XIX. AK until dying of a heart attack on 20 July 1917 following the Messines disaster.
5 *Fighting the Kaiser's War* (p. 209).
6 *Fighting the Kaiser's War* (p. 207).
7 Böttger, op. cit. (pp. 44–45).
8 A *korpstagesbefehl* (corps order of the day) of XXVII. RK for 11.12.1914 (Hauptstaatsarchiv Dresden Bestand 11358) reveals that the supply of Christmas trees for entire units was organised at corps level by the *intendantur* (see p. 119).
9 Böttger, op. cit. (p. 46).
10 Zehmisch was awarded the MStHO for his leadership of 1./134 in the defence of the Butte de Warlencourt in October 1916 and survived the war. A typescript of his diary is preserved at the In Flanders' Fields Museum in Ypres.
11 Wolff, op. cit. (vol.I p. 122).
12 Wolff, op. cit. (vol.I pp. 112–113).
13 Schatz, op. cit. (p. 57).
14 Schatz, op. cit. (pp. 57–58).
15 Hptm. Facius had previously commanded III. / 104 at Le Touquet. He returned to the regiment in January 1918 as commander of II. / 104, was promoted to *major* in April and is the officer misidentified as H.M. the King in the photo on p. 21 of *Fighting the Kaiser's War*.
16 Jung, Goslarer Jäger im Weltkrieg, 1.Band – *Das Hannoversche Jägerbataillon Nr. 10* (p. 150).
17 Maj. Max Dörffel (born 23 August 1873) originally came from IR 139, and served at the Unteroffiziersschule (NCO school) Marienberg before the war. He was a battalion commander with IR 104 from February 1915 to September 1916, and was killed in action leading II. / RIR 241 at Germakowka on 31 July 1917. Oltn. Bernhard Ehrhardt was 'donated' to IR 183 in May 1915, was awarded the MStHO in November 1915 and ended the war in captivity as a *hauptmann* and commander of II. / 183.
18 Wolff, op. cit. (vol.I pp. 210–211); the unit (mis-)identified here is the 34th Btn. CEF, a training battalion based in England which provided reinforcements to the 1st Canadian Division in the field.
19 Wolff, op. cit. (vol.I p. 209).

CHAPTER 4 – The First Battle of Ypres | Reserve-Infanterie-Regiment 245

1 i.e. officers and NCOs from the 'active' (peacetime regular) army. XXVII. RK relied initially on NCOs of the older reserve categories and on officers reactivated from semi (z. D.) or full (a. D.) retirement.
2 Oberst z.D. Hesse was severely wounded leading III. Batl. / RIR 245 in the first assault on Becelaere on 21 October. The regiment's original commander Oberst z. D. Artur Baumgarten-Crusius (later author of the Saxon quasi-official history *Sachsen in Grosser Zeit*) was hit by German artillery fire the next day. Oberstltn. z. D. Haeser of I. Batl. / RIR 245 was killed on 23 October. All had been semi-retired in peacetime. The surviving battalion commander Maj. a. D. Johannes von Wachsmann had been fully retired since 1910.
3 Maj. Artur Franz had been the most senior active *hauptmann* in the Saxon infantry at the beginning of 1914 (promoted to that rank on 18 August 1905). He was transferred from IR 179 to IR 139 and promoted to *major* shortly before the war, which he survived to retire as an *oberstleutnant a. D.*
4 Von Heygendorff frequently refers to time in colloquial terms still commonly used in Saxony but surely counterintuitive to English speakers. "¼ 9" = 8:15; "½ 9" = 8:30; "¾ 9" = 8:45 etc.
5 The shelling of Becelaere church is described in *Fighting the Kaiser's War* (pp. 30 and 184).
6 Originally 54. RD only had one brigade commander, Württemberg Genltn. a. D. Karl von Reinhardt. On 22 October he was killed by a stray bullet in the lines of RIR 245 and Oberst a. D. von Roschmann of RIR 246 took temporary command. Oberst Georg Mühry (an active Prussian officer) arrived to replace von Reinhardt on 26 October.
7 Maj. z.D. Ernst Holtzhausen (III. / 246) was killed leading an assault at Reutel on 24 October 1914. We could not identify 'Leutnant von Uslar' – it is possible that the name and/or rank may have been misreported.
8 Officially the minimum age for volunteer military service was 17. Under-aged *pfadfinder* were permitted (with parental approval) only as volunteer messengers with rear-echelon units and staffs. On 12 November 1914 the Berlin newspaper *Der Tag* lauded Fritz Lehmann and 14-year-old fellow *pfadfinder* Karl Belz from Berlin, both recommended for the Iron Cross. The article states that Lehmann was wounded at Dinant (with XII. AK) in August 1914, had 'barely recovered' when he returned to the field and was credited with rescuing a wounded major. We have found no other mention of him.
9 Regarding the change of corps commander (see p. 98).
10 For the attack on 29 October, the II. Bataillon of Kgl. Bayer. Reserve-Infanterie-Regiment 16 (the famous Bavarian *Regiment List*) was assigned to *Gruppe Mühry* (together with RIR 245, RIR 246 and RJB 26) and the rest of bRIR 16 to *Gruppe von Bendler* further left.
11 Von Heygendorff intermittently omits the 'reserve' from unit designations, as does Hauptmann John in the following chapter.
12 Hptm. Horst Kaeubler (5./245, formerly an instructor at Unteroffiziersvorschule Marienberg) fell on 29 October 1914. Ltn. d. R. Paulus Otto Halbauer (6./245) was only lightly wounded. Oltn. d. R. Hans Gerhard Arnold (7./245) was retrieved but died of wounds at the dressing station in Molenhoek and is now buried at the *soldatenfriedhof* Menen.
13 Presumably an NCO responsible for the regimental war diary (*kriegstagebuch*).
14 Hptm. a. D. Gustav von Aspern, in that rank since 1898 and retired since 19 April 1901 from IR 139. Perhaps due to his seniority and appointment as battalion commander he was promoted to *major* in October 1914.
15 See Note 11 above.
16 Two Austro-Hungarian siege batteries armed with the 30.5cm Skoda Motor Mörser were briefly employed in the attack on Ypres after their successes against the Belgian forts and in the siege of Antwerp.
17 III. RK, then engaged at Langemarck on the right of XXVI. RK.
18 The composite *Garde-Infanterie-Division Winckler. Nonnenwald* (Nun's Wood) is a Germanisation of the Flemish name Nonne Bosschen.
19 Prussian MG-Abteilung 9, as mentioned on p. 75. An *MG-abteilung* was a horse-drawn machine-gun detachment intended to support a cavalry division.
20 Oltn. d. R. Karl Ende, acting commander of 2./245.
21 Protestant Feldgeistliche (chaplain) von Funcke was official divisional pastor (*etatsmässige divisionspfarrer*) of the 53. RD, but was replaced before April 1915 by Dr. Specht. According to Aster there was bitter rivalry between von Funcke and the popular Protestant volunteer chaplain (*hilfsgeistliche* or *hilfspfarrer*) Weichelt. As was typical, a second volunteer chaplain, Pfarrer Kneschke, attended to the division's Roman Catholic minority.
22 See Chapter 1, Note 3.
23 '*Brummer*' – a nickname for heavy howitzers.

CHAPTER 5 – The Second Battle of Ypres | Reserve-Infanterie-Regiment 245

1 Kramer, Max, *Geschichte des Reserve-Infanterie-Regiments 245* (p. 23). The *diskushandgranate* relied on impact fuzes around its rim and would only explode if it struck a hard surface side-on.
2 Hptm. John is mistaken here; it was in fact the III. Bataillon.
3 Clearly an allusion to the gas attack on 22 April 1915.
4 John refers to time in the same way as von Heygendorff (c.f. Chapter 4, Note 4).
5. Generalmajor Gotthold von Erpf, commander of 107. Reserve-Infanterie-Brigade (RIR 245, RIR 247 and RJB 26).
6 Again von Heygendorff omits the 'reserve' from the unit designation.
7 Gefreiter Artur Mälzer (8./245), born 10 August 1889 at Dobitschen in Saxe-Altenburg and killed in action on 3 May 1915 at Wallemolen; von Heygendorff quotes the traditional German soldier's funeral song *Ich hatt' einen Kameraden.*

8 Genmaj. Bernhard von Hülsen was actually chief of the staff to Marinekorps Flandern.
9 c.f. Chapter 1, Note 6.
10 Every battalion and regiment had a *zahlmeister* (paymaster), a uniformed civil servant responsible not only for the soldier's pay but also other aspects of the unit's economy such as the canteen and stores.
11 Major Felix Ingenbrand served with FAR 48 in peacetime and commanded II. Abt. / RFAR 53 until at least 1917, winning the MStHO in October 1916 and ending the war as commander of FAR 64. (Ltn.?) Donner remains unidentified.
12 Very possibly Rittmeister von Gabelentz, commander of the leichte Fussartillerie Munitionskolonne des XXVII. Reservekorps (see p. 146 and Chapter 7, Note 5).
13 Although allied by treaty with the Central Powers, Italy initially remained neutral and then joined the war on the Entente side on 23 May 1915.

CHAPTER 6 – The Second Battle of Ypres | XXVII. Reservekorps

1 Literally 'General through-the-rear', an ingenious pun alluding to von Schubert's shrapnel wound in the backside in autumn 1914. According to chief of the staff of 53. RD, the neighbouring XXVI. RK called him *'General Hintendurch mit dem Angriffspipps'* ('...with the offensive bug') for his relentless attacks in the same period. See Beyer and Richter, *Tagebuch des Kgl. Sächs. Generalstaboffiziers Gotthold Ernst Aster im Ersten Weltkrieg in Flandern und Frankreich* (p. 104).
2 Knoppe, *Die Geschichte des Königlich Sächsischen Reserve-Infanterie-Regiments Nr. 241* (p. 119).
3 *Fighting the Kaiser's War* (p. 214).
4 Herkenrath, *Das Württembergische Reserve-Inf.-Regiment Nr. 247 im Weltkrieg 1914–1918* (p. 39).
5 Knoppe, op. cit. (pp. 107–108).
6 Orgeldinger, *Das Württembergische Reserve-Infanterie-Regiment Nr. 246* (pp. 86–87).
7 Knoppe, op. cit. (p. 109).
8 Herkenrath, op. cit. (p. 47).

CHAPTER 7 – In the rear of XXVII. Reservekorps

1 *Korpstagesbefehl* for 6.2.1915 (Hauptstaatsarchiv Dresden Bestand 11358). The corps orders of the day and Aster (op. cit.) provided many of the details in this chapter.
2 Lehmann, H., *Das Königlich Sächsische Reserve-Jäger-Bataillon Nr. 26* (p. 54).
3 Ulbricht, W., *Die Geschichte des Königlich Sächsischen Reserve-Infanterie-Regiments 244 im Weltkriege 1914–1918* (p. 57).
4 Lehmann, op. cit. (p. 50).
5 Properly leichte Reserve-Fußartillerie-Munitionskolonne 27, which had accompanied schwere Reserve-Feldhaubitze-Batterie 27 since mobilisation; in November 1914 its 15cm howitzers were deployed just south of Waterdamhoek. The column commander was either Rittm. d.R Albrecht von der Gabelentz (of the Karabinier-Regt.) or Rittm. z. D. Georg von der Gabelentz-Linsingen (of the Gardereiter-Regt.). Both column and battery were absorbed into the Saxon/Prussian Reserve-Fussartillerie-Bataillon 27 later in 1915, and fought at Verdun in 1916.
6 i.e. the lavatory.
7 This unit was I. Batl. / bayer. Res. FußA. Regt. 3, a 15cm howitzer battalion of four batteries which supported XXVII.RK from February to May 1915. Acting commander was Hptm. Wilhelm Bothof (severely wounded on 3 May). Oltn. d. R. Friedrich Wilhelm Dürr was in fact head of a vocational school in civilian life.
8 Salvator is a traditional brand of doppelbock (a strong malty lager) originally brewed by the Paulaner Friars of Munich for the feast of St. Francis of Paola on 2 April.
9 Ltn. d. L. Egon Kienzle from Stuttgart was wounded in action with 5. / RFAR 54 at Polderhoek on 1 November 1914. After his convalescence he was given command of the regiment's newly formed *fliegerabwehr-batterie* near Ledegem at the beginning of March 1915. The regimental history claims that this battery shot down the French aviator Roland Garros on 18 April, after which Kienzle was promoted to *oberleutnant*. Their claim was disputed by members of Landsturm-Bataillon Wurzen XIX.9, who had engaged Garros with a machine-gun from Lendelede station.
10 Evidently Major von Heygendorff served as a tutor to the three young princes during his long career with the Dresden garrison, presumably following his service as personal adjutant to their father. Prince Johann Georg was the king's younger brother and *chef* of IR 107.

CHAPTER 8 – In the Wytschaete Salient 1915–1916 | Infanterie-Regiment 182

1 *Buß- und Bettag* (Day of Repentance and Prayer) is celebrated on the penultimate Wednesday before advent by German Protestants, and today remains a public holiday only in Saxony.
2 "Toothpick Wood".
3 Rittmeister d.R. Theodor Walter Coccius (originally from UR 17); born in Leipzig 13 October 1878, KIA 27 January 1916.
4 Light low-wheeled carriages with a removable folding hood.
5 'Shovellers' – a nickname for the *armierungstruppen* (unarmed labour units).
6 Although *Fastnacht* (pre-Lenten carnival) died out in much of Saxony at the reformation, regional traditions persisted in the Oberlausitz and Erzgebirge.
7 A quotation from Schiller's play William Tell (1804).
8 Baron Raymond Pecsteen (4 December 1867–5 September 1965), a post-war mayor of Ruddervoorde. The chateau (also known as "Kasteel Pecsteen") was in his family's possession since 1800.
9 The second quotation is from Schiller's poem *An die Freunde* (1802).

CHAPTER 9 – A Summer in Flanders: 1917 | 23. Reserve-Division

1 Martin, *Das Kgl. Sächs. Grenadier-Reserve-Regiment Nr. 100* (p. 81–82). 'Cylinder', 'finned' and 'ball' mines are evidently various kinds of trench mortar projectile, but the meaning of 'chain mines' (*ketten-minen*) is unclear. In naval contexts, this could refer to a chain of sea-mines.
2 Martin, op. cit. (pp. 86–87).
3 Trümper-Bödemann, *Das Königl. Sächs. Reserve-Infanterie-Regiment Nr. 102* (p. 125).
4 *'Feuerrädel'* (Catherine wheels), *'nagelkisten'* (boxes of nails) and *'sturmvögel'* (petrels) are presumably slang terms, which we could not further identify.
5 Trümper-Bödemann, op. cit. (pp. 140–141).

CHAPTER 10 – The Third Battle of Ypres | Infanterie-Regiment 133

1 47th Bde. report to 16th Div. dated 9 March 1917. [WO 95/1955/4]
2 Original letter from the collection of Andrew Lucas.
3 As noted on p. 201 the British sources mention no such raid on 1 September, but describe an identical event on the night of 30–31 August.
4 The ribbon of the Iron Cross 2nd Class (EK2), usually worn after its award in a buttonhole or on a bar in place of the actual medal.
5 'Softly, quite softly' – a popular number from *Ein Walzertraum* (1907), an operetta by Oscar Straus.
6 Niemann, op. cit. (pp. 71).
7 Niemann, op. cit. (pp. 72–73).
8 In this sense, an enlisted man attached to a battalion or higher HQ to run errands or carry messages as required.
9 Niemann, op. cit. (p. 72).
10 Leutnant d.R. Erich Fritzsche from Zwickau was an attorney in peacetime. On 31 August 1916 he received the MStHO(R) for his leadership of 6. / 133 at Pozières on the Somme, during which he had been repeatedly wounded.
11 Niemann, op. cit. (p. 73–74).
12 Major Hans Wittich had been awarded the MStHO(R) on 11 March 1915 specifically for his part in the storming of Gheluvelt on 30–31 October 1914 as commander of II. / RIR 242. As commander of IR 133 (since August 1917) he was granted the *Komturkreuz 2. Klasse* of the same order on 2 December 1917 for the village's defence described in Chapter 10. One can surmise that Major Wittich felt a particularly strong responsibility to keep it in German hands due to his personal awareness of the grave cost of its capture in 1914.
13 48th Bde. report to 16th Div. dated 9 March 1917. [WO 95/1955/4]
14 Each company had a reported trench strength of only sixty rifles. One of the two in line that day was the unique Jersey Company ('D' Coy. / 7th RIR), formed in December 1914 with volunteers from the Royal Militia of the Channel Island of Jersey.
15 Report of 7th Royal Irish Rifles included in 48th Bde. report to 16th Div. dated 9 March 1917 [WO 95/1955/4].
16 Message from IX Corps to 16th Div. dated 9 March 1917. [WO 95/1955/4]
17 This and following quotes from war diary of 2nd Btn. Wiltshire Regt. for 24 August 1917. [WO 95/2329/1]
18 War diary of 21st Bde. for night of 30–31 August 1917. [WO 95/2328/1]
19 War diary of 2nd Btn. Wiltshire Regt. for 30 August 1917. [WO 95/2329/1]
20 War diary of 21st Bde. for night of 29–30 September 1917. [WO 95/2328/1]

CHAPTER 11 – The 58. Infanterie-Division 1917 / 1918

1 Possibly named after the Bayerischer Bahnhof in Leipzig, which opened in 1842 and is now Germany's oldest preserved railway station.
2 Böttger, op. cit. (pp. 222–223).
3 Presumably from 1st Black Watch or 1st Cameron Highlanders of 1st Guards Brigade.
4 Böttger, op. cit. (p. 243).
5 Böttger, op. cit. (p. 257).
6 Genmaj. Woldemar Graf Vitzthum von Eckstädt belonged to a noble house which had served the Saxon electorate and crown since the sixteenth Century, producing numerous Saxon generals. He began the war as an oberst commanding Schützen-Regiment 108, but was soon promoted to brigade command and won the *Ritterkreuz and Komturkreuz 2. Klasse* of the MStHO, the latter while leading 192. ID at Verdun. He commanded 58. ID from April 1917 to demobilisation.
7 *"Eine windige Ecke"* – German soldier's slang for a dangerous spot.
8 Literally 'claw guns', an obscure slang term for super-heavy artillery.
9 s.K.H. Prinz Ernst Heinrich von Sachsen, *Mein Lebensweg vom Königsschloss zum Bauernhof* (pp. 98–101).

CHAPTER 12 – Those who remained in Flanders

1 On this see also the thoughts of Oltn. Pache on p. 163.
2 c.f. Chapter 1, Note 6.
3 c.f. Chapter 5, Note 10.
4 c.f. Chapter 4, Note 21.
5 *Pfefferland* (or 'the place where pepper comes from') is a figurative distant location used by Germans in mild curses since the sixteenth century. To wish someone in *Pfefferland* is to wish them in Hell without the religious connotations.
6 German generals from the rank of generalleutnant upwards were addressed as *'eure Excellenz'* (your excellency). A generalmajor was simply *'Herr General'*.
7 *'Ross und Reisige'* – a line from the imperial anthem *Heil dir im Siegerkranz*.
8 Lehmann, H., *Das Königlich Sächsische Reserve-Jäger-Bataillon Nr. 26* (p. 34).
9 Major Lucas Kirsten, born 21 May 1874 in Crimmitschau, was originally a cavalry officer with UR 21. In 1900 he volunteered for the Chinese expedition and won the *Ritterkreuz* of the MStHO with the Ostasiatisches Reiter-Regiment. He again served overseas in Southwest Africa in 1904–1906 and was semi-retired in January 1914. Reactivated in WW1, he was awarded the *Komturkreuz 2. Klasse* in October 1916 for his leadership of IR 103 on the Somme.

INDEX

PERSONS

PLACES (in the area covered by this book)

GERMAN UNITS

CORPS

DIVISIONS

BRIGADES

INFANTRY

CAVALRY

ARTILLERY

ENGINEERS

TECHNICAL TROOPS

TRAIN

---

* page(s) contain one or more relevant images
° index of places only; page(s) contain one or more relevant maps

PICTURE CREDITS

Sächsisches Hauptstaatsarchiv Dresden 55, 63

Archiv Arbeitskreis Sächsische Militärgeschichte e.V. Dresden 30 top

Andrew Lucas Collection 46-47, 50 bottom, 57, 68, 98, 128 bottom, 150 top, 215, 222 top, 243 bottom

Uwe Hänel Collection 64 bottom right

Jürgen Schmieschek Collection 4-18, 19-29, 30 bottom, 31-34, 36-39, 42-45, 49, 50 top, 51-54, 56, 58-62, 64 top and bottom left, 65-66, 69-70, 71 top, 72-79, 81-96, 97, 99-116, 117-127, 128 top, 129-149, 150 bottom, 151-156, 157-176, 177-188, 189-202, 203-227, 222 bottom, 223-242, 243 top, 244-246, 247, 256

Jan Vancoillie Collection 35, 40, 71 bottom, 247 top right

Bibliography

UNPUBLISHED SOURCES

The National Archives, London – British Army war diaries 1914–1922 (series WO95)

Sächsisches Hauptstaatsarchiv Dresden – records filed under the following shelfmarks (*signaturen*): 11300 (Sanitätskompanien); 11351 (Generalkommando des XIX. Armeekorps); 11356 (Generalkommando des XII. Reservekorps); 11358 (Generalkommando des XXVII. Reservekorps); 11359 (Infanteriedivisionen, Infanterieregimenter, Infanteriebataillone); 11362 (Feldartilleriebrigaden /Artilleriekommandeure); 13180-13245 (artillery, individually shelfmarked by unit)

Original diaries, correspondence and photographs from the authors' collections.

Gerhard, O., *Auszug aus dem Kriegstagebuch von Otto Gerhard, Lt. im Res. Reg. 201 und ab März 15 bei den Gastruppen* (unpublished manuscript held by the Württembergische Landesbibliothek Stuttgart)

Kaden, R., typescript of personal diary, 1916

PUBLISHED SOURCES

AEF General Staff, *Histories of Two Hundred and Fifty-One Divisions of the German Army Which Participated in the War*, Washington, 1920

Albrecht, O., *Das Königlich Sächsische Reserve-Jäger-Bataillon Nr. 25 im Weltkriege*, Dresden, 1927

Arbeistkreis Sächsische Militargeschichte e.V., *Begleitheft zur Wanderausstellung Christmas Truce*, Dresden, 2014

Ashworth, T., *Trench Warfare 1914-1918: The Live and Let Live System*, London, 2004

Backhaus, W., *245er Kameraden-Taschenbuch*, Leipzig, 1926

Bamberg, G., *Das Reserve-Infanterie-Regiment Nr. 106 (kgl. sächs.) im Weltkrieg*, Dresden, 1925

Barton, P., Doyle, P & Vandewalle J., *Beneath Flanders Fields – The Tunnellers' War 1914-18*, Stroud, 2007

Baumgaertel, M., *Das Kgl. Sächs. 14. Infanterie-Regt. 179*, Leipzig, 1931

Baumgarten-Crusius, A., *Das Königlich-Sächsische 11. Infanterie-Regiment Nr. 139 (1914-1918)*, Dresden, 1927

Baumgarten-Crusius, A. & Hottenroth, J.E., *Sachsen in großer Zeit*, Leipzig, 1918-1920

Beumelburg, W., *Die Schlacht um Flandern 1917*, Oldenburg, 1928

Beumelburg, W., *Ypern 1914*, Oldenburg, 1925

Bolze, W., *Das Kgl. Sächs. 7. Feldartillerie-Regiment Nr. 77*, Dresden, 1924

Böttger, K., *Das Kgl. Sächs. 7. Infanterie-Regiment König Georg Nr. 106*, Dresden, 1927

Bucher, *Dienstunterricht des Königlich Sächsischen Infanteristen*, Dresden, 1915 / 16

Busche, H., *Formationsgeschichte der Deutschen Infanterie im Ersten Weltkrieg 1914-1918*, Owschlag, 1998

Cron, H., *Die Organisation des Deutschen Heeres im Weltkrieg*, Berlin, 1923

Cron, H., *Imperial German Army 1914-18: Organisation, Structure, Orders-of-Battle*, Solihull, 2006

Deutschen Offizier-Bund, *Ehrenrangliste des ehemaligen Deutschen Heeres auf Grund der Ranglisten von 1914 mit den inzwischen eingetretenen Veränderungen*, Berlin, 1926

Duguid, A.F., *Official History of the Canadian Forces in the Great War 1914-1919* (vol. I), Ottawa, 1938

von Funke, A., *Unser tapferes Regiment. Das Kgl. Sächs. 8. Feldartillerie-Regiment Nr. 78 im Großen Kriege*, Dresden, 1931

Grill, Dr. A., *Das Sächsische Reserve-Infanterie-Regiment 241 im Weltkriege 1914 / 1918: Kriegserinnerungen eines Truppenarztes*, Dresden, 1922

Herkenrath, A., *Das Württembergische Reserve-Inf.-Regiment Nr. 247 im Weltkrieg 1914-1918*, Stuttgart, 1923

Heydenreich, F., *Das Kgl. Sächs. Feldartillerie-Regiment Nr. 245*, Dresden, 1921

Hitchcock, F.C., *„Stand To" A Diary of the Trenches 1915-1918*, London, 1937

Jones, S., *World War I Gas Warfare Tactics and Equipment*, Oxford, 2007

Jung, Fritz, *Goslarer Jäger im Weltkrieg, 1. Band – Das Hannoversche Jägerbataillon Nr. 10*, Hildesheim, 1938

K.S. Kriegsministerium, *Rangliste der Königlich Sächsischen Armee für das Jahr 1914*, Dresden, 1914

Kastner, H., *Geschichte des Königlich Sächsischen Reserve Infanterie-Regiments 242*, Zittau, 1924

Kees, H., *Das Kgl. Sächs. Feldartillerie-Regiment Nr. 115*, Dresden, 1928-1934

Klotz, D., *Das Württembergische Reserve-Feldartillerie-Regiment Nr. 54 im Weltkrieg 1914-1918*, Stuttgart, 1929

Knies, L., *Das Württembergische Pionier-Bataillon Nr. 13 im Weltkrieg 1914-1918*, Stuttgart, 1927

Knoppe, P., *Die Geschichte des Königlich Sächsischen Reserve-Infanterie-Regiments Nr. 241*, Dresden, 1936

Krämer, M., *Geschichte des Reserve-Infanterie-Regiment Nr. 245 im Weltkrieg 1914-1918*, Leipzig, 1923

Lee, J., *The Gas Attacks – Ypres 1915*, Barnsley, 2009

Lehmann, H., *Das Königlich Sächsische Reserve-Jäger-Bataillon Nr. 26*, Dresden, 1923

Lucas, A.R. & Lucas, M.J. – *„Loos to St. Eloi – the Experience of the Saxon 123. Infanterie-Division on the Western Front, 1915-16 Part 3: Winter in the Wytschaete Salient" in „Stand To!" Nr. 98*, Macclesfield, 2013

Lucas, A.R. & Schmieschek, J., *Fighting the Kaiser's War*. Barnsley, 2015

Martin, A., *Das Kgl. Sächs. Grenadier-Reserve-Regiment Nr. 100*, Dresden, 1924

Members of the regiment, *Kgl. Sächs. Infanterie-Regiment Nr. 178*, Dresden / Kamenz, 1935

Monse, R., *Das 4. Königl. Sächsische Infanterie-Regiment Nr. 103 im Kriege 1914-18*, Dresden, 1930

Niemann, J., *Das 9. Königlich Sächsische Infanterie-Regiment Nr. 133 im Weltkrieg, 1914-18*, Hamburg, 1969

Orgeldinger, L., *Das Württembergische Reserve-Infanterie-Regiment Nr. 246*, Stuttgart, 1931

Otto, K., *Das Kgl. Sächs. Feldartillerie-Regiment Nr. 246*, Dresden, 1928

Pache, A., *Das Kgl. Sächs. 16. Infanterie-Regiment Nr. 182*, Dresden, 1924

Pflugbeil, H., *Das Kgl. Sächs. 15. Infanterie-Regiment Nr. 181*, Dresden, 1923

Pohland, F.T., *Das Kgl. Sächs. Reserve-Infanterie-Regiment Nr. 103*, Dresden, 1922

Regiments-Zeitung für die Angehörigen des ehemaligen Landwehr-Infanterie-Regiments Nr. 77, Nr. 21, Osnabrück, 1930

Reichsarchiv, *Ruhmeshalle unserer alten Armee*, Berlin, 1927

Reimer, K., *Geschichte der Abteilung Reimer: sächs. Ers. Abt. FAR 68, I. sächs. Res. FAR 54 u. III. sächs. Res. FAR 32*, Dresden, 1927

Reinhardt, E., *Das Württembergische Reserve-Inf.-Regiment Nr. 248 im Weltkrieg 1914-1918*, Stuttgart, 1924

Richter, G., *Der Königlich Sächsische Militär-St. Heinrichs-Orden 1736-1918*, Frankfurt, 1964

Richter, Dr. J., Beyer, M., Hrsg., *Tagebuch des Kgl. Sächs. Generalstaboffiziers Gotthold Ernst Aster im Ersten Weltkrieg in Flandern und Frankreich*, Würzburg, Dresden, 2018

Richter, W., *Das Danziger Infanterie-Regiment Nr. 128, 1. Teil*, Zeulenroda, 1931

Robinson, J. & Robinson, J., *Handbook of Imperial Germany*, Bloomington, 2009

Robinson, J., Robinson, J. & Buchholz, F., *Great War Dawning*, Vienna, 2013

Sachse, J., *Die Sächsische Pioniere*, Dresden, 1923

Sächsischer Feldkameradenbund e.V., *Der Feldkamerad*, issues for the years 1930-1932, Leipzig

s.K.H. Prinz Ernst Heinrich von Sachsen, *Mein Lebensweg vom Königsschloss zum Bauernhof*, Dresden / Basel, 1995

Schatz, *Das 10. Kgl. Sächs. Infanterie Regiment Nr. 134*, Dresden, 1922

Schmidt, O. E., *Eine Fahrt zu den Sachsen an die Front*, Leipzig/Berlin, 1915

v. Schoenermarck, A., *Helden-Gedenkmappe des deutschen Adels*, Stuttgart, 1921

Freiherr von Seckendorff-Gudent, E., *Das Königlich Sächsische 8. Infanterie-Regiment „Prinz Johann Georg" Nr. 107 während des Weltkrieges 1914-1918*, Dresden, 1928

Seeßelberg, F., *Der Stellungskrieg, 1914-1918*, Berlin, 1926

Sheldon, J., *The German Army at Passchendaele*, Barnsley, 2007

Sheldon, J., *The German Army on the Western Front 1915*, Barnsley, 2012

Sheldon, J., *The German Army at Ypres – 1914*, Barnsley, 2011

Solleder, Dr., Fridolin, *Vier Jahre Westfront, Geschichte des Regiments List R.I.R. 16*, München, 1932

Stuhlmann, F., *Das Kgl. Sächs. 6. Feldartillerie-Regiment Nr. 68*, Dresden, 1927

Tennyson, B. *Merry Hell: The Story of the 25th Battalion (Nova Scotia Regiment), Canadian Expeditionary Force 1914-1919*, Toronto, 2013

Tiessen, M., *Königlich Preußisches Reserve-Infanterie-Regiment 213*, Glückstadt-Hamburg-New York, 1937

Trümper-Bödemann, M., *Das Königl. Sächs. Reserve-Infanterie-Regiment Nr. 102*, Dresden, 1929

Ulbricht, W., *Die Geschichte des Königlich Sächsischen Reserve-Infanterie-Regiments 244 im Weltkriege 1914-1918*, Chemnitz, 1920

Freiherr von Uslar-Gleichen, K., *Das Kgl. Sächs. 2. Jäger-Bataillon Nr. 13 im Weltkriege*, Dresden, 1927

Vancoillie, J., *De Duitse militaire begraafplaatsen Menen Wald*, Wevelgem, 2013

Vancoillie, J., *De Duitse militaire begraafplaatsen van de Eerste Wereldoorlog in Moorslede*, Wevelgem, 2015

Various authors, *Was wir erlebten – 245er Erinnerungen*, Leipzig, 1921-1942

Verein ehemaliger Offiziere – *Das Kgl. Preußische (Westfälische) Jäger-Bataillon Nr. 7 im Weltkrieg 1914-18*, Oldenburg / Berlin, 1929

Winzer, R., *Das Königlich Sächsische Reserve Infanterie-Regiment Nr. 243 im Weltkrieg 1914-1918*, Dresden, 1927

Wilkens, Christian, *Ulanen-Regiment Nr. 17*, Dresden, 1931

Wolff, L., *Das Kgl. Sächs. 5. Inf.-Regiment „Kronprinz" Nr. 104*, Dresden, 1925

Zipfel, G., *Das 3. Kgl. Sächs. Infanterie-Regiment Nr. 102 „König Ludwig III. von Bayern" im Weltkriege 1914-1918*, Dresden, 1925

ONLINE SOURCES

Canadian Great War Project – http://www.canadiangreatwarproject.com/

Commonwealth War Graves Commission – http://www.cwgc.org/

Deutsches Historisches Museum – www.dhm.de/lemo/biografie/friedrich-olbricht

Friedhof Hamburg-Ohlsdorf – https://www.fof-ohlsdorf.de/134s21_soldaten

GenWiki – http://wiki-de.genealogy.net

Great War Forum – https://www.greatwarforum.org/

Jan Vancoillie – https://vcjan.wordpress.com/2013/11/30/german-medical-services-1914-1918/

Library and Archives Canada – https://www.collectionscanada.gc.ca/archivianet/020152_e.html

Menenwald – www.menenwald.be

Molenechos – http://www.molenechos.org/verdwenen/

Onlineprojekt Gefallenendenkmaler – http://denkmalprojekt.org

Sächsische Feldlazarette 1914-1918 – https://feldlazarette-sachsen.jimdo.com/

Stammreihen – www.stammreihen.de

That's Nothing Compared to Passchendaele – https://getjackback.wordpress.com/

The Long, Long Trail – http://www.longlongtrail.co.uk

The National Archives (UK) – http://www.nationalarchives.gov.uk

Volksbund Deutscher Kriegsgräberfürsorge e.V. – www.volksbund.de

War Diary of the 18th Battalion CEF – https://18thbattalioncef.wordpress.com/

Leather-clad *kraftradfahrer* (motorcyclists) of Generalkommando XXVII. Reserve-korps during the transfer of the corps staff and 53. RD to Galicia in November 1916. The division returned to Flanders in December 1917, while the *generalkommando* spent the rest of the war in Ukraine.

Glossary

TIME

German time is used as standard throughout this book. Due to the adoption of different daylight saving schemes during the war, the British-German time difference varied significantly from 1916 onwards. To convert British to German time apply the following modifiers:

+1 hour: Until 1 May 1916, 14 June to 30 September 1916, 1 October 1916 to 24 March 1917, 16 April to 17 September 1917, 7 October 1917 to 9 March 1918, 15 April to 16 September 1918, 6 October 1918 onwards

+2 hour: 1 May to 14 June 1916

nil: 30 September to 1 October 1916, 24 March to 16 April 1917, 17 September to 7 October 1917, 9 March to 15 April 1918, 16 September to 6 October 1918

RANK

Rank	Abbreviation	British Equivalent
GENERALE (generals)		
Generalfeldmarschall	GFM	Field Marshal
Generaloberst		'Colonel-General'
General der Infanterie (... Artillerie / ... Kavallerie)	Gen. der Inf. (... Art., ... Kav.)	General
Generalleutnant	Genltn.	Lieutenant-General
Generalmajor	Genmaj.	Major-General
STABSOFFIZIERE (staff officers)		
Oberst	Oberst	Colonel
Oberstleutnant	Oberstltn.	Lieutenant-Colonel
Major	Maj.	Major
HAUPTLEUTE UND SUBALTERNOFFIZIERE (captains and subalterns)		
Hauptmann/Rittmeister[1]	Hptm.	Captain
Oberleutnant	Oltn.	1st Lieutenant
Leutnant	Ltn.	2nd Lieutenant
Feldwebelleutnant[2]	Fwltn.	'Sergeant-Lieutenant'
PORTEPEE-UNTEROFFIZIERE (snr. NCOs, entitled to an officer's sword knot)		
Feldwebel / Wachtmeister[3]	Fw.	Sergeant-Major
Vizefeldwebel / Vizewachtmeister[4]	Vfw.	'Vice Sergeant-Major'
UNTEROFFIZIERE OHNE PORTEPEE (jnr. NCOs)		
Sergeant	Sergt.	Sergeant
Unteroffizier / Oberjäger[5]	Uffz.	Corporal
MANNSCHAFTEN ('other ranks'; no command authority)		
Gefreiter	Gefr.	Lance-Corporal
Soldat[6]	Sold.	Private

1 'Rittmeister' in the cavalry and train only.
2 A senior career NCO promoted to officer rank.
3 'Wachtmeister' in the cavalry, *feldartillerie* and *train* only.
4 'Vizewachtmeister' in the cavalry, *feldartillerie* and *train* only.
5 'Oberjäger' in the *jäger* only.
6 'Soldat' was the title for a private in the Saxon infantry only. Alternative titles in different units and arms of service included: *fahrer* ('driver' – artillery and *train*), *funker* (radio units), *gardist* (Garde-Reiter and Prussian Garde), *grenadier, husar, infanterist* (Bavarian infantry), *jäger, kanonier* ('gunner' – artillery), *karabinier, musketier* (Prussian infantry), *pionier, schütze* ('rifleman' – SR 108 and machine-gunners with all units), *telegraphist* and *ulan*.

SPECIAL RANKS AND SERVICE CATEGORIES

... außer Dienst (a. D.) Rank suffix for retired officers ('out of service'); often recalled in wartime; **... der Landwehr (d. L.)** Suffix for ranks in the (trained) second-line reserve; divided by age into two 'bans' (*landwehr I* and *II*). In peacetime ORs would pass into the *landsturm* at the age of 39; **... der Reserve (d. R.)** Suffix for ranks in the (trained) first-line reserve. In peacetime ORs would pass into the *landwehr* at about the age of 27; **... zur Disposition (z. D.)** Rank suffix for semi-retired officers (half pay); usually recalled in wartime; **Arzt** Medical officer; ranks included *assistenzarzt, oberarzt* and *stabsarzt*; **Beamte** Uniformed (military) civil servant; **Einjährig-Freiwilliger (Einj. Frw.)** One-year volunteer; a man who reported to a unit before his active call-up and paid for his own kit and expenses, with the aim of becoming a reserve officer. Served actively for only one year (rather than up to three) in peacetime; **Ersatz-Reservist (Ers. Res.)** An untrained man of military age, passed over for active service in peacetime (included about half of those eligible to serve before the war); **Fahnenjunker** Prospective officer (with variable rank up to uffz.); formerly *avantageur*; **Fähnrich** Prospective officer (with variable rank up to vfw.); **Hornist** Bugler; **Kapitulant** Re-engaged (career) soldier; the main source of NCOs in peacetime; **Krankenträger** Stretcher-bearer (private); **Kriegsfreiwilliger (Kr. Frw.)** War volunteer; a man who reported to a unit before his *ersatz-reserve, landsturm* or active call-up. If not immediately killed, such men often enjoyed rapid promotion; **Landsturmmann (Ldstm.)** *landsturm* infantry private (either a reservist aged 39–45 or an untrained man aged 17–45 without other military obligations); given ranks 'der Landwehr' if promoted; **Obergefreiter** Rank between *gefreiter* and *unteroffizier*, used only in the *fussartillerie* for a qualified gun-layer (*richtkanonier*); **Reservist** Infantry private in the (trained) first-line reserve; **Sanitäts- (San.)** Prefix for medical NCOs and ORs; **Tambour** Drummer; **Wehrmann** Infantry private in the (trained) second-line reserve; **Sanitäter** Medical orderly (private); often yelled as a call for medical assistance (like "stretcher bearers!" on the British side)

APPOINTMENTS

Bataillonsarzt (Batl. Arzt) Battalion medical officer; commanded a deputy (unterarzt) and numerous *sanitäter* and *krankenträger*; **Chef** Honorary colonel-in-chief (often royalty); **Etatsmässiger Feldwebel** Company sergeant-major; **Führer (Fhr.)** Leader; acting commander (if an officer); **Kommandeur (Kdr.)** Commanding officer (formally appointed); **Offiziers-Stellvertreter (Offz. Stv.)** NCO formally 'deputising' in a subaltern's post (typically a *vizefeldwebel*); **Ordonnanz (-Offizier)** Orderly officer; **Regimentsarzt (Regts. Arzt)** Regimental medical officer

DECORATIONS

Eiserne Kreuz 1. Klasse (EK1) Iron Cross 1st Class (Prussian); **Eiserne Kreuz 2. Klasse (EK2)** Iron Cross 2nd Class (Prussian); **Pour le Mérite (PLM)** Pour le Mérite ("Blue Max"; the highest Prussian gallantry award); **Militär-St. Heinrichs-Orden (MStHO)** Military St. Henry Order (highest Saxon and oldest German gallantry award); **Komturkreuz des MStHO (MStHO[K])** Commander's Cross of the above (for senior officers, two classes); **Ritterkreuz des MStHO (MStHO[R])** Knight's Cross of the above (for officers); **Militär-St. Heinrichs-Medaille (MStHM)** Medal of the above (for enlisted men, in silver and gold); **Friedrich-August-Medaille (FAM)** Friedrich August Medal (for enlisted men, in silver and bronze)

REGIMENT AND BATTALION

The basic unit of infantry, cavalry and artillery was the regiment. An infantry regiment normally comprised three battalions, designated with Roman numerals (I–III). Each battalion had four rifle companies, designated with Arabic numerals in a single regimental sequence (1–4, 5–8 and 9–12 in battalions I–III respectively); in 1914 the single machine-gun company was unnumbered; later each battalion had an MG company with a matching Arabic number (1–3 MGK). Companies in *jäger* and *pionier* battalions were likewise designated with Arabic numerals, as were the (typically four) squadrons of a cavalry regiment. Most artillery regiments in 1914 had two battalions, designated with Roman numerals and each with three (*feldartillerie*) or up to four (*fussartillerie*) batteries; like companies, these were designated with Arabic numerals in a single regimental sequence. The system for referring to sub-units is quite intuitive and best explained via examples; the prefix of the parent unit (e.g. 'IR') is only ever dropped where the context excludes any possibility of confusion.

Long form	Shortest form	Translation
II. Bataillon / Infanterie-Regiment 102	II./102	2nd Battalion, IR 102
2. Kompanie / Infanterie-Regiment 102	2./102	2nd Company, IR 102
I. Abteilung / Feldartillerie-Regiment 48	I./48	1st Battalion, FAR 48
II. Bataillon / Fußartillerie-Regiment 12	II./12	2nd Battalion, FußaR 12
4. Batterie / Feldartillerie-Regiment 48	4./48	4th Battery, FAR 48
3. Eskadron / Husaren-Regiment 19	3./19	3rd Squadron, HR 19